America's Been Good to Me

America's Been Good to Me

Hermann Gammeter

Rick,
Thanks for being
a friend.
all the best
Herman

Deeds Publishing | Athens

Published by Deeds Publishing in Athens, GA
www.deedspublishing.com

Printed in The United States of America

Cover design by Mark Babcock. Text layout by Matt King.

ISBN 978-1-947309-64-7

Books are available in quantity for promotional or premium use. For information, email info@deedspublishing.com.

First Edition, 2019

10 9 8 7 6 5 4 3 2 1

CONTENTS

FOREWORD AND DEDICATION

All my life people would say, "Hermann, you had such an interesting life. You should write a book". "Yeah, yeah. Okay someday I will," I used to say. Then one Christmas evening when I was telling our grandkids some story from my younger days, they seemed to have an interest in hearing what their Swiss Pa had to say. The next Christmas, Andrea, my older daughter, gave me a nice empty book and asked me to write down some things about my life. Two years later, I found the book but had not written down one word. Suddenly surprised by my neglect, I decided to start writing.

This book is dedicated to my wife, Audrey, my two daughters, Andrea and Christina, and their families, of course the grandchildren. I do hope one day they will love to read about their grandfather and the Gammeter family. I also dedicate this book to all the wonderful people I have had the pleasure to work with and the people who have helped me in my life. Some names have been changed to protect the innocent. The names of the people I have changed are wonderful folks but I might not have agreed with all their philosophy and thus I changed their names. I have the greatest respect for these professionals but, as noted, our philosophy was not always the same.

Not everything might be nice in this book; however, it is my strong belief when you write your own bio you should be honest and should not hesitate to show how it really happened. Like one of my bosses used to say, we all have our pimples and he was absolutely correct. What is important is that you admit your mistakes and correct them when you can.

ACKNOWLEDGEMENTS

There are so many people I should acknowledge and say thank you to for what they have done for me. From my parents to the teachers in Switzerland; from the neighbors to friends of the family such as the Pauli family who gave me the opportunity to make my apprenticeship. Walter Roth who helped me come to the United States. Beat Richei who took me under his wing when I arrived. Thanks to the people with Westin Hotels like Joe Callahan and Joe Mogush who believed in me and helped me in my career. Mother Andrea who was a wonderful partner and whom I did not totally appreciate during our marriage, and of course my present wife, Audrey who has been such a terrific partner. I should also thank my daughters Andrea and Christina and Lena for their support. They have made me proud so often. My grandchildren have been a delight over the years. Kathy Godwin who has patiently helped me write my story and has been wonderful in putting everything together. Special thanks to Bill Hulett who probably has helped me more than anyone else in pursing my career goals.

It was a wonderful journey over the years and all I can say is I am a lucky fellow to have had so many good times and successes. America's been good to me.

1. HOW IT ALL BEGAN

MY YOUNGER YEARS

It was a beautiful day in May at 6:30am when I entered this world. The date was May 31, 1940, at the Kantonspital Aarau (State Hospital) in Switzerland. According to the priest, the doctor, and an infamous fortune teller, I was supposed to be a girl; a little girl named Susane. But surprise, out came a boy instead. Since my mother had no name prepared, she called me Hermann, after my dad. My mother had just turned 20, was naive and inexperienced, believing whatever my dad told her. She thought he was so wise since he was thirteen years her senior. At the time, I think my father was still married to his first wife with whom he had six other children—three boys and three girls.

Times were hard since Hitler was trying to take over the world and it was the beginning of World War II. We always had something to eat; however, occasionally the food was slightly spoiled. My grandfather worked in the Army as a valet/butler cleaning the officer's boots and uniforms. This position gave him the opportunity to bring home leftover food to feed the family. Both my grandfathers were cheese makers and both were named Fritz. I always found this ironic since I did not eat cheese—cannot even stand the smell of cheese. My dad was strong willed and insisted that I learn how to eat cheese. So for three days, all he served me was cheese. I got hungry and finally tried to eat it; however, I gagged and could not keep it down. Until today, cheese smells like "old socks"—certainly not for me.

1

Until I was three years old, we lived in Messen, a quaint farm village. It was on the border of the state of Solothurn and Bern. An unusual farmhouse was located there that was split in the middle of the master bedroom by the two states — the husband slept in the state of Bern and the wife in the state of Solothurn. I believe the first three years of a child's life are important as they form the character and the moral fiber of a human being, thus I feel living in Messen had a tremendous influence on me later in life.

My maternal grandfather was a farmer and was always very protective of me and instilled in me a feeling of security; hopefully I will do the same for my grandchildren. On the other hand, quite often Uncle Otto and Uncle Max, my mother's brothers, scared me with horror stories. As you can imagine, living on a country farm, we had no running water or indoor facilities. When paying a visit to the family's outhouse, they told me the devil would come and bite me on the butt. Or when we had a strong wind or rainstorm, they said it was the devil or ghosts running through the farm. Grandfather would hug me and say, "Don't worry, Hermann; it's going to be fine." His wife, my grandmother, was sick, totally helpless, and confined to a wheelchair. Grandfather would always say, "At least she's still with us." When she passed away, I was six years old and I can still remember that sad day.

My dad was diagnosed with tuberculosis three times and when he was 33, he was told that he had just six months to live. As the world's greatest optimist, he would not accept this diagnosis. Whenever he heard of a way to heal tuberculosis, he would try it. One time he was told to drink petroleum; so each morning he had a shot glass of pure petroleum. Later, he and I were both confined at the same time for the same ailment to the same sanatorium in Heiligenschwendi, a hospital in the mountains for treating people with TB. Luckily, my dad's six months of life were extended. He passed away decades later when he was 85. It appears to me that his positive thinking definitely worked for him. It was in this facility that as a five-year old I was molested by another patient who was in his mid-twenties. I had to rub him and it was very uncomfortable for me. I swore at the time if anybody ever did this to my children or grand-children I would kill them.

On the weekend, sometimes mother would come to visit. She would travel first by train, then bus, and the last kilometer she had to walk to visit my dad and me. During the week, she worked in a factory to sup-port us and my dad's other six kids. They lived in a foster home since his first wife did not take care of the children, out of laziness I guess. Rather than wash their clothes, she actually threw them away and purchased new ones.

Finally, the day came that my parents could pick me up from the clinic. On the way home, we stopped by the hospital to see my grand-mother. Sadly though, when we arrived she fell asleep, forever. In one sense, it was a happy day because I got out of the hospital, and a sad day because grandmother had passed away.

Grandfather Vogt, mother's dad was born out of wedlock. His moth-er, my great grandmother, was a midwife and an absolute work horse. She would go by bicycle from farm to farm bringing the babies into the world. She would cook and wash for the family and go on to the next farm to do the same thing over again. She was unusual, to say the least. I remember peeing on a neighbor's land one time and she scolded me for it. Not for the usual reasons, but because she wanted me to pee on her land so her land would be fertilized and not the neighbor's.

When we worked on the farm, she would bring a picnic lunch along. She would take out the bacon, unwrap it and show it to us, then re-wrap it, pack it back and serve us bread, nuts, and apples. She raised my grand-father on her own because she was never married. We never learned who his father was, but my mom always had her suspicions about who she thought it could have been. My grandfather's house had no indoor plumbing or electric stove. They cooked on a wood burning stove. It was a hard life living on the farm, but it was a happy life. We made do with whatever we had. We were a family who supported each other and shared what little we did have. No toys or money and not many clothes or shoes except for our wooden shoes. But ultimately, somehow, we survived without all the luxuries. Growing up on the farm was fantastic — the horses, cows, chickens, fresh fruit trees, vegetables, flowers, etc. It was so nice.

The best day was always when my father came to visit us. It was about every two to three weeks. We got so excited when he came driving this shiny black Ford, the only car around. Dad was still married to his first wife, so he had an obligation to take care of two families. Although the visits were short, they sure were special. He drove us around town with that little black Ford, and I felt like a celebrity. All the people would watch us go by. Folks on the street would stand still and wave at us.

My two uncles constantly teased me and made fun of me but granddad was still my protection. For my first haircut, Uncle Otto took me to the barber. Uncle Otto was born the same day as me, but nine years earlier. Later I learned my cowboy hero from spaghetti westerns, Clint Eastwood, and I also shared the same birthday, although he was born 10 years earlier than me. At the barber shop after half an hour trying to cut my hair, in frustration Uncle Otto took me home crying. I had always heard when they cut your hair they could cut off your ears so I was justifiably scared and screamed and wiggled. This made it impossible for the barber to do his job. Mother took me back later and stood next to me with a stick — that did the trick. My first long blonde curls landed on the floor and were gone forever.

When I was about three, my dad got a divorce from his first wife and could finally move with us to Rombach, near Aarau. We moved into an apartment building which had twelve families. Above us resided Mr. and Mrs. Wyss, a young couple about my parent's age. They had no kids so I kind of became their kid, too. They were very good to me and it was fun to be with them. Often they would have a little bucket on a string and they would lower it down to us from their balcony, filled with candy or chocolates. My parents got me a little play telephone and I would play for hours — "Hello, Mrs. Wyss, how are you, yes I am doing well. OK, Mr. Wyss, thank you for your gifts, etc." So one day when they were visiting us, dad was going to show off. He asked me to play with the phone and act as I normally did. Being shy, I refused. This infuriated my dad and he screamed, "Hermann, either you call the Wyss's or I'm going to spank you." Shaking and scared, I picked up the phone, ring, ring, ring, and said, "Sorry, the line's busy." Well, everyone had to laugh and I was saved from a spanking. Then thirty years later, I had a similar incident. I took my two-year old daughter to the zoo in San Francisco. I identified the animals — tiger, lion, zebra, giraffe, and elephant. Andrea always said "doggie" with each animal. So when we stood in front of a big elephant, I kept saying "elephant", she kept saying "doggie". So like my father I got impatient and said, "Andrea, say elephant or you get a spanking." She looked at me and said "doggiephant". What could I do but hug her and love her.

BACK IN AARAU

When my parents got married, I was about three years old. I was so happy and knew that Dad would stay with us forever. Even today I remember my parent's wedding which was held in the Hotel Ochsen in Lenzburg. We had good food and music and my parents looked fabulous. Mom had a black and white dress, while my dad wore a black suit and, of course, his usual cigar. He looked like Winston Churchill. Dad was never without a cigar when he was young.

At the time when we lived in the apartment complex, Mr. Wyss started his own business; dad was asked to sign a note with the bank for him to guarantee a loan. Mom was so scared and cried and Dad said not to worry, he will make it a success. Mr. Wyss started a radio and TV business which was just beginning to take off in Switzerland. I remember we used to go to a restaurant to watch television or we would stand outside a TV shop in the cold and watch the programs. In black and white of course; it was a new and exciting era. Mr. Wyss built a great company and made a great deal of money. He bought an old farmhouse and made it into an absolute dream house; elegant would be an understatement. He had a Rittersaal (that is a room like you would only find in castles, like a smoking lounge. This is where the men would sit, drink port and smoke cigars, and discuss strategies). For many years, we visited the Wyss's. My parents were such good friends with them and of course they never forgot father had helped them to start their business. Whenever I had a chance, I would go with my folks to visit them because I was so in love with their exquisite home.

THE GREAT SALESMAN

My dad always had a sense of making money and was a natural salesman. When he was in his early 20s, he decided to go to Australia to visit his brother; as a stowaway on a banana boat, he started his trip. After eating nothing but bananas, he and his friend got caught and the police sent them back to Switzerland. The fellow who caught him was a big black man and he just grinned at the two kids. Not to be deterred, Dad always found a way to survive and bring in money to take care of the family. He sold insurance once, as well as cars at one point. He also started a washing machine business, but that did not pan out. I remember when they had to close out my small savings account because my parents got in some financial difficulty. I guess Dad had such a drive because he lost his mother as a small child and his older sisters had to take care of him. He did not like that and eventually left one day when he was very young to begin working.

After World War II ended, he began purchasing Army surplus material and sold it to his customers. He would go to different markets most every day. But when there were no markets to visit, he would go to farms and sell his merchandise. At the time, there were no big supermarkets or big shops. When "Marketing Man" Gammeter showed up, he was welcomed with open arms and was highly respected. He gave cigars to farmers and chocolate to the kids. After the war, many items were scarce and since he had the items, he could sell them easily. His pockets were full of money, loose change. When he put his hand in his pocket and gave the farmer the exact change, they thought it was like magic. Business was so good, he hired the two Zehnders brothers to work for him and they did the same thing. Since there were no big department stores only small neighborhood shops, Dad's business flourished. In the early 50s he opened a store in Aarau and my mom worked there as well with another sales lady. The shop was called Textil-Gammeter and it was quite successful. Mother, of course, first cried and said she could not run a shop. Dad just reassured her that she was capable of putting together a package and collecting money and eventually she proved very capable of being a good sales person.

In 1946, my parents were able to purchase a home in Graenichen, near Aarau. In the fall, we moved there and my parents lived there the remainder of their lives. Before we moved in, the three of us made a trip through Switzerland. We visited many passes in the mountains and it was extremely exciting. We had a convertible Ford and each of us was wearing our white hats; we thought we were "high class people". I remember driving through the mountains where kids would stand on the street at a curve and try to sell us Alpine roses, Enzians, or Edelweiss. If we did not stop and buy them, they would run down the hill to the next curve and wait for us. I learned a good lesson from the farm kids who worked hard and never gave up. This is similar to Vince Lombardi's motto about giving the second effort and determination.

My school years were fabulous. I was a happy kid growing up in the country. Our home was beautiful with flowers and fruit trees, plus we had a generally happy family. My mother had the nicest geraniums and when the village people walked by they would stop and take photographs.

DREAMING OF AMERICA

I always played cowboys and Indians and dreamed about the United States. Whenever I played, I always wanted to be the leader or the cop or mobster boss—the one who gave the orders. One time while playing in the woods with my friend, I tied him to a tree and walked away to scare him. It was deep in the forest and unfortunately, I forgot where I left him. I ran home crying and enlisted the help of some neighbors. We went back and finally found the poor kid. As a little boy, I would constantly say—do not make me mad or I will go to America. One day I was asked to pick up our monthly food stamps for butter and milk. On the way back home, I got sidetracked playing on the sidewalk with a neighbor girl and lost the food stamps. When I got home my dad asked for the stamps and I told him the story. Oh, my God—all hell broke loose. After a spanking he said okay, go to America now. With big tears, I left and walked down the street alone. Along the way, Mrs. Wyss met me and asked me what was going on so I told her I was leaving and going to America. She was so nice, consoled me, and brought me back to my parents.

Since the business was good, we made several trips with the Wyss's to Genoa, Italy and Vienna, Austria. It was fascinating for me to be in a foreign country. After the war, the city of Vienna was divided into Russian, American, English, and French sections and we were able to visit all four sections. I must say the American section was the best. We even got chewing gum from the soldiers. This was a fantastic trip. We visited Schloss Schoenbrunn, the castle where Emperor Franz Joseph lived with Sissi Schoenbrunn. It is the former emperor's summer residence of the Habsburg Monarchs. The 1,441 room Baroque Palace is one of the most famous architectural, cultural, and historical monuments in Austria. It is quite unique and fantastic with gardens which are beautifully landscaped and encompass many acres. We also went to Felden at the beautiful Lake Wortersee. Then we went over to the Wolfgangsee, the famous Lake the Musical Weisses Roessel started. Next on our trip was a visit to Salzburg. This is the magnificent area, all gorgeously landscaped, which afterward became famous in the movie *The Sound of Music*. Later in life, I was able to revisit Salzburg while the Pope was making an appearance there. His Pope Mobile, which was specially designed by Mercedes with bullet proof windows, drove by within a few feet of me. It was a very special experience with a feeling of real radiation from the Holy Father.

When we were settled in our new home in Granichen, next door to us lived the Luethy family. Mrs. Luethy was a mom with three kids and Mr. Luethy (Hugo) was a school teacher who taught me in the 5th grade. He was involved in politics, on many committees and boards. We all thought Mr. Luethy was a "big shot". Their three children were very good friends of mine. Rolf, the older son, who later became a doctor with a private practice, still reminisces about the crazy things we did. He tells the story how I tried to lift him up by his ears. Because I had always been wild about the circus, I had my own circus set-up in the backyard of our house. For summer training, I had installed a trapeze on a tree in our yard and another trapeze was installed in the attic of our house. I would cut myself in the arm until blood came to show that I was an Indian Fakir. As a wild kid, I used to say if I have a son who is brave but quiet, I will go with him to a neighbor's house and show him how to break a window and make a rascal out of him, just like his father. In the winter, I continued as a fearless nut. With my bobsled, I was the terror of the village. Skiing had no limits and with my sled I was the king. I would go higher and higher with villagers standing on the street watching and saying he's going to kill himself. As wild as I was, I would always help and try to protect the underdog. In my mind, I wanted to be a Robin Hood — take from the rich and give to the poor. I remember when Guliano, the infamous Italian bandit, was shot by the police, I cried for days. In my eyes, he was an Italian Robin Hood whom I admired from afar. Today I would not agree with all the nasty things I did, but I was just a boy — a wild kid, a real scoundrel.

It's no wonder our teacher, Mr. Lauppi, was hard on us, or at least I thought so since I got in so much trouble. One day, my friend Willie and I provoked Mr. Lauppi one more time so he hit us on our hands with a ruler. I had planned on this, so I brought some onions to school with me that day. After he hit us on our hands with the ruler, I rubbed my hands with onions as I had heard that would make my hands swell. When I got home I showed Dad my hands and he asked what had happened. Eagerly I told him that the teacher hit me and that he should go and talk to him, maybe even notify the police. He just looked at me, hit me on both sides of my face and told me to go ahead and rub my face with some onions to see if I got any swelling! The 1940s were quite different from today, but I was fortunate to have experienced in my younger years a great life in the Swiss countryside among farms, fields, and a healthy although adventurous way of life.

EXCITING MOTORBIKES AND CAMPING

Motorbikes and bicycles had always fascinated me and I attended quite a lot of races with my brother Harry. One evening with my friend

Hermann riding on the back of my bike, we unfortunately had an accident and ran into Dr. Knittel. Hermann ended up in the hospital for 12 weeks while I got a cast on my left arm. After two days, I had to go back to Dr. Knittel and he replaced the cast. It was broken so he made the second cast much thicker and stronger. Four days later, I returned again as my cast was broken and he placed the third cast on my arm. Dr. Knittel said that after practicing medicine for over 30 years, this was the first time someone needed three casts in one week. He told me he thought I needed to slow down a little.

Camping was yet another experience that I was lucky enough to enjoy as a kid. My parents bought me a small tent when I was ten years old. I wanted to go camp on Lake Hallwil, but Mother felt I would be scared so I was only allowed to sleep in our garden. Mother was up all night peeking out from behind the window shades and where she waited for me to come back into the house, afraid of the dark. But I didn't, I slept like a baby. I passed my test and was allowed to go camping at the lake. I was only ten years old and spent ten days alone camping. Later on, my cousin, Peter, came with me. We camped each summer until we were about fifteen years old. When I first started to camp, many people helped me, especially the wives who were so nice to me. I helped them clean their dishes and they gave me money or food. My ulterior motive was to save my grocery money which my parents had given me to buy flippers and goggles to swim. A young couple from Zurich was especially nice to me. This couple had no children so I was their substitute child. They even invited me to their home in Zurich to visit them; we had the greatest time. Our baker in Granichen made me a cake and he decorated it with a tent, bike, and swimming pool made out of Marzipan. The couple was so happy when I went to Zurich alone on the train and I brought them the sweets. About the same time when I was somewhere between ten to fifteen years old, I would ride all over with my bike and visit the gypsies who had a carousel which I would help them set up. I would even help collect the tickets for them. I was obsessed with their lifestyle. My fantasy was living in a trailer, moving from village to village. What a grand life that would be, I thought.

OUR FAMILY CONTINUES TO GROW

In June 1950, my dad got a phone call from the owner of a shop in Locarno, the Italian part of Switzerland. The shop owner told dad that someone had given birth to a baby. The little boy, Peter, was ten days old when we went to Locarno to pick him up. Mother who was so giving and kind, right away said no problem, we will take care of the boy. Mother took care of the other kids from my dad's first marriage as well as her own brother. My mother was a saint, but I will talk more about her kindness later. So now I had a brother, Peter who was ten years younger than me, so not exactly a playmate for a wild kid like me. We got along fine, especially later in life after I left home. Often I said God wanted Peter to come in our home so my parents would let me go and see the world. It worked out OK as Peter always stayed in the area and lived near our parents.

One day, totally not expecting him, there was my stepbrother Harry standing at the door. When I asked him what brought him here, he replied that he had left home and wanted to live with us. Mom took him in and helped him change his lifestyle. Harry, like his two brothers and three sisters, did not get much guidance from their mother so eventually they had been put in a home for kids in the Bernese Oberland. My other stepbrother Heinz died when he was only 20 of leukemia, which was unfortunate; I hardly got to know him. Two of my stepsisters I never got to know very well either until later in life. Years later, Kathy and her husband Ruedi visited me in Atlanta where I was managing a large hotel. My stepbrother Harry was only nine years younger than my mom so they related well. She helped build his confidence and supported him in his endeavors. She even encouraged him to get a truck driver's license and loaned him 8,000 sfr. That loan was utilized to purchase a used truck and start his own business. Quite often I went with Harry on his route, which I thought was fun and assisted in delivering goods. Harry was a reliable, hard worker and people seemed to like him, which enabled him to build a good delivery business.

History repeated itself a short time later when my other stepbrother Emil was found standing at our front door. Like Harry, he needed help and of course, my mother took him in. We had a house full by that time as our paternal grandfather was also living with us. One of my fondest memories of him was each night as a kid I would go to him and say that I needed a little more gasoline. He would slap me on my butt and I would run to bed giggling. Emil was a bicycle racer whose friends would come over on Saturdays and stay with us, although sometimes sleeping in tents outside. Mother would get up at 3am to make breakfast for them, cooking liver for the racers. Dad and I would go with Emil and the other racers to the village where the races took place. Emil had many accidents which mother had to nurse, never complaining. Dad spent a fortune on these stupid bike races because he wanted Emil to become a star; however, he never did. Brother Harry eventually got married and moved out. His family grew to include a set of twins, Sylvia and Harry, plus two more girls. Sadly daughter, Ursula, the second oldest, passed away from leukemia when she was only 25. It was a shame too as she was such a nice kid, always jolly and happy. Harry and his family used to come every Sunday afternoon and Mother played hostess serving food, tea, beer, etc. Often there were between 14 and 16 people at our house. Mother did this for years every Sunday like a ritual Harry would come home. Harry was never sick, never went to see a doctor for a check-up. He always dreamed of getting old but in 1992 he got sick. I had planned a trip to Switzerland, but was one day too late. Harry had passed away from stomach cancer. It only took three weeks and he was gone. This was sad for me as I liked Harry very much and we got along great. Harry's wife, Martha, who grew up in the same village as my mother, passed away soon after her daughter Ursula's death. She and Harry did not have a very good marriage due to a lot of fighting and bickering; he was rough but she was no saint either.

After Harry got married and left the house, we had a free bed at home so of course mother took in her brother Otto who, if you will remember from earlier, had the same birthday as me. Otto was a nice fellow but did not have much education; however, he had a good job as a driver for a steel company. He was a lot like my mother; he was pessimistic all the time. This was inherited from my maternal grandmother, a farm girl from the state of Bern. My dad was the opposite — an optimist — his glass was always half full, never half empty. People used to ask me which parent I took after and I always replied my mom but I got my mouth from my dad. Indeed, I was optimistic my whole life. An old proverb was "an Indian knows no pain" and I sure lived my life like that. How my mother was able to work so hard I do not know, especially when she had a house full of men and since we did not have the technology which we enjoy today. She would wash the clothes by hand and scrub them, then boil them. We had no refrigeration until the middle 50s so the milk and meats had to be kept cold in the cellar until the winter when we could put the meat outside the window. Thank God for Aunt Heidi, mother's sister. She was the oldest of her siblings. Once a week she would come by our house and help clean, wash, do yard work, etc. Of course my dad paid her as she needed extra money with three kids of her own at home. Aunt Heidi was wonderful I thought as she was so helpful, full of good humor, a great cook, and best of all, she liked to spoil me. She would invite me to spend my vacation with her and her three boys. Her son Peter was my camping companion; Alexander was the same age as me; and her baby, Fritz who was the tallest of them all. Our relationship and friendship lasted for many years.

MY FUTURE AMBITIONS AND APPRENTICESHIP

To become a musician or a chef, that was the question I posed to myself in 1954. Like many teenagers in that era, I was a fan of the popular singers and entertainers and desperately wanted to become a famous singer. When I was in my early teens, I made the decision that I would become a musician and singer and learned to play the harmonica, guitar, and trumpet. At 16 I went alone to Salzburg, Austria and interviewed at the Mozart School of Music and was accepted. I jumped on the next train back to Switzerland and excitedly told my parents I had been accepted at the school in Salzburg to study music. However, they felt I should first learn a real job so I could support myself and make a living. My dad always said that musicians are "fantasy" people, just dreamers. You can't depend on them what with all the drinking and girls. He felt there was no future; that first I should learn a trade, build a solid existence, and have an income. After that, if I still wanted to become a musician, there would be ample time to do so. So I decided I would become a chef, although knowing my father wanted me to take over his business someday.

He asked a friend of his who was a famous restaurateur if he would hire me as a dishwasher and a kitchen helper. He said okay if I would agree to work long hours, plus Saturday and Sunday work. Over the holidays, I would gladly come home and get involved with dad's business. Finally, in 1956, I started working in the kitchen, making $12.50 a month — yes, a month! Because I was good at any work I was given and proved to be dependable, I was given the chance to apprentice as a chef. It was a great time which had its ups and downs. However, since I was the youngest apprentice, the other guys on the staff heckled me — they made me look stupid and teased me a lot. For example, they would ask me to chop flour and if I didn't do it I would get scolded. The first day on the job, I had to cook spinach and put it in plastic bags and freeze it. I ended up green from my feet to my head, even my hair was green. We all enjoyed good camaraderie in the kitchen, even though the experienced staff would invent other tricks that were not so pleasant. Because it was so hot, we got beer twice a day, even though I was only 16. Since I did not like beer, I would sell it to the others for a dime.

Some of my fellow apprentices made it big in our business, like myself, while others got out of the restaurant and hotel business and found other jobs. Our saucier was Lothar, a German fellow who was nice and even tempered. One day I spilled a full bowl of salad over his head. He looked at me, grinned, and asked if I was cooking again. If I had done this to another German, he would have hit me. He used to drink fresh blood from calves which he said made him strong and aggressive. He was an excellent chef, but a nut. He would stand next to me and if I had to debone some meat and made a wrong move with my knife, he would hit me with a bone. He was a real mean person.

TIME TO MOVE OUT ON MY OWN

At the time, I was 16 and I lived in a nice room with my parents but I asked Mrs. Pauli, the restaurant owner, if I could have a room at the restaurant. She agreed and I went home and began packing. My mother asked what I was doing and I announced that I was going to live in Aarau. She could not believe it since my parents had a nice home I could live in but I would be leaving that comfort to live with one or two other chefs in a small room above the railway stations with trains coming and going all night long.

My apprenticeship as a chef was interesting and I enjoyed it. Full of fun and excitement, we were all young men and full of mischief. Time after time we got in trouble, but somehow we always got out of it. We were a group of many different nationalities from different countries, but mostly Italians. To enable me to communicate with my fellow co-workers, I learned to speak Italian. Of course, like every other male at the time, I fell in love with Sophia Loren; only I knew that—she never learned of my love for her. One of the pot washers was from Naples who spent hours teaching me to sing "O Solo Mio" in the original Naples dialect.

We did a lot of unusual things; in the cellar we even had a fish pond where we kept fresh fish. When someone ordered a trout, I was sent down to pick it up but I was such a softy I did not like having to kill the trout. I figured if someone would do that to me, I would not like it; so I came back up and told the chef there were no more trout left. He went down, brought one up, and kicked me in the butt. Mr. Pauli, the owner of the restaurant, invited me to go to Lake Hallwil where I used to camp as a youngster. We went there to fish for crawfish, which was fascinating. At night, we looked for crawfish with a flashlight. When we saw one we slowly moved the light in as they would follow it and when they were close enough, we caught them with a net.

One time I got into an argument with another apprentice so I put him in a big cooking kettle, put the heat on and left. Boy was that a stupid idea, but we stayed good friends after his survival and recovery. He later moved to Norway and enjoyed a successful hotel career.

When a new employee started to work, they too were abused, told to do dumb things like chopping flour, and set the machine to pump up sausages. Not unlike the abuse I was subjected to when I began my apprenticeship. But when you're young and naïve, afraid of losing your position, you just do what you're told to do, even when you think it is wrong.

Once we had a cooking contest and I was asked to make twelve omelets and different kinds of dishes, of course. I used almost a case of eggs because when the omelet was not perfect I threw it out and started over. With it I made a display of a nest, chickens, grass, and flowers. Well it paid off as I won first prize in the cooking contest. Once, after the contest, my mother wanted to give me some cooking advice. I put my arm around her, looked at her, and said, "You have no clue about cooking." She took it very hard and cried. She said she had been cooking for me all my life and now I'm telling her she had no clue about cooking. The rest of my life she reminded me about this incident, but because she was proud of me, it became a joke between us.

YOUNG LOVE

With my job as an apprentice, my first love came along—Desiree was her name. She was six years older than me and a very good teacher. I thought I had died and gone to heaven. We went out all the time dancing, dining, etc. She made a lot of money and I was poor, but we had fun. Plus, she had a car. When I graduated, I moved to Lausanne, the French part of Switzerland. I worked at the Hotel de la Paix in Lausanne and loved my job. At first Desiree and I wrote each other and on her day off she would come to see me. We went to France for the night and all was good. However, she found an older man and dumped me. At the time I was devastated but, like they say, time heals all wounds. Our relationship really had no future. But at the time of the breakup it hurt so much I can't describe how lousy and sad I felt. I thought it was the end of the world. I am sure other people go through these same lost loves; if only we could tell them not to worry—that life works out for the best in the long run. The lesson learned should be to get over it. Mother used to say when the good Lord closes one door, he opens a window, but at the time I did not understand that. Needless to say, I had other girl friends in Lausanne and many happy moments.

LIFE GOES ON

I purchased a Moped, which is basically a bicycle with a motor. On my days off, I would drive through the vineyards at Lake Geneva. This is one of the most beautiful places in the world. It is so romantic with castles, lakes, villages, and farms. Farmers were working in the sun across from Lake Geneva with the French Alps in the background. It is stunningly beautiful. Quite a few famous stars used to live in this area such as Charlie Chaplin, Audrey Hepburn, Richard Burton, and many, many more. Years after I left Lausanne, I went to find Richard Burton's grave, which is in a small village on Lake Geneva. I went to the new cemetery and but could not find his grave whereupon I learned from an older gentleman that he was buried in the old cemetery. This was hard for me to believe, it didn't make sense to me that such a famous star with so much success would have a simple grave with a wooden cross. I would have expected a big celebrity monument, but that is not what he wanted. He liked to have a simple grave in the village he had loved so much. He used to frequent the local restaurant and sit with the local people sharing the bull where he could be himself and did not have to pretend or be the big Hollywood star. There is another lesson to be learned from Richard Burton's simple philosophy.

LENZERHEIDE HERE I COME

After working in Lausanne, I moved to Lenzerheide, a resort in the Canton Graubünden. As a kid, I used to go there for summer camp. Graubünden is a beautiful state with famous resorts like Arosa, Davos, and St. Moritz. What a great area where I have many fond memories of my youth camps. We would go hiking, walking, and going through the river looking for crystals; what a super time we had. However, now I was there as a professional, working in a nice hotel, Post Hotel Valbella. First thing we did in the morning was start a fire in the wood burning stove where we cooked. I used to take an empty can, punch a hole in it, then put the leftover oil and grease in it. This would keep the fire burning and I did not have to constantly add wood chips. In our employee rooms where we stayed, there was no heat except for a small wood burning stove. At night when we came home we made a fire to heat the room. On top of the stove we had a bucket with water in it to heat so we could bathe ourselves. Another bucket had holes in it so we could take a shower. To do that, another employee had to hold the bucket and we would stand under it and take a shower. One night I had a hot date, was bragging so I asked my buddy to hold the bucket for me to take my shower. The bum put blue ink in the water and my skin was blue all over, especially my hair — it was terrible. So then he tells me he will go meet my date for me where he told her I was sick with a new virus — the blue flu! What a disappointment for me. We were always playing tricks on each other, but we were good friends.

ENJOYING LIFE AT A SKI RESORT

I have many great memories from Valbella. It was a winter of fun and play with lots of skiing. We would hit the slopes and I would run downhill close to a pretty girl and scare her. When she fell, I would apologize and ask if I could invite her for tea and cake in a café. Often it worked, but sometimes I was told to go to hell. Well you win a few and you lose a few, but it was worth the try. Nightlife in a Swiss ski resort is great with lots of music, singing, and dancing — just fabulous. I met many new friends and everyone was in such a good mood. After a few days, their vacation ends and they go home and the next day, new ones arrive.

The saddest memory from Lenzerheide occurred when we had an

avalanche. It buried a dozen kids, mostly girls from a school in Zurich. I will never forget the kids who died in that accident. What a horrible experience.

I had a girl friend who worked in a sports shop across from our hotel. She had dark hair and was very, very nice. Then her blonde girl friend came to visit her, so I hooked up with the blonde. While visiting there she broke her leg. We were an item for a few months; she even went with me and visited with my parents in Granichen. Dad liked her and said I should keep her, but I told him she is just temporary.

I loved to work seasonal work that comes to Switzerland. There I worked the summer season and winter season in resorts and between seasons I would take temporary jobs. That's when I took the opportunity to take courses in the famous hotel school, the Swiss National Hotel Business School in Lucerne. We had students from all corners of the globe; however, most came from Europe, Germany, Austria, Holland, Denmark, and Sweden. About 40% of the students were Swiss, the rest foreigners.

One semester I met Hanna Katrina Smith Petersen, a terrific young lady from Denmark. A tall Scandinavian with a great figure and pleasant personality, she was just a fine young lady. The first time away from home in a foreign country, I took her under my wing and showed her my home country. We became very good friends. Hanna was going to be a stewardess with Scandinavian Airlines, which is why she visited the hotel school. After our last semester ended, she went back to Denmark so I visited her in Sued Jutland. She lived with her parents on a large farm called Voiens Gard. They were a large family and extremely nice people. It was interesting to learn that Denmark has high taxes for alcohol and gasoline and the farmers had special gasoline for their trucks and farm machinery. The gas was blue in color and was not allowed to be used in cars. Hanna and I went to Copenhagen to visit her sister who was staying there. Copenhagen is a beautiful city with parks, museums, side walk cafes, restaurants, and hotels. We went to a famous restaurant which was quite expensive. We both had a drink but because of the costs, we were nursing the libation for over an hour. The waiter showed up with two more drinks and I was startled. He said the gentleman at the next table invited us for drinks. He was a distinguished fellow with a pretty lady. I thanked them and decided when I grow up and have money I would do the same thing. Since that time, I have made many random acts of kindness and helped people I have met, making many happy people because I never forgot the kindness of this gentleman in Copenhagen.

The only disappointment in Copenhagen was Edward Eriksen's Little Mermaid. It is so famous and I expected the bronze statue to be a large monument. It is only about 4 feet tall and weighs 385 lbs. He was fascinated by a ballet about the fairy tale Copenhagen's Royal Theater and he asked the ballerina Ellen Price to model in the nude. She was not willing to pose nude so they just used her head and the model's body used was that of the sculptor's wife, Elaine Eriksen. Copenhagen's famous Tivoli Garden is a colorful, beautiful place, full of lights — simply charming. There are more bikes in Copenhagen than cars, where they enjoy a very different way of life. Unfortunately, after hotel school, the relationship between Hanna and me ended.

EXPERIENCES WITH JACKY WOLF AND LA ROMANTICA

My next stop was Melide, Ticino the Italian part of Switzerland. I wrote a letter to Jacky Wolf who, according to his reputation, was a famous but crazy restaurant and hotel expert. He was just what I was looking for. In the summer of 1959, I started to work in the La Romantica, a villa at Lake Lugano. Jacky Wolf purchased the place at a fair price and transformed it into a romantic hotel, just an exquisite establishment. Famous people stayed there, including Hollywood stars, industrialists from Italy, and entertainers such as Peter Kraus, the German Elvis who actually lived close to us. There was also a famous night club with exotic dancers. One of them was Mimi — a dark-haired beauty from Germany with whom I had a fling. One night she and I went to Campione, the Italian enclave close to Melide. At 3:00 in the morning, just as we were "*learning how to speak Swiss*", there was a knock on the door and the manager of the hotel, Mr. Conti, who was married with kids, wanted to visit Mimi. He was so embarrassed and the rest of the summer season, Mr. Conti was so nice to me, I could do no wrong.

Jacky Wolf was a musician in his youth and played the violin. When we had groups arrive at the hotel, we all had to go out in the garden and welcome the guests. He would play romantic music and the employees, all in uniform, had to sing and give the guests a warm welcome. Sometimes my parents visited me. They saw me singing with my guitar in the night club, hoping I would be discovered, but it never happened.

Jacky's character deserves a few words. When he witnessed a waiter pouring the wine the wrong way, he grabbed the waiter, took him to the grill and put his arm on the grill. Once when our fish basin was broken, the plumber was called in to fix it. In the afternoon, Mr. Wolf came by and inquired if the fish basin had been fixed and I replied it had been. Then he wanted to know what was wrong with it and I replied that I was his chef, not his plumber. Boy, was that the wrong answer. He grabbed me, shook me, and looked me straight in the eyes, cursed and said that if he showed me how to hit somebody tomorrow I would know how to do it. It was a good lesson to me — from then on, I learned and listened when someone talked to me.

One night, guests ordered fish and complained because it took so long. I happened to be off that night and was down fishing at the pier. Jacky told the customer not to complain and to look at that young man fishing on the pier. He lied and said that fish is for you as our fish is the freshest you can have. On another day, some English guests walked into the garden and looked with curiosity at the trees. I asked if I could assist them and they said Mr. Wolf told him that spaghetti would grow on trees. Fast thinking, I told them that presently they are not in season, which is why you can't see them. They looked at me and said in typical British manner, "Oh, is that so".

There was an airplane crash in Belgium so Jacky Wolf started a rumor that he was in the plane and was one of the casualties. The story in Ticino got around even before the press wrote about it. He figured it was a great advertisement for La Romantica. Later we learned that he had missed the plane, which is why he was spared from the disaster. I acquired a great deal of knowledge from him, his famous fillet mignons flambé, and the Crepe Redox, a dessert. What a happy, carefree person he was. They just don't make them like him anymore. La Romantica and the time I had there will always be in my heart.

2. THE SWISS ARMY

DRAFTED INTO THE SWISS ARMY

When most people hear about the Swiss Army there are usually two things that come to mind — the Swiss Army Knife and, of course, the joke about the Swiss Navy. Having served in the Swiss Army, I think a bit of history is in order. Don't be confused by the famous Swiss Guard. The Swiss Guard is the soldiers who have served as guards at foreign European courts since the late 15th century. In addition to small household and palace units, the Swiss mercenary regiment has served as regular line troopers in various armies, notably those of France, Spain, and Naples, Italy. The Swiss were famous mercenaries for hundreds of years at a time when Switzerland was a poor country. That is contrary to today, since Switzerland is now one of the richest countries on the planet. To be a guardsman was a recognized profession where the young men often sought their fortunes abroad. The Swiss troops had a reputation for discipline and loyalty. They were considered the most effective mercenaries of the 15th century. The Papal Swiss Guard, now located in the Vatican City, was founded in 1506 and their role is like that of a body guard unit. The recruits to the guards must be Catholic, single males with Swiss citizenship, they must have completed their service in the Swiss Army, and need to have received a certificate of good conduct. They need to have a professional degree and must be between 19 and 30 years old and be at least 5 foot 8.5 inches tall. The official dress uniform is blue, red, orange, and yellow with a distinctly Renaissance appearance. After the assassination attempt on Pope John Paul II on May 13, 1981, they have been trained in unarmed combat. They use traditional weapons such as a sword and halberd as well as modern weapons such as pistols, machine pistols, and submachine guns.

The real Swiss Army operates on land, in the air, and in international waters. Under the country's military system, professional soldiers constitute about 5% of the military, the rest are conscripts or volunteers between the ages of 19-34. Because of the long history of neutrality, the Army does not take part in armed conflicts of other countries. However, it does participate in international peacekeeping missions since Switzerland is part of the NATO Partnership for peace programs.

The structure of the Swiss militia system stipulates that the soldiers keep their equipment, including all their own personally assigned weapons, at home. When I served, it also included 40 bullets. About two-thirds of young men drafted are found suitable for service; for all others, there is some alternative service available if they are not suitable. Today some women serve in the armed forces. Annually, approximately 20,000 persons are trained in basic training for a term of 18-21 weeks. This training is tough and as hard as it is grueling. While in the service, we could not wear our personal clothes, only the uniform. From hair cut to posture, everything is specified. The armed forces consist of about 135,000 people. After basic training, soldiers go for three weeks of annual training for the first few years, followed by two weeks annually for a few years, then finally only one week each year training for the last few years. Usually when a person reaches about 35, they are released from active duty. At the time of release, the soldier can keep all the gear, including weapons and ammunition. However, each soldier is still obligated to do compulsory annual shooting practice with the weapon. During peace time, the head of the armed forces is the Chief, part of the Federal Department of Defense. In time of crisis or war, the Federal Assembly elects a General. Throughout its history, Switzerland has had only four Generals. The last one was Henri Guisan from 1939-1945, during World War II. I remember him well as a kid because his photo was in all federal buildings and in most class rooms. Also, when I played military with other kids I was the self-declared General Henri Guisan.

During my conscription, Switzerland had mandatory military service for all able-bodied male citizens who are conscripted when they reach the age of majority. People are determined fit for service after satisfying physical, intellectual, and psychological requirements for military service and capable of accomplishing these services without harming oneself or others. If one is exempt from service, they have to pay 3% of their annual income tax until age 30, unless they are affected by disability.

I was 19 years old when I was drafted. I was interviewed, followed by a physical exam, then they asked me what group of the Army I wanted to join. The basic troops are considered the infantry, we used to call them the "flat foot Indians". They were not considered to be the smartest people in the world which was not really fair. We also had the Air Force and Artillery Mountain Brigade. The Brigade hiked a lot and in the winter skied. Just watch one of the James Bond movies which were filmed in Switzerland and you will understand what I am talking about. We had troops for intelligence gathering, telephone service, bridge builders, and a lake flotilla. Several sizeable lakes which lie across international borders are patrolled by a flotilla of military patrol boats. This maritime branch of the Army not only maintains the patrols but also serves in search and rescue missions. At the time I was drafted, one of the most romantic troops was the Gavallerie. They had horses and most of the members were from a farm so they brought their own horses. Our toughest elite troops were the Grenadines. They would be compared to the Marines in the United States. Most importantly, the Swiss Army can be mobilized in two hours. Each soldier had a secret envelope at home and in case of mobilization, in an emergency you would open the envelope and it would tell you where to report immediately.

When it came to my conscription choice, the officer asked me where I would like to serve. Without hesitation, I said I wanted to work in procurement. Looking at me, he asked me why this interested me. I told him I was a great chef, I would like to feed your troops, they would be happy, and I would save you a lot of money. The soldiers would like my food and morale would be high. The officer looked at me and asked me what is it you don't like to do. I answered anything mechanical, for example I hate to touch snow chains or work on a car. When I have to touch metal or car grease, I get goose bumps. The officer picked up my paper, made a stamp on it and assigned me as an artillery motor driver. He grinned and commented it was about time I learned to touch snow chains, metals, and grease. After the recruitment, I went home and literally cried at my mother's home. Just think what a total idiot he was. Rather than make the troops happy with my food and beverage expertise, he assigned me to drive a truck with soldiers in the back of the vehicle. At the beginning, I would shiver when I had to drive the truck, the responsibility weighed heavily on my mind.

Early spring 1960 came and I had to start my basic training. I was assigned to Monte Generi, a small mountain between Cadenazzo and Lugano. I used to come here with my parents and loved the Canton Ticino, it was my favorite spot. The area is so romantic with the stone houses or "rusticas"; these are little old barns or shacks which they used to store hay. Many of these rusticas have been turned into vacation homes. Ticino is a subtropical climate with lots of palm trees and exotic flowers. The Brissago Islands are two small islands located at Lake Maggiore near Ascona. In the 19th century, they were the property of an Anglo-Irishman of the St. Leger family. Richard Fleming, who was married to a Russian born lady, Antonietta, developed the gardens at a great expense. Today, the islands are the property of the Canton Ticino. Yearly, thousands of tourists visit the gardens and the palatial home. If you are in the area, a visit to the Brissago Islands is a must. So this part of the recruitment was okay with me as I was in my most favorite part of Switzerland. The first day I arrived in the military camp there were a lot of new impressions — a new environment and new faces with others who were in the same situation. It was a very memorable experience. We had to strip and get rid of our civilian clothes, which they put in a plastic bag and we said goodbye to them until the end of training. We received army clothes which included green shirts, pants, jackets, and caps, army belts, shoes, back packs, and a blanket. Needless to say, we all looked the same, the only difference between us boys was our size, weight, and posture. Nor suffice it to say we did not look like models from Ralph Lauren or Hugo Boss. Next, we received the assignment of our quarters where we were crammed 16 to 20 recruits to a room. Thanks to my mother's training, I had no problem making my bed. For others, it took hours to produce an acceptable sleeping place.

ROUTINES

I still remember the first meal we had, and of course, I had it many more times during my tenure with the army. They called it spaghetti with meat sauce, but it had more flour in it than meat, to keep it thick. The next step was to learn the basic rules (and believe you me, rules we had) such as how to speak to an officer, how to salute, how to be on time, and basic cleanliness. Each morning we were expected to be up by 6am. When the corporal called, we had 15 seconds to get out of the bed; there was no option to say just another minute or to turn over in bed. You either got up or all hell broke loose.

Within the first week, we got assigned our first vehicles. My desire was to get a Jeep but that dream was short lived. I was assigned to a Saurer truck which had a big loading bench in the back of the vehicle. Me, Hermann, the man who never had dirty hands; the man who washed his hands dozens of times a day was now forced to take over the responsibility of a big, stupid truck. Oh God, what a disaster that was. I tried to talk to an officer to get me a smaller vehicle but he said if I didn't shut up about it, I would have to take over a larger truck. I got that message real fast.

My first duty was to learn about the truck; simple things, like how to start a truck and how to drive it. I had never driven a truck in my life. I was a maniac driving and had several accidents because it was faster than I could control it. I was pretty good driving on ice with my little Renau car; I even tried driving it on two wheels. However, driving a truck was new territory for me.

The first three weeks of training was fairly routine—get up early in the morning, have breakfast, basic check of the truck, learn how to drive the truck, and then actually drive it. Changing the oil, changing tires, and installing snow chains was the worst for me. I began shivering whenever I had to touch the bloody snow chains. The only basic training that did not bother me was working with the rifle. I was very good with it and learned to be the fastest at dismantling the mechanics and mechanisms of the weapon then putting it back together. I was able to do this in 13 seconds, which was close to the record. Mr. Maucher, our corporal, always wanted to know how I did that. Mr. Maucher was a tall, lanky fellow who had a face that looked like a crater on the moon; he was full of acne and had scars all over. I always felt sorry for him, but he was a very nice man. Contrary to the other corporal, he did not abuse us and tried to provide proper leadership. He was keenly aware of my frustration with the truck.

THE THREE MUSKETEERS

There were many soldiers but for some reason the "Three Musketeers" developed. Not the ones from the famous Alexander Dumas novel, the classic tale of the soldiers who lived in the 17th century and lived on the streets of Paris and the French countryside. This was the new three Swiss Army Musketeers who lived in 1960 at the army base Monte Generi. It consisted of Fred Kocher, a good-looking fellow, me, and a third fellow named Fredy Bachman, a flamboyant young man. Fred stayed with us for the whole training, but he did not continue service after that. After the training was completed, Fred moved to Australia. I did not hear from him for years, then one day I learned that he was married and with a successful farm with a winery and still lives "down under". Fredy, the third Musketeer, and I remained musketeers and continued on to do another term to become corporals. Fredy was a year older than Fred and because I was sick the previous year, I was forced to complete my service a year later. Fredy had style and his bragging was endless. Needless to say, the three of us got along great. Fredy the man with all the answers, Fred the shy, good looking one, and me who was in between the others; kind of a mixture of both.

After three weeks of service, we got our first weekend off. We were dismissed Friday night at 4pm and did not have to be back until Sunday by 7pm. Fredy suggested that rather than make the long train ride to the German side of Switzerland, we should instead go with him to his home in Lugano, a 20-minute train ride. I inquired about what his parents would say and he laughed, explaining that his dad had been killed in World War II, when Fredy was five years old, and his mama is okay with us coming, she enjoys company. So off we went to Lugano, and Mama, as we affectionately called her, picked us up at the train station. We went to his home in Viganello where they had a large nursery with beautiful plants. Fred and I were quite impressed. Since Mrs. Bachman was a widow, she had a business partner, his name was Guseppi DeChecchi. Fredy's sister was there too, she was three years younger. The weekend was absolutely great. Out of this meeting started a wonderful relationship that lasted for years. Even today, over 50 years later, Fredy, his sister Verena, and I are still very close.

That first weekend came to an end too fast and we had to go back to our camp. The following weeks we began our exercises, including night maneuvers. We practiced moving troops, setting up cannons, and shooting them. Whenever we got time off, Fredy, Fred, and I were always together, visiting the local taverns and having a great time. When our training exercises included long walks, we would sing army songs, many in Italian. The camaraderie was fabulous with bonding that resulted in team work. We all helped each other; if one could not make it, the others were there to support them.

Many more weekends were spent at Mama's house. I felt sometimes that my mother was a bit jealous because Frau Bachman had taken a liking to me. I think she wanted me to date her daughter Vreneli, but we had our own interests. As a friend, she was great, a very nice person, but I was more interested in "bad girls". We used to say the good girls are the bad girls and the bad girls are the good girls. So for us soldiers, we were attracted to the "bad girls". Often I took Vreneli out at night, dropped her off in town to meet a friend of hers, then I went out for my own hunt, returning later in the evening to bring her home and her mama was happy.

One of our favorite places to frequent was La Canva in Lugano, a night club with dancing. Or sometimes we went to Capo San Martina, a gorgeous restaurant which had a club located on a cliff overlooking Lugano and the lake. They also had dancing and, of course, a casino in Lugano. This is how we were able to meet people, enjoy dancing, and see if we could get lucky for the evening. Fred, the good looking one, would attract the ladies, then Fredy and I would go into action. Fred was too stiff to participate.

Finally, after 12 weeks of training, we left the base camp and traveled all over the state; sometimes just one night in one place and the next night somewhere else. Often we had no place to sleep so we just slept out in the cold car. When we got lucky, we got invited by the farmers to sleep in their barns with the animals, but this was much better than freezing in the car. The good part of this type of visit was the farmers often fed us; but the very best part was when we were given Schnapps, a strong liquor that keeps you warm. Switzerland is famous for Grappa made from grapes; Kirsch, made from cherries, and Cours Zwetschgen and Pfluemli, made from prunes or plums.

One of the exercises we had to do was complete a 50 km walk in full gear, uniforms, helmet, rifles, etc. It was grueling; some of the soldiers did not make it. We had a saying, a male is not a man in Switzerland until he finished the army and completed the 50 km walk. Well, needless to say, Fred, Fredy, and I did it. We sure celebrated the next day we had off. When we had a long weekend, I would bring Fredy home to Granichen to stay with my parents. While we did many wild and crazy things, one of the best was when I challenged a friend to drive with his Jeep down a staircase in a railroad station. Not only is this a place where you're not supposed to drive, but driving down a staircase was unheard of. He accepted my challenge, rode down the staircase, and everything ended up okay; however, all hell broke out when a civilian reported it to our commander. We were lucky that Mr. Maucher stood up for us and spoke to the commander, because of that we did not have to go to jail. We always said a good soldier spends a few days in jail, so I guess maybe I was not too good a soldier because somehow I always escaped jail.

The food in the army was generally good; except we had too much cheese and that was not good for me. The number one Swiss National Army dish was "Spatz", a boiled beef, and I sure loved it. You start with a brisket of beef, salt, pepper, and herbs, add onions, chive, and boil till about two-thirds done. Then add carrots, cabbage, celery, and maybe some turnips when available. Continue cooking until done. When served with the excellent beef bouillon, tender meat, vegetables, and maybe some boiled potatoes—what a feast! Especially when out in the country, with the cold and dreary weather—you will think you're in heaven. We also had a lot of rations to eat, pre-packaged food which needed to be reconstituted. For their meat loaf, we had another name for it that I can't use right now because it is too offensive. The biscuits, chocolates, and spaghetti were in plastic envelopes which had to be heated in hot water. We had to eat this food and be prepared in the event of a nuclear attack.

The government leader at the time was obsessed with nuclear attacks. They passed a law that all newly built houses had to have a bomb shelter constructed. Existing homes and apartment buildings had to be revised to have a cellar that was to protect the citizens in case of an atomic bomb. Switzerland also has hospitals, kitchens, bakeries, sleeping quarters, etc. in the mountains and underground for protection. The general public safety is a number one issue in the country. Airplanes are parked in the mountains. Many bridges and dams are charged with dynamite so they could be blown up in case of an emergency. The reason Hitler did not attack Switzerland was because he knew the losses would be too big for the gain. The country has no ore, steel, coal, oil, or commodities, practically no natural resources. It is for this reason that the country developed into a highly technical country; producing watches, jewelry, machinery, high tech instruments. There are no moon rockets without Swiss products. Pharmaceutical companies from Switzerland are leaders in the world.

While in the army, our officers and Mr. Heizman, our training leader, had it pretty good compared to us. When we were dismissed for the weekend, they were provided with a ride to the train station. Not us, we had to run like hell about 4 km down the hill to Rivera Bironica to catch the train. It would stop specifically for us, even if it was just a village of about 1,200 people because they knew the soldiers were there to spend time visiting their families. After our war games were over, we got back to Monte Generi and by now we could all see the light at the end of the tunnel. It was time to go home and stay home. The last week of service was cleaning, cleaning, and cleaning again. I had to prepare my truck before I could return it so the next poor bastard could get it. Everything had to be in top shape. Even our own personal equipment was inspected. The inspections were more than difficult sometimes because the leaders just tried to give us a hard time. By now it was time to decide if I wanted to continue or wanted to call it quits, like Fred did. However, Fredy and I decided to go on to corporal school. It was time to say goodbye. While we were glad, our thoughts were filled with great memories, a time of fun and games. For most of us, another aspect of our life came to an end while another one was just beginning.

Fredy and I were off for four weeks before we had to report to Frauenfeld for additional training to become a corporal. Now we figured it will be our turn to give some orders. Frauenfeld is a nice town in the German part of Switzerland. Our training went well without any major problems; after all, by now we knew the basic tricks. After the training, we got off and went right back to Monte Generi. Before the new training began, I received a premonition like I often experienced in my life. I was telling Fredy, Frau Bachman, and my mother that I didn't think I would finish the 17 weeks of service. My first premonition was when I worked at La Romantica, I knew something was wrong; I just knew it, so I called home. Dad told me that Mom was in the hospital and had an emergency operation. I was not trying to be a "mentalist or fortune teller" but I just felt I would not be able to finish the training. Fredy thought I was crazy and Frau Bachman dismissed it; if she did not like something, it just did not exist in her world.

It was time for our first day of the second round of new recruits. As they arrived, more or less it was the same "spiel" which we had gone through a few months earlier, except now we were leading the new soldiers. Also, we did not have to get a vehicle ourselves, which meant less dirty hands for Hermann. We were strictly there to lead the troops. Fredy and I each had about twelve men we were in charge of, reporting to a lieutenant and our instructor, Mr. Heizman. He was a professional soldier who we knew well since we had worked with him previously. Most interesting was that our lieutenant had a great career with the Swiss Government. He moved all the way up to "Bundersrat". Switzerland has seven Bundersrat, each has a department; for example, Secretary of Defense, Secretary of State, etc. The seven Bundersrats make up the government leadership and each year a different person becomes president for one year only. They rotate that honorary position of President and are not elected by the people. Bundersrat Fillinger was a fine fellow who was a personal lieutenant for us. Nobody would have dreamed at the time that he would end up in Bern, the Capitol of Switzerland.

In our training camp, we had a cafeteria which was separate from the mess hall. There we could purchase coffee, drinks, chocolate, and goodies. There was a nice young girl and hundreds of soldiers who all had an eye on her. I told Fredy that I was going to take her out. He doubted me and said I was no "Fred", plus reminded me that I had a hundred competitors. I could not believe it myself, but we started dating and I even invited her to meet my parents during my off time on the weekends. It was fun while it lasted, but nothing lasts forever. The following weeks were routine with trips with trucks, cannons, and mountain rides. Weekends we went to see Mama and Vreneli. Fredy and I went dancing, and then back to Generi as we affectionately called the camp. The last long free weekend we had before the weeks of the war games were scheduled to begin again, we went home to see my folks. Sunday night Mother reminded me that I was wrong with my "mentalist forecast", the one predicting that I would not be participating in those exercises. I agreed with her that she was probably right as tomorrow was the big day and later that night I went back to the camp.

The next morning, I was going to rattle the troops by loudly announcing that we were going to war — but that was the last of my shouting. I got sick as a dog and was lying on the floor screaming. It took the doctor about three minutes to determine that I had appendicitis. They packed me in a Jeep and started down the winding road to Gotthard Pass, about 60 km to the city of Bellinzona. This is the capitol of the Canton Ticino, has three castles and a large hospital. Right away I was operated on and in the afternoon I woke up. I was very lucky that the appendix did not burst. The nurses here were very nice. Normally you were supposed to stay about ten days in the hospital. However, after five days I got bored. With my stitches still in, I snuck out of the hospital down to the train and visited Frau Bachman in Lugano for coffee and cake. In the early evening as I got back, the nurses informed me they were worried and had looked all over for me. I told them I was in the garden, got tired, and I took a nap on a bench so I was saved from being scolded by them. When they finally released me, I went back home.

Because I could not finish my army duty at that time, I went for a semester to a hotel school. After that I took a job as a chef in St. Moritz, a jet set resort in the Canton Graubünden. It is famous for its ski slopes, hotels, night clubs, and restaurants. It is one of the world's most famous holiday resorts. St. Moritz is chic, elegant, and exclusive, with a cosmopolitan ambiance. St. Moritz has hosted the Winter Olympics twice and is known as one of the most famous ski resorts in the world. It is the home of the Palace Hotel St. Moritz. The town has a lake. In the summer, they have famous sailing regattas. In the winter the frozen lake is well known for its horse races on the ice. Even more spectacular are the car races the rich and famous produce on the frozen lake. Porsches, Ferraris, Lamborghinis are used to race each other. They can easily crash a few hundred thousand dollar cars in an afternoon and call it fun. The rich kids like to show off.

I got a job at the Hotel La Margna. Mr. Ray was our chef, an older gentleman who has been there for years. We called him Papa Ray. The owner was a real gentleman with class, but his daughter was something else—always whining and complaining. One day she came in the kitchen whining and moaning as usual. I guess I had had enough, got mad, and tried to throw a bowl of salad at her; thankfully Papa Ray stopped me in time. I could be a "hot head" in the kitchen.

We were not supposed to ski so our work at the hotel would not be interrupted by a skiing accident. However, every afternoon I hit the slopes. It was fabulous. The beautiful white trails, the sun, the cabins with hot wine and other goodies. Just great! Early in the season I went skiing on my day off and had an accident up at Corvilla. I went to the doctor and had a cast put on my left leg. Fortunately, the cast was from my ankle halfway up to my butt, so I could walk okay. By dragging my leg, I did not miss one day of work so the chef forgave me for my mistake of going skiing. I guess he was young once, too. The winter season was great, but before they closed the hotel until the summer season, I asked Papa Ray if he could help me to get a job in America. I knew he had some connections with a famous chef in Seattle. He said he can't help, we need good people in Switzerland and presented me with a contract for the upcoming summer season. I signed the contract since everyone said how beautiful St. Moritz is in the summer.

My next step was to go back to hotel school Lucerne again for a semester. There I found my big love—her name was Therisa and her parents owned a hotel. Since she looked like she would be Asian with slanted eyes and a deep voice like a man, I called her Sui Moi. She was really nice. The first night she visited me in my room which I rented, the owner kicked us out. In 1961, you were not supposed to "shack up". We had to find a hotel at 2:00 in the morning. Our relationship was great with lots of fun and play. Sui Moi and I got very close. I met her family, which included two brothers, one who was in the oil business. The younger brother was still in school and her older sister was a stewardess with the Swiss Airlines. She was a "prima donna" traveling all over the world. I liked her parents as they were down-to-earth people.

Time came to end the school semester and I went back to St. Moritz. What a beautiful place when the weather is good. Summer season went okay at work with lots of hiking and trips to Lugano to see the Bachmans. I had a Moped and would go the four-hour trip, passing the Maloya Pass and going down through Italy to Lugano. Of course I stayed in contact with Sui Moi and for once had no other girlfriend.

At the end of the summer season, I asked Papa Ray again if he could help me to go to America. He presented the contract for the winter season, said sign here; we need good people in Switzerland. I did not sign that time and told him I would go to the US without his help. Right away he gave me the address of a contact in Seattle. I wrote to the Olympic Hotel in Seattle and asked for a job. Walter Roth, the Executive Chef, offered me a job at $17.65 a day. They would pay half my airfare but would expect me to stay with them for 18 months. Walter said we can't really hold you if you don't stay the entire 18 months; however, we had a gentleman's agreement. I thought I had died and gone to heaven. I was so excited and accepted immediately. Western International Hotels, the operator of the Olympic Hotel, helped me get a work permit, and within a few months I had a green card. When I told Sui Moi, she was not too happy. We talked about how we would run their parent's hotel one day. I had lots of ideas, how to market and promote the hotel and restaurant. She was disappointed, but I just had the urge to go to America. I said it is just a few months to learn English and then I would be back. My dad was supporting me to go and mother of course would have liked to have her boy stay in Switzerland.

Since I did not finish my training because of the illness, I had to go back the next year and finish. In the spring of 1961, I went back to Monte Generi and completed my duty. This time I was the lonely musketeer since Fred was in Australia and Fredy had finished the year before. The five weeks of training went fast with the usual army stuff without any major incidents. On my weekends, I went to Lugano to visit Mama, Fredy, and Vreneli.

3. COMING TO AMERICA

My big dream of moving to America was moving closer. It was time to go to the US Consulate in Zurich for an interview. I learned it was important to bring an x-ray of my chest with me when going through immigration in Seattle. It was hard for me to believe that being only 22 years old I now had the chance to visit "the land of opportunity, the land of milk and honey" as we called it in Switzerland. It was a country where everybody would be rich or at least they lived like they were rich. America was a dream land for most Europeans at that time. We regarded it as the almighty power on the planet under the leadership of John F. Kennedy.

In early 1963, I received my green card and was ready to book my flight to Seattle. Sui Moi and I enjoyed some vacation time together and spent the last evening with my parents. It was April 23, 1963. Sui Moi, my parents, and I went to Zurich airport which was under construction. Today, more than 54 years later, they are still building the airport and it's still under construction. My flight was from Zurich to London by Swiss Air, then I flew via Pan Am over the North Pole to Seattle. Flying today is certainly quite different from 1963. Women wore dresses and most men were in coat and tie, including me. We also had much more space to our seats, the service was excellent with real china and silverware, cloth napkins, plus they offered free liquor and wine. The cabin crew was attractive and neatly uniformed. After the ten and a half hour flight from London, we got ready to land. I got scared because when I looked down and saw the big airfield, I thought we had missed the airport. Later I learned that it was the Boeing Airfield that we had passed. The immigration process in Seattle was relatively quick, although I was a bit apprehensive. I knew my x-ray would show a scar on my lung from the tuberculosis I had as a kid. When I handed the envelope to the Immigration Officer, he looked at me and asked what this was. I told him and he looked at me like I had lost my mind. He grabbed the envelope and dropped it in the garbage without even opening it. A feeling of great relief came over my entire body.

I remember my first day in America like it was yesterday, even though it was more than 54 years ago. I slept in the plane so I was wide awake, even due to a time difference of nine hours. As I got off the plane I was picked up by Joe Heudorf, the Sous Chef of the Olympic Hotel. He was driving a red Buick convertible which impressed me because I figured he must be rich. The check-in at the hotel was efficient and friendly, with a very nice room. Since I had been flying all day, I thought I should go for a walk. It was the first time in my life that I was in a city with square blocks. I walked down toward the water from 5th Street to 1st Avenue. How was I to know 1st Avenue at the time was skid row. Every few yards I saw someone laying or sitting on the floor. They saw me in my suit and asked if I would give them a nickel for a cup of coffee. Of course, I thought, sure, no problem. Within a few minutes I was short $2.00. The problem was I only had $200 when I arrived and barely spoke any English. Oh, my God, I thought, I just arrived in the richest country in the world and everybody is begging. I learned fast though and the next fellow who asked me for a dime, I told him to go to work like me, then he could buy his own coffee. After this experience, I went back to the hotel and was asked to go to the Grill Room and enjoy dinner. I ordered a ham steak with French fries. I did not know what a ham steak was but I ordered it because it was the cheapest item on the menu at $2.90, including salad. Later I went to bed and slept like a baby; slept two hours and cried for twenty minutes, slept two hours and cried for twenty minutes.

The next day I reported to the kitchen. My first impression was so different from the crews I was accustomed to working with in Switzerland. There every person was a Caucasian. In Seattle we had whites, blacks, Indians, Mexicans, Puerto Ricans, a lot of Asians, West Indians from Alaska—a total mixture of cultures. The white chefs were mostly from Switzerland or other Europeans. I was directed to go to the Accounting Office and register as a new employee where I had to fill out only three forms for Social Security, taxes, and payroll information. Today, thanks to our fine geniuses in Washington, DC, we have close to twenty forms to complete. Back in the kitchen, Joe Huedorf said to go over to the butcher, get some fresh bones, and make a demi glace. I knew what a demi glace was and how to make it; however, where is the kettle to roast the bones, where would I find the mirepoix (that is the vegetable you need such as onions, carrots, celery, etc.). I figured I would get an organized introduction to my job, but I was faced with disappointment. The introduction was what we would say in Switzerland as *"bird eat or die"*. In America, I later learned it's called *"sink or swim"*. The end of that first day couldn't come too soon; I was ready to go to bed and rest. The next day before my shift began, I started to look for a place to stay. Walking around Seattle I saw a lot of signs that said, "Apt. for Rent" I thought Mr. Apt. must be a rich man, he has so many houses. Later I learned "Apt. for Rent" is a place you rent and stay. Some of the other Swiss fellows told me that an old lady on Cherry Street had some rooms for rent. I went to see her and got a room for $25 a month. Silvio, one of my Swiss coworkers, lived there, too. After I received my first paycheck, I put $175 under my mattress. I figured that would be my traveling money to go home in case it didn't work out for me. Since I only planned to be in America for 18 months, I did not buy a TV, not much at all except clothes and just the minimum I needed. The rest of the money I saved. After all, I only had $200 to start with when I came here. I worked for two weeks, either from 6am to 2pm or from 2pm to 10pm. While in Europe, you worked 8am to about 2pm then three hours to rest and you came back 5pm to 10pm. With my new American hours, I thought it was a waste of my time, so I got a second job at the Seattle Town and Country Club, which was a piece of cake. The Chef was a German fellow and in my opinion not a very good chef. He bought mostly convenience food and was a "world champion" at opening cans, fixing pre-fab food, tearing open food boxes, preparing convenience foods, and defrosting frozen food. It was unbelievable to me. I was used to making everything fresh, including mayonnaise, sauces, vanilla crème, consommé, bullion, soups, whatever it was, I was accustomed to preparing it fresh. This included even cutting fresh potatoes for French fries. I figured Otto, that was the chef's name, thought that as long as customers are happy, it did not matter that we served this crap. However, Otto made the most fantastic desserts by buying pre-fab food. He would put it together like a master pastry chef. Altogether, the time I spent with Otto was good. We got along well as he needed some European support and I made some extra money working this second job.

Working at the Olympic Hotel had become fantastic for me. I could learn so much and each day I learned something new. Because I did not speak much English, my work was in the Main Kitchen. One night, because one of the fellows was sick, I had to work in the Marine Room, one of the restaurants. Me, the European trained chef, extremely conscientious, I felt so lost. A waitress came with an order for Prime Rib, a baked potato with chives, sour cream, and bacon. Then a server had an order for apple pie with cheddar cheese toasted. I almost cried. I had no clue what these people were talking about; never heard of baked potatoes with sour cream, bacon, and chives. Who the hell would put cheddar on apple pie? They had to take me out of the room and replace me with someone else. It was so humiliating and embarrassing for me. All the chefs wondered what I had done now because they knew the General Manager was looking for me. Bob Lindquist, the General Manager, was telling me that he was flying first class with Swiss Air and the stewardess, Heidi, was serving him. When they made small talk, he found out that I was currently working at the Olympic Hotel. Heidi was the sister of Sui Moi. What a small world it is. Bob always remembered me during my career with Westin and has always been fond of me.

Another unusual experience for me was when I was drafted by the US Army. I got my advice from the Swiss boys on how to behave so I would not qualify. I went to the draft office where we were all asked to sit in a large room. I brought a Swiss Newspaper and was reading when a sergeant came over and shouted, "Gaemeter, Gumeter, Gamter." I knew he meant me, but did not react. He then came to me and asked me what my name was. In a very heavy Swiss accent, I said Hermann Gammeter and he told me to come with him. We had to fill out some forms and I acted like I could not understand so he helped me and filled out the paperwork for me. He asked me what my mother's name was and I said yes. Again, he asked me what my mother's name was, and again I said yes. So very slowly he said, "YOUR MOTHER'S NAME." I looked at him and said, "Yes, mother me, my mother yes, she is Switzerland." After that, the officer gave up and sent me to the next stop with Dr. Traying to check my eyesight. As I read the chart I pronounced the letters in German rather than English, i.e. E is Ehh, and a is Ahh. The officer looked at me and said, "Next one, this one is dumb." We then were all asked to undress, bend over and the doctor checked us out. Everyone else was naked and there I stood in the room fully dressed. The officer came and told me to show him my ass. I looked at him and said, "I no have." By now they had enough of me and took me out of the room and told me to wait. After about an hour, a gentleman came by and in broken German explained to me that I did not qualify. My category was 1Y, which meant slightly retarded, the same classification as Cassius Clay.

He continued and explained that I would be given another chance in a year or so. Shortly after his apology and announcement that I did not qualify, I left the room and went into the mess hall. There were young people who wanted to be in the army because they had no jobs. One of them cried because he did not make it. I felt so bad for him. But my plan was to stay in the US for 18 months. After all, I had just finished the Swiss Army so why should I go back in the army again. At that time, many of the young soldiers were being sent to Vietnam. Boy, was I glad that was over.

Back at the Olympic Hotel, our Executive Chef was Walter Roth, the fellow who brought me over to America. He was a crazy man, drinking too much, but he was one of the best professionals I had ever met. Walter was so inventive and had a new idea every minute. He would put on the greatest banquets and parties. One time we had to make a special presentation for a sports fishing company. Walter set-up a pond with a little boat in the ball room and he had an Indian sit in the boat and pretend to fish. The fresh caught fish would then be cooked on the side table. The buffets he orchestrated with lights, fountains, and with fantastic decorations. We had chafing stations and I always enjoyed working in front of the public; what a pleasure it was for me. However, it was also agonizing and often I said I was going back to Europe tomorrow. These Americans are heathens; no class, no style. They came to the buffet line, in one hand a cigarette and a martini. I presented nice carved beef or fish or whatever, and then they put sauerkraut, cheese, Jell-o, and a vegetable on top. What a mess. What a bunch of uneducated peasants they were. What I did not think about at the time was that they were paying my salary.

Walter was something else when he was drunk. Nothing could stop him from how he misbehaved or from what he would say. One time he was going to throw a room service table out the window. When he had a new steward in the kitchen and he was unhappy with him, he shouted that he should be made a General Manager as he will never be able to be a good steward. In the afternoon, Walter would go down to the butcher and stamp the beef sides and other big pieces of meat. He would only accept deliveries of meat that he had personally selected and stamped. One day I was with him and he started to drink. He began to tell me how stupid I was, that it would take three years until I would have an idea of what America was all about. I just figured he's crazy and drunk. I had just finished my apprenticeship as number one in the state, I had finished hotel school as number three, and finally had completed my army service. I was so, so, so smart why would it take me three years for me to figure out what America was all about. In reality, I must say it took me five years to get the pulse and feeling of what was going on in American business. The lesson, learned later on, was that you are not as smart as you think you are. Today, I have come to the conclusion that the more I know, I realize how little I know. My conclusion was being humble pays off.

Another unusual experience with Walter was a dinner with President Eisenhower. After the gala, Eisenhower wanted to thank the people who put on the event. When Walter met Eisenhower as he was being introduced, the President jokingly said, "Well, another foreigner." Walter took it wrong. He looked at Eisenhower and said, "You sure don't look like a god damn Indian to me," meaning Eisenhower was a foreigner, too.

One afternoon I went meat stamping with Walter and he started his drinking program. He got meaner and meaner. Finally, he looked at me and said, "Hermann, you are a dumb bell, stupid, don't know anything, you are fired." I was so crushed and disappointed, I went home and told Hans Mueller, who also was a Swiss, that I had been terminated. He told me not to worry, that I would find another job in Seattle. The next day when I did not report to work, I got a phone call and Walter was on the other line. He wanted to know where I was, if I was sick or else why I had not come to work. I informed him that he had fired me yesterday. Walter's comment was not to believe what people say after a few whiskeys. Happy and elated, I ran down to the Olympic Hotel and went back to work. This is how creative and innovative Walter was. One night we sat at the dinner table in the kitchen. The Catering Manager came by and said we have to come up with a very special dinner for the visit of the Italian Ambassador from Washington, DC. Walter looked at the oblong sugar holder that was on the table. His idea was to take the sugar holder and on the bottom we put in some green spinach mousse, then a mousse of white fish. Next was a red tomato mousse, and at the end of the sugar holder, we put a shrimp that we shaped round. This way we had a food item that looked like a gondola representing Venice and the colors of the dish represented the Italian flag. Walter was extremely creative. He came up with something new in a New York minute. His creativity is why he was able to get away with his crazy behavior; the managers, hotel vice presidents, etc. all knew of his capabilities. The eighteen months I spent at the Olympic were fantastic from a professional stand point; I learned so much.

Now as far as my private life was concerned—that was a blast, too. We had a group of Swiss guys and ladies. We did a lot together. Every Saturday night there was a dance in the Swiss Club. At midnight, there was no more alcohol service until Monday at 6am. Shortly before midnight, we purchased some extra beers. One night I got two bottles of beer and opened them. I was wearing a sports shirt that had two pockets on the chest, which is where I stored my beers. I went over to this girl, bowed to her in the European manner to ask her to dance. The beer poured all over her. She looked at me, said no thank you and said she better go to the restroom and clean up and maybe we could dance the next weekend.

That reminds me about a relationship I had during my first few months in America. Not speaking much English, it took me ten minutes with hand and feet to figure out that we would meet at 8:00 at a certain café downtown. Her name was Dee; she was from Scotland and a few years older than me. Dee worked for Saint-Gobain Company, a large French organization from France. She was Administrative Assistant to the boss in the Seattle offices. She was quite well educated and I was the kid who just got off the boat. For some reason, we hit it off well. For months while we were dating, I picked her up from work. When we got home I cooked for her, which she loved, and we both enjoyed our evenings together. Dee was responsible for me learning English. For hours, I would watch TV shows such as Greatest Show on Earth with Jack Palance, who was one of my heroes. Others were the Patty Duke Show, Leave It to Beaver, The Saint, Ed the Talking Horse, Beverly Hillbillies, and many more. At that time, most of the shows were still in black and white.

For Thanksgiving, we went to see Dee's Aunt and Uncle. Roy and Eve were their names and their young daughter, Carol. It was a fascinating experience for me; first to learn about Thanksgiving, but also because Roy and Eve acted as the perfect hosts. Roy was in the Canadian Army. He had one of his uniforms with the red jacket and the bush head gear like they have at the Tower of London. Then Roy took me to an Indian Reservation, that was the highlight of my trip. I saw real Indians, with feathers, dressed in Indian clothes, etc. Today looking back, I must say these people were poor, smoking, drinking, sitting around lazy, and looking forward to being supported by the government. Dee and I had a nice relationship for a long time which ended when I went back to Europe. While dating Dee, I received a letter from Sui Moi telling me that she had gotten married to a Dutch fellow. While I was crushed, life had to go on. Later I learned she was divorced after only two years.

Out of all the Swiss fellows I worked with, I had two special friends. One was Hans Mueller. He was 20 years old and could not legally drink, but he had a fake ID. We did a lot of bar-hopping together. One night we sat at a bar on First Avenue. Next to me sat an Eskimo woman and we both kept drinking. I was on my soap box telling her how I disliked America; that the people had no culture and they were all peasants. After a while I guess she had had enough. She looked at me and said, "Where do you come from, Sonny." She said, "Why the f--- don't you go back to where you came from." Boy I felt like I had been hit over the head with a 2x4. I suddenly realized that 350 million people don't have to adapt to me and that I had better change my tune and adapt to the people in the country where I'm currently living. Instantly, I became an American.

My other friend was Beat Richei, a wonderful young man, stable, smart, and a good worker. He had his feet on the ground, contrary to my craziness. Beat had a car and a boat and loved outdoor living. I figured I would not be staying in America more than 18 months, then I would go back to the old country, marry Sui Moi, and run her father's hotel. So why should I purchase a car. I would rather save my money. Whenever I went with Beat, I would pay for the gas. At the time, it was 32 cents a gallon and cigarettes cost about the same, although I did not smoke. Beat and I were really buddies, good buddies. We went skiing together at Chrystal Mountain and White Pass Mount Baker. For only $5.00 we had an all-day pass. What an experience that was. In the summer, we ran all over Lake Washington with Beat's boat. Seattle, when the weather is nice, is gorgeous; but when it rains, it really rains. The whole Northwest is like Switzerland with mountains, lakes, and fantastic vegetation. I will never forget all the nice trips Beat and I made.

Also, I must say he always protected me. Upon my arrival, the American chefs played tricks on me. I loved Walgreens and would go there 4-5 times a week, have my cup of coffee, and study the world. One chef told me once that I should bring him some candy bars and that I should tell the sales girl that you want chocolate bars for boys, the ones with nuts. When I did, the sales lady got mad at me; I had no clue why. It was Beat who explained the joke they played on me. Hans Mueller and I went to the taverns together to have our beer. I would sit at the bar for hours with one beer. They had a special glass called a scooner. A beer was only 25 cents. Contrary to Hans, Beat was not one to go in a bar or tavern and hang out. He would rather go home, read a book, or work on his car or boat. Beat and I drove all over Washington, visited county fairs, and went boating. Seattle has what is called the Sea Fair in the summer. The festivities include hydroplane races, parades, farm product shows, and exhibits. There was also a large park with all the carousels and rides. I will never be able to thank Beat enough for what he did for me as a young lad during my first few months spent in America. Thank God, our paths crossed again later in life.

In the summer of 1964, there was talk of a new hotel in Los Angeles, called the Century Plaza. All the best people at Western International were supposed to go and work there. It was the biggest investment the company had ever made. At the same time, they were also stepping out of Western's usual league and comfort zone, as most of the hotels up to this date were in the northwest, Canada, and Alaska. Walter said I should go there where he will be appointed the Executive Chef at this new property and Beat was to join Walter as well. Henry Mulligan was supposed to be the General Manager, a young up and coming hotelier who at the time was the General Manager of the Space Needle in Seattle. I told Walter I would be going back to Switzerland in the fall. He said for me to come to Los Angeles in 1966 when the Century Plaza would open, but I was not convinced.

Then one day Walter asked if I would be interested in going to work on a private yacht. An oil company was looking for a young chef who had to cook three meals a day for four people; the boss of the company, the captain, a deck boy, and myself. The yacht was a Grand Banks and the salary would be $750 a month. Without hesitation, I accepted the job. So, in August 1964 we took off with our boat, which was the lead ship, then there were three other boats; a dynamite boat and two accessory boats with laboratories. Our job was to go out in the ocean and look for oil. The dynamite boat would explode dynamite in the ocean and they would check to see if there was oil in the water. The horrible result was the resulting dead fish that came floating up around after each explosion. The most beautiful salmon and other fish were killed with these experiments. One night we were in a horrible storm and I was so terribly seasick, I thought it was killing me. I wanted to die and if I had had a gun that day, I think I would have shot myself. Most of the people on all four ships were sick, except our captain who just stood there smoking his pipe and grinning. He told us not to worry, that he had gone through many storms in his life — it's just part of life on the high seas. When we finally got on land the next day, my legs were still shaking and I felt as though I was still moving while standing on the solid ground.

One day I visited the dynamite boat where one of the guys was smoking a cigarette. I knew we had 10,000 lbs. of dynamite on board and I asked him if he ever had an accident with his job. He smiled at me and said, "Son, in my job you have only one accident in life and then you're gone." All this while, he continued smoking his cigarette. I could not wait to get back to our yacht. My time during the oil exploration was great except one time when I was hitchhiking and I met a former Korean veteran who told me about killing people, which I will write about later. What a job I had cruising the Pacific Ocean, cooking three meals a day for four people. Luckily, I was able to save most all of my money earned since my time on the yacht included room and board. We visited many ports at night and went to the pubs with the deck man; we had a super time. However, all good things must come to an end. We made the trip back to Seattle and my next adventure was to plan my journey through the United States.

4. FAR AWAY — STILL SO CLOSE

Most Europeans who immigrated to the United States eventually lost touch with the homeland. I knew many who would write home once a year or not even that often. Most of the immigrants in the early years, after the turn of the century, never went back. For example, like my uncle who moved to Australia and never returned to Switzerland. Often Swiss people would say they forgot to speak German, French, or Italian. These are the three national languages of Switzerland; actually we have a fourth language, which is Romanisch. There are only about 250,000 people who speak Romanisch; mostly they are the older people who live in the Canton Graubünden. The language is a mixture of German, Italian, and Latin. It sounds funny to me although I can understand a few words of it because I lived in Lenzerheide Valbella and St. Moritz. All the laws in Switzerland are published in three languages and the money is written in German, Italian, and twice in French; I never knew why it is printed in French twice. Most of the population speaks German, then French, and Italian and finally just a few speak Romanisch. Once I remember a Romanisch speaking ski instructor would say if he caught that cook from the Post Hotel who always scares his girls on skis, he will hit him over the head. Luckily for me, he never caught me.

Beat Richei is another one who kind of lost touch with home. He only went to visit his parents about once every three or four years. Walter only went home about every five to six years, even though he still had quite a few relatives living there. Another who kind of lost touch with the homeland was Tony Ruegg, a real nice, humorous man. He said he still owns a cow in Switzerland and goes to the farmer who pays him for the milk. Tony acted like he was dumb, but he actually was very street-smart you could say. He suggested the next time we planned to go to Zurich we should rent a car, then dress in a chauffeur's uniform and wear a driver's hat. In Aargau, where I originally came from, he would drive and I would sit in the back of the car. When we went to the area of Zurich which was Tony's home, he would sit in the back and I would wear the uniform and play the driver. Thus, anyone who saw us would admire the two rich American kids. However, we never did actually do it as it was not my "cup of tea". Tony, though more unassuming than he looked, had more of an interest in the stock market than in cooking, even though he was an excellent chef. He was a real wheeler dealer and always had something going on the side.

Like I said, so many immigrants lost touch with the old country; but for all the years I was gone, I constantly stayed close to home. I guess one reason that helped was I wrote to my parents every single day, if only one or two paragraphs. Basic things that had happened during the day or week and experiences I had. I kept then updated about my work, which of course was extremely interesting to my parents. Every day I wrote and on Saturday I would mail the letter to my parents. Back in Europe, my mom did the same thing, daily she would write in a journal, about her neighbors, local or national politics, or about the price of milk—just whatever was happening. She wrote me with news about a neighbor who was sick or had passed away. Through the intense communication, we stayed close as a family and kept united with each other. Another way I kept connected with my family was each year I went home for vacation; no matter where I lived, I made a trip. Sometimes I went two or three times the same year. Mom had saved all my letters in an office file and had them sorted year by year. The only letter I ever received from my dad was when I sent him $100. He wrote to tell me that he got 4.32 Swiss Francs for each US Dollar. Today you get 99 cents Swiss money for a dollar; that's an indication of how the world has changed. Our leaders all over the world do not do what is right but what brings them votes to keep them in power. The waste in our government is atrocious. This happens not only in America but all over the world, plus the cheating and favoritism. A lot of what can be described as "you scratch my back, I'll scratch yours". Then the baloney about political correctness is another huge waste. But since I cannot control it, I try not to worry about it.

My vacations in Europe are priceless. The time we spent with our kids in Switzerland and Austria is memorable and the opportunity to see the enjoyment their grandparents experienced cannot be described. In Granichen, we usually went jogging and the girls would follow me on their bikes. We went hiking in the mountains with fresh air and pastures full of cows — just outstanding. We also had many relatives and they all wanted to see me and the kids so they could spoil them. Back in those days, the milkman came every day by the house with a car and a shop inside. The kids could not wait to go with Grosi, as they called my mother, their grandmother; Grosi is slang for Grandma in Swiss. Mom would put her wallet in her bra to hide it. Christina would ask her grandmother in broken German why she put your money on her chest and she said it was to keep it safe and she would know she still had it. The garden at Mom's home was nice, with fruit trees, vegetables, grapes, and flowers. Having grown up on a farm, Mom was an outstanding gardener. The kids would enjoy playing in the garden where Christina would take snails and put them on her chest and let them crawl up her body to see which one was the fastest.

In Austria, their grandparents were called Oma and Opa, who were wonderful people. They had gone through an awful lot during the war and were thus very appreciative of not only their lives but for whatever they had. We were fortunate whenever we were in Europe to make the trip to visit them by car so the kids could spend half their time in Switzerland and half in Austria.

Over the years with all the moves I had with our company, in each city I would join the Swiss Club, which kept me close to home. Some of the clubs are fabulous and the camaraderie is great. It keeps you connected. The most elaborate Swiss Club I was involved with was the club in Singapore. This club was founded by a rich Swiss donating a large piece of land with the stipulation that it could only be used for the purpose of establishing a Swiss club. The club was founded in1871 by Otto Alder and his friends. At that time, the land was inexpensive, but today the land itself would be worth millions. The club has a bowling alley, 300-meter shooting range, swimming pool, tennis courts, and play grounds. It is an enormous estate. Something a developer can only dream of. Thank God it is protected forever. What fun it was to see the Chinese and Malay chefs cooking Swiss food such as Swiss hash browns, minced veal in cream sauce with mushrooms, noodles, and boiled Swiss beef. There was no difference in their presentation of these dishes than from the same dishes served in one of the finest restaurants in Zurich.

Switzerland has what is called the Fifth Parliament. It is an organization to represent the Swiss abroad. They meet twice a year, usually in the spring they meet in Bern, the Swiss Capital. The meetings include food that is excellent. All meals are served in up-scale hotels or specialty restaurants or in castles with famous and elegant banquet rooms. White and red wines are normally served. The members of the Swiss Parliament are selected by the Consul General of the foreign country then they are elected by the Swiss who live in the area. Each country has members according to the population who live in that country. The United States for example has six delegates and I was chosen as a delegate for many years. The delegates are assigned according to the geographic area of the country. Programs around the world which we were working on were finances, Swiss schools, Swiss Clubs, Swiss charities in foreign countries, programs for or to help Swiss people who are stranded in an emergency, or summer camps where kids spend several weeks in Switzerland each year. First time I participated for about eight years and then three years later I was again selected as a delegate for six years. I am fortunate to be able to meet so many executives from around the world. Many delegates have to be financially sound as the delegate is required to bear the cost for participating. Although each delegate receives 100 Swiss Francs per meeting, this would not even cover the cost for meals, much less lodging or airline flights. It is definitely a financial commitment to participate in the Fifth Parliament program. My reason for giving up my parliament duties was because I was retiring. The involvement of the Swiss Abroad Organization is another reason I stayed close to home. Although I was Swiss, in general my friends were mostly Americans or people from other European countries. I knew to be successful you needed to be international and not just Swiss oriented. One last point I would like to make about my closeness to Europe and America of course is the fact that I lived in Europe, then the US, then back to Europe, back to the US. After retirement, Audrey and I would spend six months in the summer at Lake Lucerne and the six winter months in Atlanta. I will go into more detail about these adventures later.

5. MY 1964 TRIP HOME

After the cruise trip, we went back to Seattle where I picked up my suitcase and clothes that I had left with Dee. Then my big tour started from Canada down to Mexico, straight across the country, then back up north to New York. At the time, I decided I would travel mostly by hitchhiking or by Greyhound Bus at night. Very simple since I was from the Israeli or Scottish side of Switzerland and felt this was most economical. Hitchhiking was free and Greyhound Bus traveled at night so I had no costs for a hotel room and I could sleep on the bus.

The first leg was on the boat Princess Margaret from Seattle to Victoria, Canada, the most charming little city you can imagine, with hanging flower pots all over the city. They had a fascinating idea invented by the tourist board which enabled a visitor to take different tours throughout the city. They had lines of different colors painted on the pavement and whatever tour you selected, all you had to do was follow the color chosen. Two distinctive attractions in Victoria stand out in my memory. One was the Empress Hotel and the other was the Butchart Gardens. The hotel is located at Government Street, facing the inner harbor. It is an iconic symbol for the city. The Edwardian Francis Rattenburgh was commissioned by Canadian Pacific Hotels. As a terminus hotel for the Canadian Pacific Steamship Line, construction of the hotel began in 1904 and was completed in 1908. The property played hostess to kings, queens, movie stars, and many other famous and infamous people. The hotel had several great restaurants and banquet facilities. It was very elegant and fancy I must say when I was there in 1964; however, I felt that it required quite a lot of money to bring it back to its former glory. It looked tired and was missing a good manager who could provide some TLC — tender loving care.

As I said previously, the other place that caught my attention was Butchart Gardens. In my younger days, I had seen many elaborate gardens, mostly when I visited castles or parks in Europe, but this one was something else. It is easy to understand why Butchart Gardens is a tourist attraction, not just in Victoria but in the whole Canadian West. Over a million tourists visit this site each year. Robert Pim Butchart (1856-1943) and his wife, Jennie (1866-1950), who owned a cement manufacturing company, moved to Western Canada because of the area's rich limestone deposits which are necessary in the production of cement. From what I can determine, they must have made an enormous amount of money at that time. There was a great deal of construction going on with building commercially as well as residentially. In 1907, a 65-year old garden designer from Yokohama, Japan, Mr. Isaburo Kishida was summoned to Victoria to build a tea garden. This garden became widely popular, which attracted people to view it. Several prominent citizens, among them Jennie Butchart, commissioned Mr. Kishida to build Japanese Gardens. In 1909, when the limestone had been exhausted, Jennie felt she would turn the sunken area left from the limestone excavations into a garden. This first garden's work was completed in 1921. It was at this time they decided to receive guests who enjoyed admiring the gardens. Later, the Butchart's decided to reinvent their tennis courts and turned them into an Italian garden. Their next decision was to renovate their kitchen's vegetable garden which resulted in a fabulous rose garden. Their home was renamed "Benvenuto" which in Italian means "welcome". While getting older in 1939, the Butchart's decided to make a great gift to their grandson Ian Ross (1918-1997) and gave the gardens to him. Ross was involved in the operation and promotion of the

Butchart Gardens until his death 58 years later. The development and expansion of the gardens continued under his leadership. The ownership of this botanical jewel remains in the Butchart family to this day. The great granddaughter, Robin Lee Clark, is currently the Managing Director. Should you ever visit Western Canada, a visit to Victoria's Empress Hotel and Butchart Gardens is a must.

The next leg on my trip was to Portland, Oregon. Walter Roth gave me the names of people who I should visit along the way. As my reference, Walter contacted some of the people and told them I was a young Swiss chef whom he would appreciate hosting should I come by. In Portland, I had lunch at the Benson Hotel, another Western property, where the General Manager was my host. The Benson was founded in 1913 and is another great European style hotel with a fine reputation. In 1964, the famous London Grill was known all over the Northwest. While traveling Highway 1 down the coast, I found it to be one of the most scenic highways in the world. Along the way are quaint fishing villages, entertainment parks, restaurants, boutiques, and shops. People were strolling, walking, bike riding—it was just lovely. The magnificent Pacific Ocean, the cliffs, Monterey, and Carmel are all breathtaking. Americans probably may not realize it, but they don't have to go to Europe to see beautiful scenery—they have it all right here in the good old USA.

While hitchhiking south on Highway 5 below Portland, a police car stopped and the officer asked where I was going. I told him my destination was San Francisco. He gave me a puzzled look and told me I was not allowed to hitchhike on Interstate highways. He inquired this time as to where I was from and when I said Switzerland he gave me another funny look, then told me to climb into his car. He began driving further south while we enjoyed a very interesting conversation. He wanted more information about my homeland and he told me his father had been stationed in Germany during the war. The time flowed very fast because of our intense conversation, but eventually he stopped the car. He said I had to get out of "his taxi" because the sign in front of us said "California" and that is where his jurisdiction ended. I could not believe it; this policeman drove me almost the whole length from Washington through Oregon to California. What a deal I had. I learned that day not all cops are bad. Because of this event, all my life I have had a great respect and affection for law enforcement. Through my work with the Rotary Club and other organizations, I have continued to support them.

The trip continued south and my eyes opened wide when I saw the Golden Gate Bridge for the first time. Luckily for me, it was an incredibly beautiful day with the blue Pacific Ocean and the red bridge with the city of San Francisco in the background. Later on in life, I had the pleasure of living and working there so just a few remarks from my 1964 trip to the "city by the bay".

I went to the St. Francis Hotel on Union Square. There were people everywhere since the Democratic National Convention took place there. With "McGovern for President" signs hanging all over the place. This was my first exposure to American politics and I thought it was more like a three-ring circus. Not having been exposed to politics previously, I once asked my dad when I was about 10 years old what politics was. He simply looked at me and explained that it is the art of lying. While at the St. Francis Hotel, I asked for the Executive Chef, Clovis Soubrand. He knew from Walter I would be coming and he was truly something else; trying to show off, he gave me a tour of the hotel. When he introduced a secretary, he would make a comment, addressing her as honey and asking her if she had a date that weekend. Each following woman would get the same greeting. I was not even embarrassed as I did not know at the time what he meant by these rude comments. In the main kitchen, he prepared the following fabulous meal for me:

CELERY VICTOR

Wash large stalks of celery. Make a chicken stock in the usual manner with carrots, onions, bay leaves, parsley, salt and whole pepper. Place celery in the pot and boil until soft. Allow to cool in the broth. When cold, press the broth out of the celery gently with hands and place on a plate. Season with salt and pepper, chervil and add wine tarragon vinegar and olive oil.

TOURNEDOS VAUDEVILLE

Season two small tournedos (filet of beef) with salt and pepper, then broil the beer or sauté in a pan with butter. When done, place on a platter, lay on each a fresh warm poached egg. Garnish the plate with stuffed tomatoes. Cover the tournedos with a Sauce Madere, which is a brown sauce with Madeira wine flavor. Serve with a side dish of rice, noodles, or potatoes.

COUPE ST. JACQUES

Slice some fresh fruits, such as oranges, pineapples, pears, and bananas, add fresh berries in season. Put in a bowl with sugar and add Kirshwasser or Maraschino. Let it stand for about 2 hours then fill a coupe glass about half full with the fruit and fill the remainder with two kinds of sorbet raspberry and lemon. Smooth the top with a knife. Decorate with some fruit and whipped cream. This is a real classic which I made hundreds of times during my apprenticeship.

Across from the St. Francis Hotel up Powel Street a short distance was the Hotel St. Francis Drake, another Western Hotel. With the legendary cable cars running in front of the hotel, crossing the street could prove to be dangerous. In front of the hotel were the regally red-suited beefeater doormen who extended a warm welcome to each arriving guest. I met with Mr. Plant, the General Manager who reminded me of an English Lord. Although a very nice gentleman with a busy schedule, unfortunately his time was limited to a short meeting with the new Swiss boy. He invited me to lunch in their fancy dining room and took care of the check. He also told me to go up to the Starlite Room at night where there was dancing, the epitome of a romantic night club. The lights of the city below, the fabulous view, and the music all made me feel as though I had died and gone to heaven, especially when the band played Tony Bennett's famous song "I Left My Heart in San Francisco".

The next day I took the opportunity to visit the city. To ensure I did not miss anything, I took a guided tour of China Town, Fleishhacker Zoo, and the beaches, the sea cliffs with the seals, a Japanese garden, and Fisherman's Wharf, plus many other wonderful sights. To this day, San Francisco remains my favorite city.

From the cultural city of San Francisco, the tour also showed me the gaudy, flashy, illuminated city in the middle of the desert—Las Vegas. Wow, what a place I thought. I had heard all the horror stories about people losing all their money there so my number one rule was right away, no gambling. The enticements were great and tempting; I made use of some of them but made sure I did not gamble. For example, they would give you a free roll of nickels to start gambling. I would put two or three nickels in the slot machine when they watched me and the rest of the money went into my pocket. I did this in several hotels. They also gave out free drinks, which I gladly accepted, along with some places that even served free sandwiches. At night, I slept in the park which was clean, warm, and most importantly, free. The only money I spent was to see some shows. Having been a trumpet player myself, I just had to go to the Harry James Show. These shows were overwhelming to me, someone who had never seen something like this before in my life. Again, later in life I visited Las Vegas many times, even went recruiting there for college students for our management program at work.

Driving through the Mojave Desert, my journey took me next to Los Angeles, the so called "City of Angels". While moving through the desert toward Los Angeles, because I had heard so much about Death Valley, I did not dare travel by hitchhiking. I was scared to be stuck out there alone so I wisely decided to splurge and spend the money on a Greyhound Bus ticket. This time however, while traveling during the day, I could not sleep on the bus. Again, my experience was a very different, interesting trip. Although we sometimes regard the desert as hopeless, unpleasant, hot and stinky, I was delighted to see desert flowers, cactus, desert animals, and many colorful areas which were fascinating to me.

Arriving in Los Angeles was yet another surprise waiting for me. The huge highways and the large size of the city were unbelievable. The three days I had to spend there were a marathon from morning to night; so much to see—so much to do. I visited places such as Disneyland, Knottsberry Farm, Sunset Strip, Santa Monica Beach, and Beverly Hills. I saw movie stars with funny cars; one even had the horns of a bull on the hood of the car. Man, what a city I thought. In the hotel where I was staying I met a nice girl, Mary, who was on vacation there with her mother. I asked her out to come with me to the Hollywood Palladium. After getting permission from her mother, off Mary and I went by taxi to the event. The attraction at the concert hall was the Lawrence Welk Show. It was the first time I had heard the band leader's name and had no clue what to expect. I was surprised to see that the whole program was filmed and would be televised. Mary and I had a great time dancing and laughing. After the show, we went back to our hotel and I invited her to come up to my room for a night cap. As it goes you start kissing and whatever, and I commented on her beautiful tan and asked her if she spent much time on the beach. With her eyes wide open, she looked at me and said she was black. Mama Mia—that was a new one for me.

I had heard many stories about Tijuana, Mexico so I figured it should be my next stop. After my visit to Tijuana, I classified the city as a sex tourist trap. It might be unfair but all I saw was based on sex entertainment. The shops and movie places were included, even walking down the street there were seven-year old boys and girls who approached asking if you wanted to sleep with mommy or if you wanted to have fun with their sister. I would find that hard to believe today, but at 24, seeing all the sailors and tourists, I felt like it was quite funny. After a couple of beers to build up my courage, I decided to visit one of the houses of pleasure. It was $5 for me which was a lot of money at the time but I figured to have this experience since you only visit Tijuana once in your lifetime. After the entertainment that I had paid for was over, I gave my story of being a poor immigrant to the hostess. With my blue eyes and blond hair, I looked at her and asked if she would give me a discount as I knew she would get $2.50 and $2.50 would go to her pimp. She was trying to believe my story and gave me $2.00; that's when the door opened and this huge Mexican Bandito came into the room with a large stiletto in his hand that he continued shining with a cloth. I thought to myself this was a good time to get the hell out of this place. Quickly grabbing my pants, I jumped out of the window, landing in a garbage can one floor below. Running as fast as I could, adios Mexico I said to myself. That was the day I learned not to play the fool.

On the road again and hitchhiking, I moved from San Diego to the Grand Canyon, to Phoenix and Tucson, Arizona, then on to New Mexico and El Paso. Since I eventually lived in Arizona later in my life, I will go into detail about this area later.

El Paso is a town in Texas but it reminded me more of a town in Mexico than one in the United States. The city was very colorful, with lots of tourist attractions. It has a great history with most of that involving Mexico. With a great number of Navajo Indians present, I was very interested in this since I originally came to America to find cowboys and Indians. The weather was great in El Paso so I could sleep in the park at night. Of course an attraction of El Paso is its close proximity to Juarez, Mexico. I guess you could call it a "Poor man's Tijuana". So I needed to see it but what a disappointment it was, especially after the first kid asked me if I wanted to sleep with mommy. I had enough since it still reminded me of my previous experience in Tijuana.

It was time to sleep in the bus again so I took a night Greyhound from El Paso to Dallas to see the real Texas. What a nice town with a lot to see. While in Dallas I met Willi Rossel whom I had met earlier at the Olympic Hotel in Seattle. Willi, one of my fellow countrymen, was the Executive Chef for Braniff Airlines. Braniff International Airways was a company who at that time had a great reputation. It was established in 1929 and unfortunately ceased operations in 1982, which was a shame. Due to high fuel prices and the Airline Deregulation Act, they lost their competitiveness in the marketplace. Willi served me a great meal and was an excellent host. We went to the Executive Dining Room of Braniff as he wanted to show me how they pamper their first class passengers with the following menu as an example:

SWEETBREADS BRAISE AU JUS (GLACE)

Place in a buttered sauté pan one slice of onion, one carrot, a little parsley, a bay leaf, a clove, and a few peppercorns. Put 3 par-boiled sweetbreads on top. Add one half cup of bouillon, some salt and bring to a boil. When reduced, place in the oven, adding a little bit of meat extract and glace by basting it continually with its own broth until it becomes browned. When done, plate up and strain broth over it. (I love sweetbreads)

CHICKEN SAUTÉ MARENGO

Joint chicken, season with salt & pepper and place into hot olive oil in sauté pan—note the olive oil has to be very hot. When nice and brown on both sides, add four chopped shallots and a little garlic allowing them to get hot, but not brown. Next, add one half glass of white wine and let it reduce. Add a cup of brown gravy, one cup of chopped tomatoes, and a can of French mushrooms. Cook for about 15 minutes or done. Dish up and garnish with chopped boiled eggs and croutons which have been fried in oil, chopped parsley, and a few slices of truffle on top.

BERLINER PFANNENKUCHEN

Make the coffee cake dough (see recipe below). Roll out into balls about the size of an egg, flatten them a little and put one half teaspoon of strawberry jam on top. Pinch the dough over the jam and lay them on a cloth, smooth side up. Cover and allow to rise to nearly double in size. Fry in hot oil. When done, dust with powdered cinnamon sugar.

COFFEE CAKE DOUGH

One pound of flour, one ounce of yeast, two eggs, two ounces of butter, two ounces of sugar, a pinch of salt, the rind and juice of one lemon and a touch of nutmeg. Put flour in a bowl. Dissolve the yeast in a half cup of lukewarm milk and add to the flour with the eggs; work it into a medium stiff dough. Cover with a cloth and let it rise to double its size. Then work in the butter, salt and lemon flavoring and mix well. Let it rise again for about one hour. This dough is the foundation for all kinds of coffee cakes. It can be flavored with vanilla, oranges, chocolate, or whatever flavor your heart desires.

The meals enjoyed with both Willi Russell and Clovis Soubrand were excellent. I must say it was quite an adjustment having to go back to the 17 cent McDonald hamburgers on the road. As my time with Willi had come to an end, my next city tour was Dallas which was very interesting. You could sense the richness of the place, a real Texas flavor fueled by the oil business and ranches. The tycoons of Dallas and Texas were prevalent everywhere. Although Dallas was still marked from the assassination of President Kennedy I was determined to visit some of these areas. At the time of my Dallas visit, I was accustomed to drinking 7/7 which is Seagram's Whiskey with 7Up. I complained to my waitress one day that the drink was too weak. She said that the liquor laws required you to get your own whiskey. I inquired as to how one accomplished that and she said to go outside and ask a taxi driver which I immediately did. To my surprise, he opened the trunk of his car and handed me a shot of whiskey and said that would be 75 cents; I could not believe it. It was not until later in life when I supervised three hotels there as the Sr. Vice President for Renaissance Hotels that I learned to appreciate both Dallas and Texas.

From there I went to Houston where I took my usual tour of the city. The weather was almost too hot but I decided to spend the night in the city park as the room rate there was good—free. I learned Houston was founded in 1836 and incorporated on June 5, 1937. June 5th was a special day to me already as it was my old Army friend, Fredy Bachman's birthday, as well as my brother Harry's birthday.

Now I knew when I arrived there, thanks would be owed to Walter Roth as another gourmet meal would await me. A grand tour with lunch at the Rice Hotel Houston hosted by Charles Finance, whom I had met previously with Walter Roth, was the highlight of my visit there.

The historic building was completed in 1913 on the site of the former capitol building of the Republic of Texas. Today however it is a luxury apartment building and is listed on the National Registry of Historic Places. While I was there in 1964, the hotel was filled with a collection of unique, beautiful antiques, and it was a thoroughly grand hotel. After the Rice Hotel closed its doors in 1977, it is hard for me to believe it remained unused for 21 years. What a shame for a piece of history to end. Finally, in 1998 the property was renovated and turned into exclusive apartments. While at the Rice Hotel, Charles Finance prepared the following lunch menu:

CONSOMMÉ CHARTREUSE

Boil one cup of chestnuts in salted water until tender then strain off the water and pass the chestnuts through a fine sieve. Put the cold chestnuts in a bowl; add four whole eggs, one pint of lukewarm consommé, season with salt and pepper, mix well. Next put in buttered timbale moulds. Set them in a bain-marie and boil for 20 minutes. When cold, they will set like custard. Turn out the moulds and cut in slices 1/8th inch thick. Serve in hot consommé.

FILET OF SOLE MEISSONIER

Trim four filets of sole, fold them in half, season with salt and pepper, and lay in a buttered sauté plan. Add half a glass of white wine and half a cup of fish broth. Cover and cook in oven for ten minutes. Put the sole filets on a platter and cover with the following sauce: Cut a carrot and a turnip in very small dices like brunoise. Put in a casserole with one once of butter. Put two ounces of butter in another casserole, add a spoonful of flour and the broth from the cooked sole, boil for five minutes, bind it with the yolks of two eggs mixed with a half cup of cream. If too thick, add a little fish stock. Bind the liquid with two egg yolks and mix with half a cup of cream. Strain and add the carrots and turnips from which the butter has been drained. Serve with boiled potatoes and spinach.

PISTACHIO ICE CREAM

Prepare a vanilla ice cream mixture. Crush one quarter pound of pistachio nuts to a very fine paste, mix with a little orange flower water and two ounces of sugar. Infuse the vanilla ice cream mixture and strain. Wait until cold, color a very light green and freeze it.

From Houston, I hitchhiked my way to New Orleans, also known as the birthplace of jazz and the blues and the colorful city with the Mississippi steam boats. On the streets, there were many musicians where I even remember seeing a little black kid playing the trumpet in a way which I could only dream of being able to do. The French Quarter was something else to see.

The city was named after the Duke of Orleans who reigned as Regent for Louis XV and it was established by French colonists who brought their European culture. The city is well known for its French-Spanish Creole architecture. Their unique cuisine, lively music, and annual celebrations and festivals are also quite famous. While I thought it was a lovely fun city, my impression was it was filthy and dirty. When I visited there, it was summer time, and in the French Quarter, it is impossible to miss the smell of the carriage horses. I remember vaguely the tour guide was telling us something about the cemeteries in New Orleans which require everyone to be buried above ground because the city is below sea level, similar to Holland.

Walking along Canal Street, the most famous street in the city, I felt like taking a bus ride. When the bus stopped, I climbed aboard and sat in the back of the bus. Suddenly nobody moved, people looked at me strangely and finally the driver shouted for the white kid to sit in the front of the bus. I did not move whereupon a policeman was summoned, came in and removed me from the bus. After a few minutes, the same scenario was repeated in the next bus. I climbed aboard, went to the back of the second bus, and the bus driver again said for the white kid to get to the front of the bus. Again I stayed put, another policeman arrived, removed me from the bus and the bus rolled away. Perplexed I wondered what the heck was going on. Determined, I was going to show those bastards. The next bus came, I went to the back, nobody moved again, all the other passengers looked at me and someone said I must sit in front of the bus and I replied that I liked to sit in the back of the bus. By now the third policeman escorted me off the bus. Finally, I asked this policeman what was going on and very politely he explained to me that only black people sit in the back. Actually, he emphasized they *must* sit in the back. Having been brought up by my mother that all people are the same, whether white, black, yellow, or whatever their skin color was. I could not understand what had just happened to me. On my next bus ride, I sat in the first seat and guess what—the bus moved this time as soon as the last passenger was on the vehicle.

My time was getting short because I had a reservation at a hotel in New York as I had to catch an ocean liner to Europe, so I decided to take a train from New Orleans to Washington, DC, with no stops in Philadelphia. It was a lovely trip with plush train cars, a dining car, and of course I could sleep on the train. At around 4am we had a stop in Atlanta where I got out for some fresh air. At the time, I categorized Atlanta as a very backward city and unsophisticated. Of course, I had no clue I would spend many years there in the future and eventually even retire there.

Arriving in Washington, DC, the nation's capitol, it was a wonderful experience, what a lovely place I thought. While staying at the Mayflower Hotel, another grand landmark hotel, I visited Lincoln Center, the Washington Monument, and many other famous landmarks, including Arlington Cemetery where President Kennedy's grave is located. At the time, I thought this would be my only chance to experience this fabulous city so I better see everything I could. Little did I know that later in life I would visit Washington many times.

New York City was my next stop. This was the only city where I had a hotel reservation. I stayed at the Warwick Hotel at the astonishing rate of $4.50. It was the year of the World's Fair so I decided to treat myself and also thought that when you go to New York, go all the way. The World's Fair was interesting and enjoyable. It was the first telephone service where it was possible to see pictures; you could call Europe for $23.60 for three minutes and actually see the person in Paris to whom you were speaking. Technology has definitely changed since 1964. While in New York, I was able to experience the usual tours of Ellis Island, the Statue of Liberty, the Empire State Building, Broadway, etc. Fortunately, I was lucky enough to return to New York later and lived in the Big Apple for two years, which I may write about further.

The day came to board the Ocean Liner Constellation, a fabulous, proud passenger ship. It was a festive scene, with people on the ship excitedly leaving for Europe and other people on the dock waving goodbye. There was music by a big band, garlands hanging all over the ship and falling onto the dock below and in the water. Standing on the deck, I thought to myself after all this excitement and the traveling over the past few weeks with no time to sit and relax, I have an opportunity to rest and recuperate from my enormous stress. Of course my presumptions were totally wrong. There was so much to do on this ship and they don't give you a break. From meals, lectures, dancing, pool, and a casino to gyms, wine tastings, and church service; you name it, we had it. My room, or our room I should say, was very nice. I shared it with three other passengers. It was a cabin for four people, most likely the least expensive accommodations on the ship. Believe it or not, crossing the Atlantic went so fast because of all the activities they kept you busy with. There was this one lady whom I met, about twice my age, and she drove me bananas the whole trip. We were dancing, kissing, playing, and having fun. Still today I do not know why I had such affection for her and vice versa. It must have been the ocean air or the shining moon at night. Of course, we both knew it would end once we hit land. She would go back to America and I would stay in Europe, but it was fun while it lasted.

It was morning with a beautiful sunrise when our eyes first saw the Island of Madeira. It was the first time we hit land since we left New York. Madeira is a tropical paradise in the Atlantic, west of Portugal and north of Africa. The capital of this Portuguese Island is Funchal, a real jewel in the ocean. While visiting here, I was in awe discovering the gorgeous flower gardens and colorful setting of the island, which was a real paradise to explore. The region is well known for its history of making wines, especially Madeira wines, in addition to its gastronomy, history, and culture. Its endemic flora and fauna landscapes are classified as a UNESCO World Heritage Site. Madeira's wines are produced in a variety of styles ranging from dry wines to be used as an aperitif to sweet wines mostly consumed with dessert. Madeira wines are also an important part of cooking, often used in sauces. The highlight of my brief stay in Funchal was going up to the Monte Mountain and taking the ride down to Funchal in a toboggan. These rides used to be a fast means of transportation for locals to get down the hill to the city. The toboggan rides have been around since 1850; however, today it is mostly a tourist attraction. A toboggan is a basket mounted on a sled while two men dressed in all white wearing white straw hats operated the sleds. They steer it and run alongside the sled down the hill.

Our cruise continued from Madeira going south to the coast of

Africa where Casablanca was my next stop. Unfortunately, the welcoming committee was not Humphrey Bogart or Ingrid Bergman but rather an unruly hoard of beggars. So many poor people and since we were Americans, they considered us to all be rich. There were people everywhere, many of them handicapped, children, women, cats, and dogs — a very sad sight for an arriving tourist. Casablanca was the first Arab city I had visited in my life. There were so many new things to see that it was hard to take it all in and because it was so different, I felt I could not discover enough. In the stores, men were dressed in local clothing with their unusual head gear and the women wore black outfits where their faces were covered where all you could see were their two eyes peeking out. Casablanca's mystique, its atmosphere, and crazy traffic plus the people with camels and donkeys were all very unusual to this young man from Switzerland. During our entire city tour we were followed by beggars.

An old rattling bus took us along the dusty road to the city of Rabat, the capitol of Morocco. On our journey, we passed many carts pulled by donkeys and men riding on camels. Once we arrived in Rabat, we took a city tour and it was more of the same that we had seen in Casablanca. Passing a local butcher shop, I encountered meat that was black because it was totally covered by flies. When the butcher was preparing to cut the meat, first he had to shake off the insects, which would fly away. A street vendor who played a flute for his dancing snake, sold me an Arabic dagger, the kind shaped in the form of a half moon. There were lots of interesting items to buy, the kind you would take home as a souvenir before asking yourself why the hell you ever bought this item to drag around on your trip.

Another interesting experience was visiting the mosques; for a Swiss protestant kid, this was a totally different world. Because the people participating in the prayers did not wear shoes, the smell was so bad it made me gag. After prayers, we participated in an Arabic coffee ceremony, which again, was new to me. The finished product was a little metal cup filled with a strong black liquid; so thick that the spoon almost stood in the cup by itself. What an unusually different world this place was. By now I could not wait to get back to the ship, take a long hot shower, and get rid of the dirt and smell of the day's trip.

Our ship moved and after a night's journey it was time to say good-bye to the older woman I had been seeing during the trip as she went on to the Mediterranean Sea and I got off in Gibraltar, affectionately referred to as "the Big Rock". Gibraltar is a British overseas territory located on the southern end of the Iberian Peninsula. It is at the entrance to the Mediterranean Sea where it meets the Atlantic Ocean.

Around 10am, I went to the dock to inquire about my boat's departure for my next trip... Algeciras, Spain. The woman at the dock whom I asked about the departure time replied that the next boat would depart at 2:15pm. I asked her why she was there so early and she replied with a smile that she wanted to be early for the next trip from Gibraltar over to Spain. The boat ride to Algeciras was only about six miles. Slowly I realized I had enough of traveling so I booked a train from Algeciras to Madrid. I spent three days in Madrid and because I could not speak a word of Spanish, each day I ordered Sandwich con Jamon and Cervesa which means a ham sandwich with a beer. I am accustomed to eating my dinner between 6:00-8:00 but I forgot that in Spain most restaurants don't open for dinner but until much later, around 9:00. This was a disaster for me. When I visited the Hotel Ritz, which was built in 1910, I was disappointed; it appeared to have seen better days. The hotel looked tired and could have used some "lipstick and rouge", in other words, it needed money poured into it and was in dire need of a renovation. The Prado, the National Art Museum in Madrid which was established in 1819, was absolutely fantastic. This art treasure certainly made an impression on me. It was the first time I had seen paintings by the great masters such as Rembrandt, Raphael, Durer, Francisco de Goya, Diego, Velazquez, Greco, Rubens, van Gogh; you name it, they were there. The artists depicted included many sculptors as well. My day spent at the museum was a fabulous experience.

My first and last bullfight was in Madrid. Although the event itself was colorful, festive, dramatic, and spectacular, I found it sad that the bull had no chance. No matter how elegant the toreador or matador dances and excites the bull; it is definitely a one-sided game. Men on horseback with long spears gore the animals that bleed, moan and groan; it is just awful. The crowd roars and shouts while the poor bull suffers. If it were up to me, bullfights would not be allowed. Unless you could take the spectators first and put them in a ring and let them run from a herd of bulls, then maybe it would be fair.

On this first trip to Spain, I decided it was not my favorite place; however, later in life while on vacation in San Sebastian, Bilbao, Zaragoza, and Barcelona, I must say I learned to appreciate Spain and quite liked it. Time was getting short and so was the money, so I booked a train from Madrid back to Switzerland. It took many hours while I took the opportunity to sleep on the train. After traveling through Spain and France, we finally arrived at Home Sweet Home. Since I had not seen my parents, brother, family members, and friends for almost two years, it was a great reunion and a treat for all of us. I must say Mama's cooking was lovingly welcomed.

The next step was to decide what I should do now that my traveling had come to an end. My initial thought was to return to America. However, my parents suggested that if they helped me financially, I could run my own restaurant. They registered me in a course to make the "Wirte Pruefung" which is an education course which enables you to earn a license to operate a restaurant or a hotel. It only took several weeks so I began the program. Because I was already a chef, I got a break and received credits for all the subjects regarding hotel service that I had already studied. In addition, I was required to take economics and the law part of the program.

While at this school I met an old friend from hotel school, Rita Schmid, who was attending along with her sister Roesli Schmid. Roesli was two or three years older than me. We hit it off right from the start and were dating quite some time. She was extremely smart, with great experience due to her prior work, but there was always something in the back of my mind questioning if she was for real. Mama from Ticino, happy that I came back from the United States, told me about this hotel in Astano, Hotel de la Posta, which was available for rent. Roesli and I went to meet with the owner, a slick lawyer, and agreed upon a deal that we would take over the hotel.

That's when all hell broke loose. My mother cried for days because she felt I should not do this, that I should continue to travel and see the world. She said I should not tie myself down in a restaurant in a small village in the Italian part of Switzerland. Then Mr. Wyss called me and suggested that I should go to Egypt and work at the Shepard Hotel, like I did when I was younger, but stressed that I should not bury myself in Astano. Other friends also tried to convince me that it was the wrong move.

About the same time, I got a film sent to me that showed Roesli in a negligee, it came anonymously but somehow I found out that it was sent from Basel, a place Roesli visited quite often. Needless to say, it made me presume that she had led kind of a double life. So I worked up the courage to speak to her and tell her I did not think we should run the Hotel de la Posta together; she was shocked. I did not tell her about the film I had received. Her response was that if I did not run the hotel with her she would immigrate to Lambaréné in Gabon and join the staff of the Albert Schweitzer Hospital in Africa. My reaction to her was good, you should do that as they need dedicated people so off she went to Africa and worked for Dr. Schweitzer.

Again, I felt I should go back to the United States. Since I had just completed the education course, my parents convinced me to stay in

Switzerland to work for a short time, to at least give it a try. While looking for a job, a young dynamic young restaurant chain named Moevenpick caught my interest. I went to Zurich and applied. Because I had just returned from America, they were instantly interested and I began working for them immediately. Ueli Prager, the boss, was a genius in hospitality. He was young, dynamic, and open for new ideas. Even the name was unique. He got the name Moevenpick when he was walking across the bridge near Lake Zurich when he saw the seagulls fly in, pick up some food, and fly off. The word "seagull" in German is *Moeve* and then he added "pick" because of the behavior of the birds. He could already envision guests coming into his restaurant—eat and leave out again.

When I started to work, I was told they did not pay much but I would learn a lot working for them. It was certainly true, especially the learning part, which was excellent. First I worked in the regional office, writing recipes and procedures for quality control. The best was when I was out of the kitchen and in the front of the house. Part of my orientation was working in different properties for the company.

After four months, I was assigned as Assistant General Manager at the Moevenpick Ueberland in Zurich, which was a big step. I loved my job as it was interesting and versatile, never boring. Being only 25 years old and in this position was fun. It enabled me to buy a nice car; I enjoyed nice lodgings, and had a pleasant girlfriend, a secretary who worked in the head office. I figured it was great that I knew what was happening in the company. I must admit, however, that my calculation was not quite right on my part. She was pretty secretive of what was happening in the company, in other words a good confidential employee.

The company had an annual outing for the employees, a cross country run that was required by all to attend. We stopped at different stations where we had to complete a form with questions. When you answered the questions correctly, you received certain points. This gave the employees who did not run as well as others the opportunity to win. Because I was new to the company, I did not know some of the questions or history of Moevenpick, but the girls who knew me gave me the right answers. To my surprise, I won the run because I had an extremely fast run but mostly because I had answered the most questions correctly. To myself however, I questioned if I really deserved to have won this competition.

Working for Moevenpick was great, the company was growing and then there was some talk about going into the hotel business, building and managing hotels. The joint partner would be Holiday Inn. Eventually it did grow as anticipated and today Moevenpick has many hotels and is an international company.

In the summer of 1965, Walter Roth wrote me a letter asking me to work for him again, this time in Los Angeles. He said he would be in Zurich the end of September and wanted to meet with me. Since I felt I owed him this courtesy, I replied that I would meet with him. September came fast and as I picked up Walter at the Zurich Airport, I noticed a roll of plans under his arm. As I greeted Walter, he said he wanted to go over the kitchen plans, he did not even take the time to shake my hand. We immediately went over to the café to review the plans. There was no discussion of how my family was, if I was enjoying my job — nothing; just the business at hand that Walter was interested in at the time. He announced that the hotel would open June 1st and he wanted me there in Los Angeles by March, or at least no later than April.

I told Walter I did not want to go back to work in the kitchen, that I was an Assistant General Manager and thus no longer cooked in kitchens. Walter pleaded with me to come and help him open the goddamned hotel and he would help get me out of the kitchen with Western International hotels. I told him I would think about it. After discussing it with my parents and Mr. Wyss, plus enduring a couple of sleepless nights, I met with Walter again. Before his departure, I committed to join him in Los Angeles. This time he shook my hand and left on the plane.

The next few months went fast. My work was great. I was able to spend time with my girl friend and members of our family. I was able to take a vacation to Belgium, Holland, Germany, and Luxembourg. While in Holland, I visited the Rijksmuseum in Amsterdam. This museum is absolutely fantastic, with over one million objects on display. It was originally founded in The Hague at the royal palace in 1800, but then it was moved to Amsterdam as the National Museum in 1808. The building itself is a piece of art. Frans Hals was my favorite painter in the museum because he painted people as they actually are — a drunk with a big red nose; a man smoking a pipe, or a hard-working woman with a scarf on her hair. He painted realistic people compared to many of the old masters who express themselves in paintings of holy people like religious icons, not the way people really are. The other thing I specifically remember of my 1965 Amsterdam trip is the red-light district. As much as I love ladies, this was not my cup of tea. There were women in sleazy outfits standing in front of their windows, making themselves available for sex. All I could feel was pity for these poor girls.

The middle of March 1966 came fast and now it was time to pack up and go back to America. This trip however was much better than the first. I had a bit more money and I also spoke much better English than in April 1963. This time my flight was direct from Zurich to Washington, DC.

6. WESTERN INTERNATIONAL HOTEL COMPANY

My flight from Zurich to Washington DC, the nation's capitol, was great where I met my Seattle friend, Beat Richei. Even though I had a long flight, Beat felt we should immediately head south, especially since he had already quit his DC job a couple of days before. Fortunately, I had decided prior to leaving Europe for the States to get my international driver's license so I would be able to drive, thus, Beat and I could alternate driving. Off we went to Miami, driving straight through, all in one night, excited because neither of us had ever been to Florida before.

While in Miami, we enjoyed the Cuban flavor, although our stay there was very brief. From there we decided to move north to Winter Haven where we visited Cypress Gardens, a theme park which began operations in 1936. With its beautifully manicured gardens and famous water ski shows, it was a wonderful diversion in the middle of Florida. They featured colorfully costumed Southern Belles who were stationed throughout the park, complete with hoop skirts and umbrellas to keep the hot sun off their delicate ivory skin. It provided a marvelous site for tourists. In 1966, Cypress Gardens had become one of the biggest attractions in Florida and Winter Haven became known as the Water Ski Capital of the World with the talented formation skiers and their elegant boats putting on dramatic shows for the tourists. We also learned that the television show, Sea Hunt starring Lloyd Bridges, had been filmed at Cypress Gardens in the early 60s. It was one of the few tourist attractions in Florida since in those days there was no Disney World, Epcot

Center, or Magic Kingdom, and no Universal Studios was in existence. Years later, the park went through several reorganizations and unfortunate bankruptcies, and eventually became Legoland Florida.

Beat and I drove north to Interstate 10, heading west past Mobile, Alabama and Baton Rouge, Louisiana, then north to Jackson, Mississippi. Interstate 20 took us west through Dallas, Texas, then we went north to Oklahoma City and finally we drove on Interstate 40 past Amarillo to Albuquerque, New Mexico. What a fun trip we experienced while traveling through the big wide open country of the United States. To quote a popular credit card commercial, the impressions were *"priceless"*.

After driving through Arizona, we had an unusual situation arise. I stopped at a local fruit stand and purchased a big bag of mixed citrus fruits for a dollar. Approaching the California state line, there was a Border Protection Station where we were required to stop. The Border Protection Inspector asked if we had oranges or grapefruits to declare and I proudly replied indeed I did. He notified me I could not bring them into the state of California as the Agriculture Department is afraid they might have insects on them or other bacteria which would endanger the citrus in their state. When I was told I would have to leave the fruits with him, my response was no way was I going to leave my fruit. So I sat down on the street curb and started to eat the oranges and grapefruits.

Fortunately, after a few had been consumed, the Inspector smiled and said he could see I was determined to keep my fruits. I told him he could bet on that. Addressing me as *"young man"*, he said I did not have to eat them, all I had to do was peel the fruits and take them with me. My friend Beat was in stitches laughing about the entire ordeal. By now it was the first week of April so we bid our adios amigos to Arizona and drove west toward Los Angeles.

When we eventually arrived in Los Angeles, we went directly to the Century Plaza Hotel to meet Walter Roth, our Executive Chef. The hotel was still under construction with a planned opening date of June 1. Since we still had time prior to the grand opening, Walter suggested we get our personal lives in order. I found a nice apartment on Beverly Glen Boulevard, only five minutes from the hotel, which was important to me. Having been told I would need transportation while living in Los Angeles, next on my agenda was car shopping for my first American car. So, I decided to purchase my first vehicle, a white Chevrolet Corvair, a really neat looking, unique car, with the engine in the rear. I had to purchase a Chevrolet since it was produced by the co-founder of the Chevrolet Motor Company, Louis Chevrolet. Louis was born on December 25, 1878 in the Bernese Jura Region; a French-speaking area of the Swiss canton of Bern, Switzerland. He learned to be a watch maker like his father and later became a famous American race car driver, car designer, and the rest is history.

When I prepared to purchase my car, the salesman said he was sorry but he could not sell the car to me because I had no credit history. I argued with him about the need for a credit history when I was prepared to pay cash. So I put my hand in my pocket and pulled out $600 cash and put it on the table. His eyes opened wide and he stammered, "*Yes sir, yes sir, right away, sir*". In just a few minutes, off I drove with my new car.

Up until this experience I had always paid cash for everything, if I did not have the cash, I did not buy something. My only bank account was a savings account as I did not even have a checking account at that point. I learned the American way of life was to get credit cards and establish credit, which I did but I never carried a balance on any credit cards more than 30 days. To this date, the only credit I ever received was for a mortgage for a home; however, now I pay cash for them, too.

Beat and I completed our paperwork in Human Resources at the Century Plaza and began to work. The first few days we were busy unpacking the equipment, organizing and setting up the different kitchens we had, and hiring the employees. The closer we got to opening the hotel, the longer the work hours became. My assignment was Sous Chef in charge of two restaurants — the 24-hour café Plaza and the Garden Room. The café Plaza, a European styled outdoor café, was located on the plaza level and open to the hotel. It was a runaway the first day as we had thousands of visitors the day the hotel opened. Naturally the hotel's guests stopped by and ate with us. For three solid weeks, we had a constant line of guests waiting to get in. I had two black short order cooks who I hired from the Beverly Hilton Hotel. For the rest of my career, I have to thank Eddy and Cherry for the outstanding job they did. I had many chefs who worked for me, but those two were the best.

The Garden Room kitchen was located one floor up on the opposite side of the hotel. It was designed as a place to have a small lunch or dinner, but mostly afternoon tea was to be served. The Garden Room had a gorgeous setting with bright lights and glass all around. Outside the hotel were beautiful gardens with plants, flowers, and little streams. Because of what this place was to be, it was totally under-designed with small limited kitchen and storage space, and side stands where everything was compact. Due to the setting of the restaurant and its location, it took off with high demand. I was running between the two places like an Olympian, wearing white Danish clogs, people could hear me coming and going. The joke was *"here comes the white speed boat"*.

On the plaza level, the Granada Grill was located. It was designed after the Olympic Grill in Seattle and since we were close to Mexico, it was named the Granada Grill. It was equipped with the finest appointments; the kitchen was first class all the way with special china, cast iron cocotes and dishes, and the uniforms were superb. The staff included many chefs, busboys, waiters, captains, an assistant manager, and a restaurant manager. Once I remember the General Manager of the hotel asking the restaurant manager what the soup of the day was, he turned and asked the assistant manager, who turned and asked the waiter, who then asked the busboy who proudly answered it was Mexican Tortilla soup. However, as nice as the restaurant was, it did not take off. I had learned another lesson... not to think just because something works in Seattle it will work in Los Angeles, too. The place bombed because people expected a Mexican restaurant due to its name and its décor. It was sad to see this beautiful eatery so utterly fail. It was an abortion.

We had an outstanding staff of people at the Century Plaza. When the hotel was originally planned, it was the biggest thing Western Hotels had ever done. The saying was this would either put the company on the map or it would break the company. So naturally all resources were put into this hotel. The strongest department heads were selected. Western had a strong philosophy of promotion from within so many workers got new job opportunities. The Vice President/Managing Director was Henry Mulligan, Don McClaskey a super fellow, was the Resident Manager. From Controller, Executive Housekeeper, Director of Food and Beverage, Director of Marketing, to the Executive Chef, Walter Roth, the best minds in the industry were put in place.

The hotel was extremely successful. Bob Hope was correct in his opening line at the official grand opening of the property *"Isn't it amazing what you can do with a bunch of old aluminum cans"*. *"Yes"* he continued, *"beer cans built this hotel"*. He was joking, referring to the Aluminum Company of America who had provided financing for the project.

One day Henry Mulligan, our top boss, asked me to come with him for lunch at the Beverly Hills Country Club. The mission was to see how they serve the spinach salad that I was to copy for the Garden Room. Of course, it was a tremendous treat for me. While having lunch, I began to eat with both hands on the table; fork in the left hand and knife in the right hand. I guess you would call it the European style. Henry thought I did not know how to properly eat. I watched Henry eat with the left hand under the table unless he was using it to cut the meat, then he switched the fork in the right hand. Watching him I figured he was a heathen; I thought to myself here is the great hotelier and he does not even know how to eat properly.

While growing up, if I did not have both hands on the table, my mother would have scolded me. I learned another lesson that each culture is different and I should not judge the other person just because they are different. As we were leaving the Beverly Hills Country Club, I saw Dean Martin's silver convertible Aston Martin parked next to Henry's car. On the dashboard he had a bunch of Dean Martin tapes and I surmised he liked his own singing.

Our employee restaurant was called Cantina. It was great and all employees ate there, from the room attendant to the Vice President/ Managing Director. One quiet night I went for coffee and Andrea, a pretty Austrian girl, was sitting there alone, so I joined her and inquired about how things were going. She sadly said she had just lost a boyfriend. I explained to her my philosophy when I lost a girlfriend in the past was I just think there's another mother somewhere who also has a nice daughter, so the same should apply for her. In other words, there's another mother somewhere who also has a nice available son. The main reason I started to talk with her was so many staff members, especially the male department heads, commented on what a pleasant person Andrea was. So I figured I better get to know her, plus she is from the old country and I already had enough wild experiences with American girls I had dated in the past to last me for a while.

After work, Andrea and I went to a Polynesian restaurant at La Cienega Boulevard. It was quite something to experience Polynesian-Hawaiian style food and all the fancy colorful drinks. The main attraction was about every twenty minutes there was this acoustic rainstorm with wind, lightning, and rain. It felt like we were in the midst of a tropical storm, but when we went outside the sky was clear, filled with twinkling stars. Andrea and I started to date and we had some very nice friends, especially Europeans from Austria, Switzerland, Germany, and other countries. Some of the other young German chefs wanted to become movie actors since we were in Los Angeles. A few got some small roles as bystanders in movies and they asked me to join them, but I had no interest as I wanted to become a hotelier and not the next Gary Cooper.

CHICAGO — JANUARY 1967

After the hotel was open for a few months, Walter Roth lived up to his promise. I was asked if I would be interested in moving to Chicago to work at the Continental Plaza Hotel, a luxury property at Michigan Avenue. My position would be restaurant manager and I would finally be out of the kitchen. The plan was to build a new restaurant replacing Café Lautrec. Happy as a lark, I accepted the job. Chicago here I come at the beginning of January 1967. I will never forget my first workday in Chicago; it was January 16, 1967. The same day the McCormick Place Convention Center burned down during the Home Show. The city was packed with convention attendees and the disaster at the Convention Center was headline news. Many buyers and exhibitors were staying at the Continental Plaza Hotel, experiencing panic and the resulting confusion which ensued.

The Café Lautrec was our all-day dining room with décor and atmosphere which patterned after the French painter, Henri de Toulouse-Lautrec. It was a nice place, but too dark and needed a facelift. Thus, we planned and did our research about the 1893 World's Fair in Chicago. Our conclusion was to rename the new restaurant Chicago Grill. It was a bright and friendly café with red décor. In the middle of the room was a Ferris wheel, a replica of the one from the World's Fair. We hired a new Sous Chef for this café, a German fellow named Wolfgang Fillinger. At the time, I did not know of him but he proved successful and was later promoted to Seattle's Space Needle as Executive Chef. I thought it was ironic that Dick Ferris, who was manager at the Olympic Grill in1963 when I worked in the kitchen there was now our general manager and I was the restaurant manager. Dick was a brilliant manager. Our executive assistant manager was Jack Vaughn, a super fellow who worked at the Century Plaza as rooms director when I was sous chef at that property.

This new restaurant did well, thanks to our director of PR for all the help she gave us to promote the place. I had a gold medallion made with a ferris wheel on a gold chain. We were working hard but having fun at the same time. I was dating the general manager's secretary for a while, even though she was a few years older than me. We had a great time skiing and visiting her parents in Indiana. She had a new Mustang car but I had decided I did not need a car in Chicago. Around that time, I started a relationship with a pretty Jewish girl, but it did not last long as her parents felt she should not be associated with a Germanic man.

Andrea and I talked about once a week on the phone and after a few months we decided she should also move to Chicago. She drove all the way from Los Angeles alone to Chicago in her little VW Beetle, making the trip in three days across the country. Once she arrived, she got her own apartment about 20 minutes from my place and began working at Marina City, a great restaurant operated by Hilton. One day she asked me if she could visit the Chicago Grill on her day off. Of course, I said yes and she came for dinner, but I was a jerk and made her pay for the food herself. I made up to her by interviewing her girlfriend's son who was desperately looking for a job. What a smart move that was to give the 16-year-old Tony a job as a busboy. He worked hard, later in life I worked with Tony at the Plaza Hotel in New York. He had worked himself up all the way to general manager and stayed with Western Hotels for many years. After a few months at the Chicago Grill, I wanted to do something else. Our director of food & beverage, a German fellow, helped me work in banquets. The catering and banquet Department was run by a Greek fellow. The whole department was mostly Greeks and it was a mafia haven. The bums got away with anything. I got cheated left and right. The department head would take tips away from me and give them to his grandson, who at times did not even show up for the events. I was smart enough not to fight city hall as I had a bigger objective, which was to become director of food & beverage. To get there, I needed more experience. This was another one of those times when one of my premonitions came true — the mentalist was at work again. I was setting up the Governor's Suite and saw on TV a speech being given by Martin Luther King. I commented to my Greek banquet captain that I wondered when he's going to get shot, as this was after JFK had been shot. I went down to the ballroom to check on something and 20 minutes later when I got back to the Governor's Suite, Nick said, your prediction just came true. I looked puzzled and asked him what he meant. He told me they just shot Martin Luther King in Memphis. I was sick to my stomach when I heard this.

The Continental Plaza had a supper club called the Consort Room, located on top of the building and it was very successful, with continental food and elegant service. However, the main attraction was a band, Franz Benteler and his Royal Strings, which did two shows each night. Franz, who owned a 1701 Stradavarius Violin, was born in Hamburg, Germany. He was an outstanding musician and had become a favorite of Chicago's Mayor Richard J. Daley. Since Franz and I both spoke German, we became very good friends. When I first arrived, our executive chef was a Swiss fellow who was transferred shortly after my arrival. That is when Tony Ruegg became our chef. Tony was a Swiss boy who said he had a cow in Switzerland and was always interested in the stock market. Tony had a knack for making money. We had a Jewish lady's luncheon one day, and Tony spent too much time studying the market rather than watching the chickens cook. As we served the lunch, some ladies began to complain about the chicken, saying it was not cooked properly and wanted to substitute it for a fruit plate. Panic broke out in the kitchen as we could not handle all the complaints. Even Tony did not have a solution. So I went to the ballroom and took the microphone and made an announcement to the ladies that, as you can see, the chicken is slightly pink, this is a new very expensive breed of chicken. We wanted you to have it first so you can experience it. The complaints stopped and we got away with the BS of a pink chicken breed. Yet another lesson was learned — this time help yourself.

One day Tony and I were talking about flying and commented that we should take lessons. So I challenged Tony that I would be able to get a private pilot's license before he could. Without letting him know, I went to Northbrook and started my lessons. About six months later, I asked him how his flying lessons were coming and sheepishly I showed him my new pilot's license. I really had fun doing this and had my first solo flight after 10 lessons. I took cross country flights to Madison, Wisconsin; Gary, Indiana; and Rockford, Illinois; plus other small cities, which was great. One day I invited Andrea to come flying with me and all went well until I turned off the engine and she got scared. I explained to her that when I was taking lessons, my instructor said if the engine ever stops, the plane doesn't necessarily crash because you just glide slowly down. Although this seems obvious, you don't think about it but planes are designed to continue even when the engine stops, thus it glides down.

The same year, Tony, his wife, plus Andrea and I spent New Year's Eve together and my plan was to ask Andrea at midnight if she would marry me. It did not work out because about 10:30 that night she and I got into an argument so I figured to hell with this proposal. It did not matter that I did not have a ring anyway. In Europe when you propose, you do not have a ring; after a couple agrees to get married, they go together to a jeweler and purchase rings. In February, we went skiing and it was cold, cold, cold. We were both bundled up and going up the ski lift when I asked Andrea if she would marry me. She replied to me that she guessed her mind was frozen enough that she said yes. In Switzerland before you can get married, your names have to be posted for two weeks at city hall, anybody who wants to object can do so. We wanted to get married in Europe but figured the legal part should be done in the US. On April 23, the anniversary of my arrival in the US, we went to City Hall in Chicago, had a blood test, got a marriage license, and a judge performed the marriage ceremony. Andrea went back to her work and I went back to my hotel to work. We had two big banquets and since it was winter, everyone had coats. As luck would have it, my cloak room girl did not show up for work, so I called Andrea to see if she could come and help me after her shift. She came and assisted. After I completed my paperwork at 12:30am, we went home to sleep. That was the end of our wedding day. We did not tell anyone that we were married.

In June 1968, Andrea and I flew to Europe to get married, this time by a priest, in church with dancing — the real McCoy. Since we had the legal marriage papers, the priest who confirmed me as a kid was able to do the ceremony. After Switzerland, we went to Austria and had a reception for the friends of Andrea and family members who could not come to Switzerland. Again, it was great and we certainly made up for what we missed in April when we got legally married in Chicago. I'll have more to share about our wedding later in another chapter titled "Three Clans — Three Marriages". I decided our wedding gift to each other should be a new Mercedes. A Chevy Camaro was about $2,300 in 1968 so I figured I might as well buy a Mercedes for $2,800. Back then the dollar was still strong against the German Mark.

In June, on our honeymoon, we picked up the new Benz in Stuttgart Germany and drove it to Switzerland. After the wedding activities, we went to Lugano and visited Mrs. Bachman, whom I called Aunt Sophie by now. We next took a trip to Cortina d'Ampezzo, the Italian Alps where they had the Winter Olympics in 1956 and subsequently a number of world winter events. It was a fantastic journey. From there we traveled to Venice, the City of Love. However, I was disappointed with

Venice as I felt it was an Italian tourist trap. I went back to Switzerland and then back to work while Andrea went to Austria to spend a few days with her parents. The car was shipped back to Baltimore and when I received confirmation that it had arrived in the US, I flew there in the morning. I picked up the new Mercedes in Baltimore and drove it the same day back to Chicago, arriving at midnight, dead tired. A few days later, I was asked to move back to Los Angeles. At first I thought I cannot go because I had applied for US citizenship in Chicago and I knew I could not complete it in Los Angeles since you had to live six months in the state where you applied for citizenship. However, my career was more important, so I took the job as Director of Restaurants at the Century Plaza Hotel.

We left Chicago in a traumatic fashion. I remember when we drove out Michigan Avenue soldiers were stationed on top of buildings with rifles and guns. It was during the 1968 riots when Mayor Richard Daley during the Democratic National Convention announced they would shoot to kill. Also, the assassination of Robert Kennedy had an influence on the protests and unrest in the city of Chicago. "So long my friends," I said to myself as we started our trip across country back to Los Angeles. It was a fun trip again across the good old USA. We visited different places I had never seen before. My visit to the Grand Canyon, the trip through Utah, and the opportunity to see the Mormon Temple in Salt Lake City were all interesting experiences. Learning the history of the Mormon Church alone was fascinating.

RETURN TO LOS ANGELES

Los Angeles here we come again. Our trip was great and once we arrived in Los Angeles we had to look for an apartment. We found a nice place and the newlywed life was good to us. Since I was Director of Restaurants now, I felt Andrea should also find a job in administration so she got a job in the Accounting Department at the Sheraton Hotel. I was told the reason they moved me to the Century Plaza was that the new Food & Beverage Director had no clue about that subject. He had previously been the Director of Human Resources, one of Henry's "boys", a yes man. The previous Food & Beverage Director, Jack Borg, left the company and moved to Carmel running his own hotel so Henry just promoted the HR person because he was one of his cronies. I felt Henry was one of the greatest hotel managers in the US; however, when it came to international issues, he was living in a dream world; he had no clue. Also, I felt his biggest problem was that he surrounded himself with yes men rather than mavericks and people who were aggressive and had their own mind.

When starting the second time working at the Century Plaza, I decided I would hire professionals who wanted my job. Several reasons formed this decision, first it keeps me moving and second, these people will be chargers and innovators. I loved my new job with all the restaurant managers and room service staff reporting to me, with the exception of Fred Bishop, who happened to be the brother of Joey Bishop, the comedian. Fred was in charge of our supper club, the Westside Room and he reported directly to Henry, another special saga. This did not bother me as I had enough work on hand as it was. After living for six months in Los Angeles, I could again apply for US Citizenship. I went to Beverly Hills High School and took citizenship classes. When the day came to complete my interview, the officer commented that I knew more about US History than most Americans do. I felt flattered and was proud to go to city hall for the naturalization ceremony. It was festive since it was me and a thousand Mexicans who were also there to get their US citizenship. For me it was a great honor and a special feeling came over me, I was so proud now to be one of them.

While Andrea and I worked hard, we felt we should have some fun too so we saved up our money and purchased a little travel camper. All my life I was crazy about camping and now we were able to enjoy our new hobby together. On the weekends, we would go to a state park and hang out. Andrea used to love to eat shrimp, crabs, and grilled pork chops; camping provided the ideal back drop for these feasts. One day she was telling me we will have no more shrimp, no crab meat, no pork and some other unusual items like no Christmas tree. At first I just dismissed it in my mind and forgot about the incident.

The Banquet Department at the hotel was very successful and since we were a new hotel, many of the charity functions moved from the Beverly Hilton to us. When working in the ballroom there would be Debbie Reynolds, Doris Day, Diane Keaton, John Wayne, Frank Sinatra, or Kim Novak. We were delighted to see so many of the Hollywood stars of the 1960s. The ladies used to be named the Honorary Chair of the balls, so naturally they would be involved with the decorations of the ballrooms. The excitement this brought to the hotel is hard to describe.

Our Lobby Court was another success story. It was a sunken cocktail lounge with pretty waitresses. Here any time of the day you could see celebrities such as seeing Buddy Hackett drive up to the front of the hotel in his Cadillac with the two long horn cow horns on the hood. He would come into the lobby for a drink and meet with other movie stars.

Our camping trips in Los Angeles did not last long. At the beginning of December 1969, I was asked to go to Singapore where the company was building the Shangri La Hotel. I was to be named the Food and Beverage Director but I was perplexed as to why they would send me since I had never been an F&B Director before, in addition to the fact that the hotel would just be opening. Of course I jumped at the opportunity and asked Henry Mulligan when I should report—next week was his answer. Henry said I better get moving.

Andrea went to Pasadena to get baptized by some new church she became involved with but because I was so busy I had no time for this. We had to sell the car and the camper plus we had to get shots for malaria and yellow fever. Actually, we received so many "poison" vaccines that we could not take them all in just a few days, so the last vaccinations we actually received were given in Hong Kong. Anyway, all was done in exactly one week. From Los Angeles, we flew to Hawaii and stayed one night. When we were standing on the balcony at the Ilikai Hotel I told Andrea someday I'm going to live here in this place. Andrea's reply was, "So you think you're going to live in the Ilikai one day," the hotel owned by Chin Ho the big financier with whom Western had a management contract. She had a great way of staying calm when I was dreaming; she would just gently say so! Andrea never argued with me about a point I was making.

From Hawaii, we flew Japan Airlines to Tokyo, the capital of Japan. This was our first trip to this country and came with many more new experiences. Western had an affiliation with the Imperial Hotels in Japan and that is where we stayed. We had a beautiful suite, overlooking the palace where the emperor stayed. We visited Tokyo Towers, enjoyed a city tour, experienced some of the Japanese Gardens and even participated in a Japanese Tea Ceremony. The Kimono clad ladies were lovely with their hair style and white faces. The food was okay as they really know how to use their resources. Just riding a train in Japan is an experience. People are stationed at the trains whose only job is to push people into the train to pack them in like sardines in a can. Japan is an absolutely interesting exotic travel destination where I wish we would have had more time to explore. I vowed I would return to this country again.

From Japan, we flew to Hong Kong for my first trip there ever. We stayed at the Miramar Hotel where our host was Ruedi Choi, a tall Chinese man looking more like an Italian than Chinese. Ruedi was very well respected in our company. We were served a wonderful Chinese dinner of eight courses. I discovered I had a lot to learn as everything was new to me. The Chinese culture is very different than I was used to. We left Hong Kong and flew directly to Singapore. Bill Ellis, who was the General Manager, picked us up at the airport. It was a few days before Christmas and our accommodations for a few days would be at the Intercontinental Hotel until we found an apartment. It did not take us long to realize that we were now the minority in a country made up of mostly Chinese ancestry, roughly 74%. While 14% were Malaysian and 9% Indians. The rest were Eurasians, and Caucasians like us were referred to as expats.   This was the first Shangri La Hotel ever built and today it is considered a high end successful international hotel chain. Finding an apartment was easy, but Singapore has different levels of pricing—local prices and prices for expats, thus we had to pay more than expected. At the hotel, we had a very small crew, since the hotel was still under construction. From Western, we had the General Manager, Director of Marketing, and me, all the others were locals. Since we had just arrived a few days prior to the Christmas holidays, Bill Ellis and his wife Doreen invited us to celebrate Christmas with them. They had two children, a daughter, Kimi, and their son, Kevin. Andrea was telling me that we could not go because her new religion did not permit Christmas. We sat down to discuss this as she explained her new beliefs to me. The new church was led by a fellow named Herbert W. Armstrong and it was called the Worldwide Church of God. The church's magazine, which I called propaganda, was named The Plain Truth. The members had strict rules such as no make-up, unleavened bread was to be eaten at certain times and specific other foods were prohibited. We were even required to throw away all the food we had and start over fresh. Needless to say, I was shocked to see my lovely bride being taken over by this new church. I will go into greater detail about this organization later; however, on that occasion I put my foot down and told Andrea that we were going to the Ellis's home for Christmas and added she was going to wear make-up and look pretty.

Since our hotel opening in Singapore was delayed, I was asked to go to Bangkok and work at the Dusit Thani Hotel. This hotel was to be the first hotel for a chain like Shangri La. At the time, I felt the bosses at Western had been taken. Shangri La opened a second hotel with Western in Hong Kong, but after that and once they established themselves, they kicked Western out, and also in Thailand.

While in Thailand I had a great time although opening the hotel was tough due to the fact that many mistakes had been made. For example, all the trays and a lot of the kitchen specs had come from Seattle and everything was done in inches. But the owners made a deal with the Germans, who had provided the financing, to build the kitchens and to supply them with German equipment. Unfortunately, all the German kitchen equipment was in centimeters not in inches. Nothing fit—it was an absolute disaster. Most of the machines had a different voltage than Thailand so would not work. In my career, I participated in many hotel openings, but Thailand was the worst. We had to take meat from our kitchen over to the Montien Hotel, where we ground it to make hamburgers then back to our hotel to cook and serve. The General Manager at the Montien Hotel was a Swiss fellow by the name of Peter Daetwiler, a real good hotelier. To add insult to injury, another problem in Thailand, and most of Asia as a matter of fact, was to get anything done you had to pay off customs officers, police, and agents under the table. It was a way of life in the Orient. We as honest Americans acted way too naïve to deal with those crooks.

At the opening gala dinner, we had certain wines to be served but none of them got through customs until days later. Lynn Himmelman, our Executive Vice President and who later became President of Western Hotels, considered himself to be a real wine connoisseur. Since I did not have the proper wine to serve, I looked for similar wines, then I wrapped the bottles in white napkins so you could not read the label and added fresh orchids to further decorate the bottles. It worked beautifully and we got away with serving the wrong wines and everyone commented on how lovely it was presented and served.

In Asia it is normal for each hotel to try to outdo the other hotels. So, someone had the great idea to have a live elephant in front of the hotel with the doorman. During the hotel's official opening ceremonies Princess Syracuse was chauffeured in her white Rolls Royce to the front of the hotel. At about that same time, as Murphy's Law would have it, the elephant came right over and made a rather large, stinking deposit right in front of the hotel. Needless to say, we were horribly embarrassed by the incident and the subsequent newspaper story and photos. This was the end of our lovely elephant welcome at the front of the hotel.

The hotel had many restaurants including a Thai place, a café, a continental dining room which specialized in flaming dishes, plus a Japanese restaurant, plus bars and lounges. So, we had huge training challenges. We had to train men and women who, until just a few weeks before were cutting pineapples and riding elephants, and now we had to bring them up to a level of international service. Not just simple service either, but elegant French service. The staff was wonderful. They would never say no but only yes; yes was their answer for everything. I tried to teach one particular group of staff members to sort silverware by putting it in a Cambro tray and thus properly store it. Before my demonstration they would all sit on the floor and rather than sort the silverware, they would just put them in a heap. I explained to them how it should be done and after I asked them if they understood, they all replied yes, yes. Good job! I patted myself on the back and went for a cup of coffee. I returned 20 minutes later and the Cambro trays were pushed in a corner and they were all sitting on the floor and doing it their way. Our training began with the very basics. The girls had hardly ever worn shoes, but we showed them how to put on silk stockings. I would tell them how to hold a tray and how to walk around tables so they could simply learn how to move around the dining room. What was so gratifying was that once they learned something they really showed appreciation for their progress. All the girls I called Susi and all the boys I called Tom. Years later, when I came back to the Dusit Thani, employees came to me and said they remembered that I was the man who had called them Susi and Tom. I really loved the Thai people as they are so gracious and sweet. I fell in love with their culture, the temples, and all the interesting things we could experience.

For the men, the many, many massage parlors in Thailand are a paradise. They give you a bath, a great massage, and take care of you. It is really a nice experience. What I did not like was that the rooms are open at the top so you could hear the discussions. Many of the Executives of the Dusit Thani were well known in these places. I never told them what I was doing in Thailand; I just told them I was a tourist. Our boys again acted naïve and I knew sooner or later the owners would use it against us. One night I came home and Andrea wanted to know how my massage was. I played dumb and said what massage? She said she knew I had gone to a massage parlor and still trying to deny I had gone there, I indignantly inquired as to why she would accuse me of that. She answered that I smelled like a pound of Johnson's Baby Powder. Alas, boys will be boys. Luckily, Andrea was very tolerant.

After the hotel's grand opening but before going back to Singapore, Andrea and I decided we would visit Cambodia since neither of us had ever been there before. With Royal Air Cambodia, an airline who had a total of three airplanes at the time, we flew to Phnom Penh, the capital of Cambodia. All went well until we arrived in Phnom Penh and learned they had lost our luggage. What an ordeal that was. We had no clothes and could not purchase any because the Cambodian people are very small compared to Andrea and me — nothing fit us. We had to make do with what we were wearing when we left Thailand. We washed our clothes and undergarments each night and tried to dry them as best we could so we could wear them again in the morning. Of course our clothes were damp and no fun to wear, as you can imagine. After a day the airline informed us our suitcases had been found. The airline representative picked us up and drove us to a Kampung (a term used in Malaysia and Asia for a village). In a shack upstairs we found an airline employee who had the key to the storeroom where the luggage was stored. It was comforting to witness the key to the storeroom was safely kept under a mattress. Once we got our belongings I thanked the employee for his help. As a reflection of the fine service provided by Royal Cambodian Airlines, he simply replied, "no problem sir." My foot, I thought, but at least we did get our clothes back.

Back we went to the Grand Hotel where we were staying. This property was like going back in time. It was old-fashioned but elegant. In the main dining room, the waiters wore white jackets with black bow ties and black pants. In the middle of the restaurant was a brown box for the tips. They all worked in teams. Each staff member according to the hierarchy of their positions had points. A busboy had the least points and the maître d' had the most points. At the end of the month the tips would be distributed according to this point system. The employees were wonderful, very cordial and appreciative. Now that we had clothes again and looked presentable, it was time to play tourist. We took a taxi to go around the city. Here the taxis have a human engine. Actually, it was a bicycle with two seats located in front of the driver who peddled the bike to drive you around. There were hundreds of these taxis. The main reason we wanted to come to Cambodia was to see the temple cities of this area. They are absolute archeological wonders. Our next move was to visit nearby Siem Reap, which is world-renowned for its temple cities.

Angkor Wat is a temple complex and is the largest religious monument in the world. It was originally constructed as a Hindu temple for the Khmer Empire but gradually was transformed into a Buddhist Temple. It is enormous and is surrounded by a moat.

Angkor Thom, our next temple city stop, was the capital of the Khmer Empire. It was built sometime in the 12th century and was given this name about four centuries later.

Through the years so many of the famous temples have experienced extensive damage and deterioration from excessive plant growth, fungi, ground movement, war damage and unfortunately, theft. The archeological restoration of the culturally unique structures began in 1908 and again in 1960 and continues still today. A visit to the temples in Cambodia is a truly unforgettable experience.

From Phnom Penh we traveled home to Singapore where the Shangri-La was waiting to be developed. I soon learned working with the local contractors was going to be a challenge. I would ask how long until we would reach a certain stage in the construction, and their answer would be five weeks. Then I asked what the sequence of events would be. They said first we need to pour the concrete. I asked how long does that take and the contractor said about three days, then it has to dry. Next, we need the plumber and he said that takes about two to three weeks, then they will need to install the electrical work which takes about ten days. That was followed by the installation of the equipment and fitting which take about a week. After hearing all this, I added it up and it came to eight to ten weeks, not five weeks, which is what I was initially told. I could see that working in Asia could be really frustrating at times. Our work and planning continued and generally it went well. At the time the Shangri-La was under construction there were several other hotels getting ready to open about the same time as us. The competition was high as everyone wanted to outdo each other. The Hilton, the Hyatt, the Ming Court and the Mandarin were our biggest competitors. All of these hotels were owned and financed by locals who were on an ego trip and had to be "the best." Typical Chinese mentality I call it.

I was determined to open the best food & beverage operation in Singapore. We planned several restaurants and lounges, but our interior designer was a gay guy from Denmark who had no idea of F&B operations. Everything he planned was based on looks and aesthetics but was not functional to work with. I fought with him for weeks to make the designs more functional. A good example was our Café Garden, which was a gorgeous garden concept. We had glass bird cages with all kinds of tropical birds. There were a variety of colorful, beautiful creatures in different sizes, different feathers, and with different colored beaks. It was a pleasure to watch the birds flying around. What no one had thought about was that the birds have to go to the bathroom. So, imagine you're sitting there in the garden as a guest having breakfast or lunch and here comes one of the birds flying over and he "*does his thing.*" The press we received on this issue could not have been worse. People would write into the newspapers or call the television station with comments suggesting the management team of the hotel should be put in the bird cages and that the birds should run the hotel. Needless to say, within weeks the bird cages and the birds left the Shangri-La. The café was redesigned and eventually became very successful.

The Golden Peacock was a continental dining room with big peacocks in the center and four booths around them, all arranged in groupings. The base plates, which were like chargers, I designed and Selangor Peter Company produced them. They were so nice that people wanted to buy them, and even our interior designed liked them. Next to the Peacock Room was the Peacock Bar with dark wood and elegant furniture which graced the lounge. On top of the building was the Tiara Room, a supper club with live entertainment, again another exquisite restaurant and lounge. The lights of the city at night gave the place a special atmosphere. The Shang Palace was our Chinese restaurant, which the owners had asked us to build and operate as the most famous Chinese restaurant in the city. It was a matter of showing off. I really studied the Chinese restaurant competition such as the Siam Intercontinental Hotel in Bangkok and the Hilton Hong Kong Chinese Restaurant, which were both flops; the Jakarta Intercontinental Chinese Restaurant, which was equally unsuccessful; and the Kuala Lumpur Sheraton Chinese Restaurant, which bombed. My conclusion was that all of these American hotel companies designed Chinese restaurants but they played around with them. In other words, they could not leave the concept original like it had to be. They added little changes in the recipes and felt they wanted to be different. For the Shang Palace I went to the local library and studied the Shang Dynasty. I went to Hong Kong, and with the help of Ruedi Choi I interviewed chefs and found Lam Chun, a Chinese chef who had a great resume. He did not speak English, so I had to speak to him with an interpreter. Following the Chinese tradition, he would decide on his own crew; Tim Sam would be his chef and he would choose any other chefs for his crew as needed. We would pay Lam Chun a fixed dollar amount and he would in turn pay his crew. Lam Chun and I had a great chemistry from the beginning and I was very confident in hiring him. Later I found a restaurant manager, Louis Ng in Hong Kong. The Shang Palace took off like a rocket. It was so successful we had a line at the door for weeks whenever the restaurant would open for lunch, dinner, and weekend Dim Sum. The owners were absolutely delighted with the success of the dining room.

At the same time all this planning was going on, Andrea discovered she was pregnant with our first child. Today I confess I am sorry I did not have more time for Andrea; for me it was work, work, and more work.

As we hired our staff I approved of each employee who joined our team. Of course, I also interviewed the department heads and made the decision to hire or not. I also talked to the other staff whom the department heads recommended. I told them how important their job would be and how they would make me look good. If they did a poor job the guest would say that the F&B Director must be lousy. But if they did a great job, the guests would think that the F&B Director was outstanding. The staff members who were hired took their jobs very seriously and it certainly showed in their performance.

Ads I placed in Swiss newspapers helped us find eight chefs whom we hired for the main kitchen. Next, I also requested Wolfgang Fillinger, who I had worked with in Chicago, to be our Executive Chef. The powers-to-be felt I was crazy since Wolfgang was Chef at the Space Needle Restaurant in Seattle, plus the fact that he had never opened a hotel. They said I needed a seasoned Executive Chef, but I was adamant about getting Wolfgang and said I would take the responsibility. Thanks to Bill Ellis, our General Manager, I prevailed in getting Wolfgang Fillinger to come to Singapore as our Executive Chef. Soon after that Wolfgang showed up with his pregnant wife.

Andrea and I purchased a speed boat and joined the Singapore Yacht Club. Our General Manager also had a boat, so Andrea and I often joined them on weekends for some boating and fun. I needed a boat since Singapore is so small. It gave me a feeling of freedom to get out on the sea and visit the different islands in the area. It was nice and relaxing. Since we were only 88 miles from the equator, we had to pay close attention to the sun as it was easy to get sunburned. We often played with Kevin Ellis, Bill's 10-year-old son.

The hotel was finally ready to open in stages, with the first to open being Kendurina, our employee dining room. It was the best in Singapore, with three different sections for food and sittings. The Malay area was for the Moslems, the Chinese section was for the locals, and finally the Western part was for whoever wanted it. Each employee was allowed to eat wherever and whatever they wanted. The next outlet to open was the Café Garden, which was a 24-hour restaurant. During the opening in the morning, Andrea said her water had broken and she needed to go to the hospital. Off we went to the Glen Eagles Hospital. At that time, you could not go into the labor room but were required to sit in a waiting room — that was too much for me. I was so involved in opening the hotel that I went back to the property to work. Then Doreen Ellis, the General Manager's wife, saw me at work and told me I better get back to the hospital. She had just paid a visit to a friend in the hospital and saw a little basket being moved and it said *"Baby Gammeter."* So I ran to the hospital and found our sweet little Andrea. It's ironic she was born on May 12 since it is also her mother Andrea's birthday. Now that we had a baby, we hired an Amha, a servant who cooks, cleans, washes, etc. She was Chinese and a wonderful woman. Andrea's gynecologist was Professor Dr. Shears until four weeks before the baby was born. Then Dr. Shears was named President of Singapore. After that happened, Dr. Ung was assigned as her new gynecologist. Dr. Ung loved horses and followed the race circuit in Penang, Kuala Lumpur and Singapore. I always wondered if she induced Andrea's labor so she would not miss a horse race.

The next openings were the Golden Peacock, the Shang Palace, the Tiara and of course, our Banquet Department. We had a great crew and within a few months we earned a great reputation in the country as being the best party facility. Lee Kuan Yew was the Prime Minister of Singapore, whom I had the pleasure to meet on several occasions. When Queen Elizabeth visited the country with Prince Phillip, Princess Ann and all her VIPs, the Prime Minister decided to have the party at the Shangri-La. I wanted to get a photo of me with the Queen but did not actually think it was possible. So I asked Francis Lee, our outstanding photographer, to position himself up in the projection room. During the reception when I walked close to the Queen and Princess Ann, he snapped the picture, which I still have to this day. However, it is not as important to me now as it was in 1971. Yet another one of my life lessons — as you get older your values change.

The Peacock Lounge was something else. We had three gypsies playing, one playing a harp, one on a violin, and the third playing the piano. They were absolutely the best I have ever heard, but managing them was another story. Almost every night they had a fight. Of course it was the alcohol that started most of the arguments. Kathy, the violinist, was "*friendly*" one night with the piano player, and the next night she was with the harpist. It was definitely a three-ring circus to keep the trio in harmony. As musicians, they were fantastic. Whether it was a waltz,

Mozart, or Viennese music, whatever the guests requested, they would play.

The Lost Horizon was our live disco lounge. We had two bands, usually from Australia or England. Members of rock bands usually have long hair but that's a no-no in Singapore. The government feels that long hair comes with drugs, so the band members had to either cut their hair or wear wigs before they even got off the plane in Singapore. If they were not willing to do so, the airlines were required to take them back to the destination from where they came. Singapore has very, very strict rules and you better follow them or you have to face the consequences. The Lost Horizon was built like a ship, all handmade with wooden carvings. It was so nice, with sexy lights, quiet booths, little tables and cozy corners, just great. The two bands played non-stop all night. When one band was leaving, the other band came on. They played the song Shangri-La written by Carl Sigman and Robert Maxwell in 1946. The term comes from "Shangri-La," the hidden valley of delight in James Hilton's 1933 novel *Lost Horizon*. Back in the 1930s and 40s it was slang for heaven or paradise and the song is said to be about the joy of being in love.

At the Shangri-La we enjoyed many successes and I can humbly say the opening of the F&B Department at the hotel was an unbelievable success. But my biggest achievement was the Dutch Food Festival. At the time it was common that American hotels in the Far East would organize food festivals to generate business. We hired a promoter, Egon Padjasalmi, who lived in Bangkok, Thailand and organized many promotions. So we decided to do a Dutch Food Festival rather than the usual Swiss, Italian, or French. We approached KLM, the Dutch airline, to partner with us since they were in the process of expanding into the Asian market and they agreed to be one of the sponsors. I then went to Holland and met with the Department of Agriculture and Fish. A meeting was set up with Heineken Beer to get promotional items. Then I went to the Delft Pottery Factory, makers of the world-famous Dutch blue china. They gave me a tour and agreed to fly some of their Delftware to Singapore for an exhibit. Table china of course was of great interest to the Chinese people. We took pictures for the press with me eating herrings in the Dutch manner, not that I liked it but it was necessary. After all the arrangements had been made in Holland, back to Singapore I headed. Uniforms were made for the waitresses with little Dutch headdresses, just as sweet as could be. They looked so nice. I also had a Dutch Drehorgel (an English barrel organ) sent to Singapore and played it in the lobby. A Dutch woodcarver would take the shoe size of VIPs and while they ate dinner, he would carve their custom wooden shoes and then present them to the guest. Ria Keuken, a Dutch singer, would entertain the customers. Very colorful promotional materials were prepared, but because they were so good they were unfortunately stolen by thieves who used them to decorate their homes. In the restaurants we had stewardesses from KLM to help with seating and assisting the guests. I had 10,000 tulips flown in from Holland, which was a story in itself. The housekeeping department had to take care of the flowers on a daily basis. Our Executive Housekeeper was Annaliese Chanchorle, a big German mama. Her assistant was Audrey Smith, a pretty fashionable Chinese lady. When the two walked through the hotel we would say "here comes the jumbo jet and her mini-mini." They were absolutely fantastic professionals. Annalisa and I would constantly argue in German, but often we would break bread together. She would say I was the most demanding, arrogant F&B Director she had ever met, but she also admitted that most of the time I was right. I would just laugh and invite her for lunch. After the end of the food festival, Egon came to me and said it was the best food festival he had ever seen, which of course made my day. Needless to say, it was the staff and wonderful people who made the festival successful; I was just the conductor.

The Dutch cuisine is more peasant or country style you could say, not fine like French or Italian, more basic like German cooking. Many Dutch recipes are from Indonesia, since it was once a Dutch colony, which I will discuss in another chapter. Following are some Dutch recipe examples:

BOERENKOOL STAMPPOT

- 3 lbs. potatoes
- 2 onions
- 1 bay leaf
- 1 lb. kale
- 1 pinch salt
- 1 pinch ground pepper
- 1 lb. smoked sausage
- ½ cup milk
- 2 tsp. butter

Peel and dice the potatoes and onions. Clean, trim, and slice the kale. Add the potatoes, onions, kale, bay leaf, salt & pepper. Add just enough water to cover all in a 3 qt. pan. Cover and boil gently for about 25 minutes. Meanwhile, steam the smoked sausage for about 20 minutes and slice it. Remove the bay leaf, drain the vegetables and mash them, add the milk and butter. Stir in the hot sliced smoked sausage, then salt and pepper to taste before serving.

ERWTENSOEP

(a thick pea soup, so thick that people say the spoon should stand in the soup.)

- 1 lb. green split peas
- 34 fl. oz. water
- 1 carrot peeled

- 1 small potato peeled
- 4 oz. of celery
- 1 small onion
- 1 bay leaf
- 1 small smoked ham hock or smoked sausage
- salt and pepper.

Rinse and wash the split peas and add them to the water. Chop the vegetables and add them to the water, plus the bay leaf and meat. Bring to a boil and simmer for about 40 minutes or until done. When the peas are soft, remove the bay leaf and stir the soup until the peas dissolve and give it a creamy consistency. Cut the meat off the bone or slice the sausage and stir back into the soup. Add salt and pepper to taste. Serve with a slice of buttered, dark rye bread.

CHANGE IS IN THE AIR

Singapore was great from the management team to the employees to the friends we made. We found pleasure in our participation in the International Food and Wine Society, with whom I did great parties at the hotel. The Swiss Club Andrea found to be a great place for her friends and children to enjoy. Everything seemed to be going along just fine, then I got the phone call asking me if I wanted to go to Kansas City. It seems the Hall family, the owners of the Hallmark Card Company, were building their first luxury hotel and Western had the management contract. We were ready to go to Kansas City after I sold the boat, our car, the furniture and had already made travel reservations, but a second phone call changed all of those plans. Now they wanted me to go to San Francisco. The St. Francis had some F&B problems and they were in the final stages of opening an addition to the hotel. They had a history of seven F&B directors in the past two years and thought maybe I could stabilize the operations. This meant I would be the eighth in only two years which also signaled something was not quite right there. After quite a bit of convincing, I took the job but first I requested two weeks of vacation before I was willing to start with my next challenge.

VACATION

We went to Jakarta and then to Bali. The island of Bali was still a bit backwards. We saw women walking around in their colorful sarongs but not wearing anything on top. It appears it was common to walk around topless. Luckily, we arrived in Bali during a big festival and natives were carrying big colorful bowls with fruit and flowers on their heads. They brought these to the temple to thank the gods for their blessings. From Bali we flew to Sidney. While in Sidney we made arrangements to meet at 4pm in the lobby with an older gentleman. We walked in and I saw him sitting in the corner. We greeted him and hugged each other. It was my father's brother, Uncle Godfried. It was such a touching moment. A picture was taken with my daughter Andrea, Uncle Godfried, and me—three generations of Gammeters. I sent a copy to him from San Francisco and he wrote back to confirm he had received the photo. He was so happy to meet someone from the old country. After all these years, he never went back to Switzerland after he had moved to Australia in the early 1900s. I learned he passed away about three weeks later.

After our visit to Sidney we headed to Tahiti. I was looking forward to visiting this paradise. We stayed at the Intercontinental Hotel in Papeete, the capital of French Polynesia. When we arrived at the hotel, the front office manager was wearing flip flops, with an unbuttoned shirt displaying all his chest hair. When we got to our room the crib we had requested for Andrea was not there and the room was only half made.

We called Room Service for some milk for the baby but we were told they were out of milk. As you can imagine, I had one of my attacks—I was so angry I began to shake. I told Andrea we're done here, we're going to check out and head for Acapulco, Mexico. When I met with the front office manager I told him we were checking out. He wanted to know where we were going, to which I replied Acapulco. He wished us luck as the next flight was not for three more days. I had to eat crow and be nice for the remainder of our stay. Fortunately, we did have some fun in Tahiti. We took a taxi around the whole island and visited the home of Paul Gauguin, the French artist. His exhibits were wonderful, and it was interesting to learn his history as he led a rather unusual life. Although we eventually did have a nice time in Tahiti, I do not think I will go back again. Hawaii is much better.

Our next stop was Acapulco, Mexico, a place that had always fascinated me. Teddy Stouffer, a famous Swiss bandleader, moved there during Hitler's time in 1943. He started a night club, restaurants and hotels. He was known as "Mr. Acapulco." He also started the cliff divers who jump from the high cliffs down to the water below. Teddy was a great promoter and helped transition Acapulco from a fishing village to an international resort. We stayed at the Caleta Hotel, a Western affiliated property. From there we went to Mexico City and stayed at the Camino Real, another Western Hotel. The colorful country of Mexico had always attracted me and I love their lively music. All their Mexican hoopla was right up my alley.

THE ST. FRANCIS IN SAN FRANCISCO

Upon arriving in San Francisco, it was right back to work. Andrea and I found a first home in Terra Linda, in Marin County. It was located on a hill with a gorgeous view. We only had one car which made it a little hard on Andrea because it left her stuck in the house. But she took the opportunity to prepare a nice garden in the yard and to make it a home for us and little Andrea. After only three days at the hotel, I already knew what the problems were. I told Andrea I did not think I would ever be able to turn the F&B Department around unless I changed the Executive Chef, Purchasing Agent and the Director of Catering. Later I found out that five former F&B Directors had made the same comment and then they were gone. So, I did not tell anyone of my perception except my wife. I remembered the old saying — *if you can't fight them, join them*. At one of my first department head meetings, I asked for help from the Engineering Department. The Chief Engineer said not to worry; after all, how long are you going to be with us? I grabbed a water pitcher prepared to throw it in his face, but the Director of Housekeeping, a German girl, gently touched my hand and stopped me, as she had obviously seen my reaction. The St. Francis had a lot of history, some of it I read or heard about and some I experienced myself. Dan London, a real gentleman, was the General Manager for years, but I don't think he was a good money manager. Supposedly, he would get a horse in the ballroom and sit on it, then the tailor would come in and measure him for his new horseback riding clothes. He was always in the news, spending each summer in London. He used to say, "in San Francisco they call me Mr. London and in London they call me Mr. San Francisco." The hotel had an employee, Arnold Batliner, who was the money washer. His job was to clean the coin money so the white gloves of the ladies would stay clean. I liked Arnold and visited him often with his money washing machine. He was born in Feldkirch, Austria, near the Swiss border, so we had many common interests. Mr. Batliner was interviewed by many national magazines and was once on the TV Show "What's My Line" and stumped the experts. A lady would go around the offices and sharpen the pencils and bring fresh ice water to the desks. All this complicated what management called traditional service and cut into the profit of the hotel. When managers tried to change something to be more efficient, the answer usually was *"We can't do this — this is the St. Francis."* I remember doing a calculation for the Dutch Kitchen, a very nice coffee shop that lost money each month. I figured the way we operated it we could have given 50 cents to each guest and tell them to go have breakfast somewhere else and our losses would have been less. The Terrace Room, a lunch and tea restaurant off the main lobby, had all Asian female staff dressed in kimonos. One time I spoke to Chris, the restaurant manager, about a service mistake one of the ladies had made. Not a problem I said, just thought she should know about it. She apologized for the service and indicated that she was a new employee, which was her excuse for her having made a mistake. When I asked her how long the staff member had been working there, her answer was 13 years. I simply turned around and went back to my office. Yeah, *"the new girl,"* I thought to myself.

The hotel never had an employee dining room. The staff would eat whatever they could get or wherever it was. It was totally out of control. I finally was able to convince management to build a cantina for the employees and I wanted everyone to eat there, including the Executive Staff. I don't think our Managing Director Vice President ever visited the place. He was a great fellow and I have to thank him a lot for my career. I loved the man but sometimes he just drove me crazy with his ideas and stubbornness. He was hard to change. His name was Bob Quince, the Vice President for the company, but when it came to the head office in Seattle, he did not want to have anything to do with it. I never understood how he got away with it. I guess the Seattle boys were naïve. Rather than sending me to the F&B conference, he said you don't need to go, so instead I went to Kansas City to help open the Crown Plaza Hotel. Bob's friend, also a Vice President General Manager, ran that place. His name was John Dunken. He had the same idea about Seattle headquarters that Bob had. The opening in Kansas City was fun. I was asked to have a drink on top of the building with the

Executive Assistant Manager whom I knew from Chicago. But as I got to the kitchen and saw the confusion and hard work the staff had, I never went back in the dining room. I was helping to get the show on the road. We had quite a few people I knew from other hotels who were there as opening assistance. It was fun to see old friends; one was Audrey Ying, whom I knew from Singapore.

Back in San Francisco, Andrea got pregnant with our second child. Bill Hulett, our manager, and I became fast friends. Bill is probably the person who helped me most in my career. He was fun, a good man who was very street smart, but I learned you had to be on his side of the street. He and his wife Penny were extremely helpful to me and Andrea. Over the years, we developed a great friendship. I will always be grateful for the help we got from them, especially Bill in his help with my career. I had to present the budget to Bill and he said we could not send this to Seattle. I told Bill this is the way the numbers are, and I didn't think personally that we could achieve them. Bill told me to change it or else. My reply to him was "or else call headquarters and tell them you need a new F&B Manager," but I was not going to change the numbers. I told him we had made too many mistakes over the years and it will take time to turn it around. I was always a bit scared of Bill and I think he knew it. Also, because of my European background, I was inhibited in public speaking and realized I needed help in this area. Over a few drinks I told Bill about my inhibitions, and the next thing I knew he told me to join Toastmasters of San Francisco. He said the hotel would pay for it since it was continuing education. I appreciated this very much and enjoyed the meetings, plus it helped my self-confidence. We had a waiter at the St. Francis named Larry who was 104 years old and not quite with it any longer; he could get out of control. He would go up to a guest and when a lady asked him how old he was, his answer would be, "Old, do you know what that word means? It means rotten, wasted, or bad. I am none of these, therefore I am not old." Or he would look at a female guest and say, "I don't like your make-up." Larry really was something else. When pouring coffee, we were afraid he would burn someone because of his shaking. Larry should have been let go years ago, but everyone was afraid of the union. One time there was a reception for Richard Nixon. Management wanted to keep Larry away from the President, but no such luck. When Nixon walked into the ballroom, he saw our ancient waiter and said, "Hi Larry, how are you?" Larry replied, "Fine, how are you Dick?" Everyone just had a surprised look on their faces. Bill told me to fire Larry. Well I did, and then we had some issues with the union, but after a while it was all settled. One night I got a call from Bill Hulett when he was General Manager of the Mayflower Hotel in Washington DC. He told me to turn on the TV and watch the Johnny Carson Show. There were Larry and Johnny. Johnny asked him why he was not working at the St. Francis anymore. Larry's answer was when they speak to you in Italian and you don't understand it, then it's time to quit. Johnny just shook his head and introduced the next guest.

As noted before, the St. Francis was a bit stiff. Thanks to Don Blum, our PR consultant, I was able to bring in some new ideas and come up with promotions. Don was great, and he loved some of my ideas because the hotel had no pizzazz. For Thanksgiving I did a big display in the lobby with a life-sized stuffed turkey, Pilgrims, straw, pumpkins, etc. It looked great and was in the newspapers. During the Jewish holiday we presented a Seder table during Passover. Each of the items arranged on the table has special significance to the retelling of the story of the exodus from Egypt, which is the focus of this ritual meal. The Jewish community loved the kindness we showed them by preparing this table.

We took a trip to Switzerland, and when I said goodbye to Bob and Bill they put a $100 bill in my coat, an act that touched me. They said we should enjoy a nice dinner on them during our vacation. Bill found out the purchasing agent was cheating and fired him, which I was glad about. A few weeks after this, the Executive Chef and Director of

Catering quit and started their own restaurant. Upper management was shocked and upset. They wanted to know how we could run the hotel without them. I said we would have to manage better and work harder. Needless to say, I went home, told Andrea what had happened and celebrated with a good bottle of wine. My lesson learned here was to have patience and all will fall into place. Now I could get a handle on the F&B Division. The joke of how long I would be staying was over and I received the respect I deserved. Also, when we needed a new Executive Chef, I was able to convince the GM and Manager and the Seattle staff that we should get Wolfgang Fillinger from the Singapore property and we did. Unfortunately, we lost Bill Hulett when he was transferred to the Mayflower Hotel in DC. I missed him, but Larry Magnan, whom I knew from the Century Plaza, came in as the new manager of the hotel. He was a good fellow and we had lots of fun together. He lived in Terra Linda like we did, so we commuted to work together. He drove and paid for the gas and I paid the toll for the Golden Gate Bridge. Many times Larry had dinner with Andrea and me. One night we came home and Larry commented that it smelled so good. He joined us and inquired as to what we were having for dinner. Andrea told him it was tripe in tomato sauce with boiled potatoes and salad, a typical European dish. He looked at me and said he suddenly remembered that his wife Ruth had to go to a PTA meeting tonight and he was due home to watch the children. I have to assume that tripe was not Larry's favorite dish. Unfortunately, it was around this time Andrea had a miscarriage, after 6 months — it was a boy. A few months later we had another miscarriage after 4 months, and again it was a boy.

We had been in San Francisco for about two years before I finally got rid of all my resort clothes from Singapore. I had to purchase dark suits, banker suits we called them, which befitted the St. Francis. We went to Switzerland and a salesman talked me into purchasing this flashy outfit. When Bob Quinze our GM saw me, he wanted to know where the rest of my band was because he thought I looked like Liberace. That was the end of that outfit.

With all the frustration I sometimes had at the hotel, all I had to do was take the cable car, go to the Fisherman's Wharf, have a glass of Chardonnay and some shrimp, go back to the hotel and work was okay again. Andrea got pregnant again and was in her eighth month. Mr. Carlson of UAL, Inc. purchased the Ilikai Hotel in Honolulu. I was told to go as the Executive Assistant Manager, which is the number two position in the hotel. We were told Bill Hulett was going to be the GM so we should take over the hotel and Westernize it. I was informed that Henry Mulligan, who I knew was president of the company, told Bill he was going to tell him who his assistant manager would be. Bill was stubborn and said he wanted to select his own man, otherwise he could not do his job. So, Henry took two pieces of paper and told Bill to write down who he wanted as his assistant and Henry would also write down who he wanted to assign as the assistant. They both turned the paper over and both had written Hermann Gammeter. So we packed up, sold the house, and Hawaii was our next step. We got to the hotel, and our reservation was supposed to be a big secret. But Hawaii was a great "Bamboo Telegraph" that worked very well. Our welcome to the hotel by the room clerk who checked us in was that the staff members were happy Western was going to run the hotel again.

The next day, Bill Hulett arrived with his wife Penny who, like my Andrea, was also eight months pregnant. Employees immediately started to bet on who was going to have the baby first, Penny or Andrea; this was typical of Hawaiians. The first few days Bill and I realized the big challenge ahead of us was turning the hotel around. It had about 800 rooms and some of them were condominiums with individual owners. There was also the Yacht Harbor building with all hotel rooms and across the street was the Marina Building with all privately held condominiums and we managed the entire complex. Chin Ho, who lived on top of the Ilikai Hotel, was born in 1904 and was an entrepreneur, businessman, philanthropist, and self-made millionaire who pioneered Asian involvement in the Hawaiian business community. Chin Ho was the man United purchased the property from but was also a friend of Western Hotels. For generations before the rise of Ho, the business community in Hawaii was controlled by a small group of white family business interests. He was able to overcome the conservative business conditions and "cracked Hawaii's bamboo curtain" and gained a toehold in the whole establishment. He was the first Asian to be named a trustee of one of Hawaii's largest estates, the huge Robinson estate. Ho founded the Capital Investment Company. He and his wife Betty were wonderful people, much easier to please than some of the other condominium owners with whom we had to deal. Eventually Bill Hulett was able to purchase several condominiums which would increase the hotel rooms and decrease the condos we had to worry about.

At the time we could live in the hotel because the new home in Hawaii Kai was under construction. Again, Andrea said her water broke and I drove fast to the Kapiolani Hospital and figured it would be another long labor so I better get back to the hotel. When I arrived there our secretary Nina told me I had become a father again, so I better get back to the hospital. I found Andrea and our healthy beautiful little girl who we named Christina. In Hawaiian Christina is Kikina, since they have fewer letters in the alphabet than we have.

The work we had to do was overwhelming for me. My new position was so different from my former job where I had all the answers. I had been the king in my prior position, but now I had to depend on other department heads who reported to me. It was a much different ballgame. On top of it all, Bill was a hard charger and I am sure at the time he had a struggle with his job as well. Everything had become overwhelming for me with all the renovation work to be done and me not having all the answers in my new position. On top of all this we were building a new home and I was worrying about how I would pay the high mortgage, plus our new baby; it was all mounting up around me. John Dunken, who used to be the General Manager at the Ilikai years before, came to help us take over the hotel. He was not much help since the locals all loved him and considered Bill and me as the "new kids on the block". This led to tension between us and John and the staff as well. Bill handled the stress better than I did. Finally, it came to the point where I almost had a nervous breakdown and could not think straight anymore. I told Bill I wanted out and requested to go back to being F&B Director. He spoke with Joe Callahan, who was one of my mentors, and told me they would see what they could do. Bill was kind and told me to go on a vacation for a few days. So Andrea, the girls and I went to Maui, a very laid back island where I was able to relax. When I got back to Honolulu, I was able to continue my job. We moved into our new home and all went well. We never talked about changing my job again.

Bill and I worked very well together. He always had new ideas. One day he told me we should build tennis courts, that no other hotel has tennis courts on the beach. Thinking it was just his idea for today, I said it was a good idea. Bill left and I did not see him until late in the evening. He walked into the building and had figured out where and how he could make the Ilikai a tennis resort. The next day, early in the morning, he started to work with our own engineering department to measure and make changes, and he developed a plan to build the tennis courts. It was to be located in the back of the hotel, outside our offices and over the parking deck of the Marina Building. It worked out just great. The Ilikai became a tennis resort, the home of Hawaii's professional tennis team. I remember having Ilie Nastase, Arthur Ashe, and many other tennis pros stay with us. This was not just a great move for the hotel but also for us who worked there. Bill and Jeff Flowers, who worked in San Francisco, played against our Controller, Ray Holmes, and me. It was a fantastic time we enjoyed and it established a unique camaraderie between us. Bill and I went to Atlanta to participate at the Annual General Manager's conference. Before our departure, at our Department Head Meeting, I gave the big speech about everybody doing a good job while we are away on the mainland. I told them there is an old Swiss saying—*"when the cat is gone the mice will dance."* The whole room broke up in laughter. I wondered what the hell was so funny and Bill explained to me that the American saying is *"when the cat is away, the mice will play."* This was another one of my great German-English translations.

The General Manager's meeting was very educational for me as it was the first one I had gone to. Joe Guilbault, the General Manager, came down the outside of the 73-story hotel in a King Kong outfit while we were enjoying breakfast. So Henry Mulligan got furious and told Joe he should be fired. Joe just laughed and told Henry he couldn't afford to fire him cause then he would have to run the hotel. The best thing about the meeting was that we finally changed the name of our company from Western International to Westin. Thus our properties became the Westin Chicago, The Westin Toronto, etc. I was so happy about this change. At every General Manager's meeting we had a fun night the last evening of the conference and at the Peachtree Plaza they had arranged an Arabian Night with music and lots of girls. There was a photographer who took pictures with some of the executives with the girls but some of them were not too flattering. As the party was going strong and the men were chasing the ladies, all of a sudden, the commandos came in. Like terrorists, they came in from the second floor of the ballroom down the balcony on ropes. They took the ladies and the party was over. It was fantastic the way they controlled the fun night without anyone getting in trouble.

After we had returned to Hawaii, Bill had to go on a business trip to the mainland. Andrea, Penny, and I went to the beach for some sun and fun. While playing in the sand and surf, my trunks had gotten filled with sand. I looked down at my pants and said, "Oh, my God. I have a breaded veal cutlet." Today Penny still smiles about that incident.

Lynn Himmelman, CEO of Westin Hotels, came to visit us at the Ilikai. Since Bill was out of town, Penny and I had to entertain him. We went with him all over to find the villa of his son-in-law who was a Japanese hotelier. After that we went to dinner where Lynn told us that his son-in-law had 30 different Mai Tai recipes which were the best. When I asked him for the recipe so we could serve it at the hotel, his reply was that he thought I was too young and would not appreciate it. I thought that was a crazy answer to my request. He was known to have told the managers at the hotel that we should walk on the outside edge of the hallways and on the side edges of the stairs so we would not wear out the carpet. He was quite a character and quite eccentric, but we all loved him.

After telling Bill that I would like to take a Dale Carnegie Course he said to go ahead as the company would pay for it. That was a fantastic experience for me and helped my self-confidence and I finally got rid of some of my Swiss shyness. After the course I continued as a graduate assistant. Nina Kealiiwahamana, our Executive Secretary, was always teasing me and correcting me when I said "Hawai" and she kept reminding me that it has two "i's". Nina was a fabulous singer who sang with Don Ho and was in many shows. She was the most gracious Hawaiian lady you could imagine. She and her husband Gordon were shining examples of the Hawaiian spirit.

I had gotten rid of all my banker suits and had accumulated a fantastic resort wardrobe. The job was going super well; we loved Hawaii and felt at home. On top of all that, the hotel was extremely successful. Then Bill called me to his office and asked me if I would like to go to New York and I said anywhere except New York. After a few minutes of talk, he convinced me it would be a great opportunity. Mr. Carlson bought the Plaza Hotel and at the time I had no concept of that particular hotel, but we had to bring it up to Westin standards. Joe Mogush, a good friend of my mentor Joe Callahan, was the Vice President and Managing Director.

Andrea and I went to Europe for a ski vacation. After that I went to New York to start my job and Andrea spent a few days with the kids with her parents in Austria. Since we lived in the hotel, we had to build a kitchen in one of our bathrooms. I wanted to have a relatively normal family life and did not want to have the kids ordering room service which would mean paying guests would have to wait because the staff was busy taking care of the manager's kids. When Andrea and the kids arrived, I went to the airport to pick them up as well as our poodle, Martini, but Martini did not arrive. Bill Hulett had taken him to the vet in Hawaii to give him a shot to keep him calm. Then in San Francisco they took him out to do his thing and unfortunately he was put on the wrong ramp and ended up in Los Angeles rather than New York. The next day he arrived but due to all the excitement and because the medication had worn off, he became blind. We originally got Martini in Singapore, and he went with us to San Francisco and then to Hawaii. When he arrived in Hawaii, we had to put him in quarantine. Of course the kids and Andrea had to visit our 5th family member every Saturday until he got to come home. Martini was certainly a well-traveled canine.

Work at the Plaza was good, however the first few weeks were a bit confusing. We had a lot of uncertainties. Joe Mogush was the MD and VP, Frank Finneran was our Manager and I was the Resident Manager. Joe Mogush was to return to Seattle as Sr. VP and supervise several hotels. Frank Finneran wanted the job but was moved to another hotel as General Manager. Frank was a great talker and could give a speech for half an hour which was elegant and interesting but when he was finished, you would scratch your head and wonder what the hell he was talking about.

For the hotel, it was good they brought in a new Managing Director. I liked Frank and his wife as they were very nice people; however, Frank left the company because he wanted to go back to Seattle. Our new Managing Director was Paul Hagen, one of Henry's boys. A great PR man and smooth operator, but the dirty job had to be done by me. The Plaza of course was a hotel with many traditions and bad habits which were hard to break. We had employees who had 40-50 years at the hotel so whenever a new manager came, they just figured management comes and goes. Also, the union rules were senseless. To make a guest room, we had different job categories such as the maid who made the bed, a hook man to handle the drapes and pictures, then a bathroom maid for the bathroom. The quota was to make 12 rooms per day, but if a maid would make nine rooms on the 10th floor and one on the 11th floor, we had to pay $2.50 travel time to use the elevator. When a maid forgot to put the soap in the guestroom, a bellman would bring up the soap and we had to pay him 50 cents to do that. The job classifications we had were absolutely ridiculous. Actually, I blamed the previous management staff who agreed to those crazy rules. They should have done better negotiations with the union. In the Oak Room we had an oyster shucker — all he did was prepare oysters in the kitchen. I tried to get him to make some salads and other pantry jobs but there was no way he would do that. I told the union I would take oysters off the menu and lay off the worker. The union said I did not have the guts to do that and I would be run out of town. So, I fired the cook and had to pay him a severance package, but the problem was solved.

One day we had a banquet luncheon at which Henry Kissinger was speaking. As he went on, we could not find an engineer whose job it was to turn on the microphone. So I went up and turned it on thinking that Mr. Kissinger would not want to wait at the Plaza to make a speech. The next day at 12:00 noon the entire engineering department walked out to teach management a lesson not to fool around with the engineers. When I came to the hotel I visited with the housekeepers and tried to give them a pep talk. I told them how important their job was and how much I appreciated their hard work. My mother was a maid, so I said I knew what they were going through. All of a sudden, a big black maid who was the union's job steward started to shout. She ranted that they had heard all this bullshit before, why the f—k didn't I go back where I came from. She was a tough cookie who had worked at the Plaza for about 25 years but six months later she was gone.

One of the first projects when Westin took over the hotel was to remodel the Persian Room. This was an entertainment room with a 12-piece orchestra and continental dining. We were losing money each month the Persian Room was open. One of the problems we encountered was the 12-piece band which could have been done with only 6 musicians. The 12-piece band quota was established in the '40s before we had all the modern electronic instruments. We had Ben Vereen as our entertainment act in the same year that he was honored as the Entertainer of the Year. We enjoyed a packed house every night, but at the end of the month we had a loss of $50,000. We talked to the unions regarding our suggestion to combine jobs and to make other changes or we would have to close the Persian Room. Their response was predictable that we could not do that as we would be run out of town. To make a long story short, we were not successful in negotiating with the union, so we laid everyone off and closed it. Maison Mandelsell, a women's boutique we had at the St. Francis came in and paid us a rather high rent each month which went straight to profit.

Another nightmare we experienced was with the employees of the many different shops we had in the hotel. Each day they would come into the Palm Court and help themselves to sweet rolls, croissants, coffee, orange juice or whatever else they desired. I called the employees of the shop to a meeting and told them this had to stop and informed them even our own staff is not allowed to eat like this. Their response was they understood and would stop this behavior. It would work for a couple of days then they would get started again. Our second meeting was held with the shop owners and the situation was explained again and they assured me they would put an end to this vexing situation. For three days all was well and again their staff members would help themselves to whatever food or drink they desired. I got so frustrated and angry I was shaking but I did not say a word. I simply walked around the hotel and stopped in the jewelry shop where I took a gold watch. Next, I went into the men's shop and found a couple of nice silk ties which I selected for myself. At the flower shop I chose the nicest arrangement and walked out with it. In the lady's boutique I found a lovely silk blouse for Andrea and the travel shop had the perfect but rather expensive travel bag which I used to put all my loot into. As you can imagine, staff members ran after me and asked me what I thought I was doing. I simply replied that I was shopping and would be coming back once each week taking advantage of our barter agreement which was orange juice, sweet rolls, croissants, etc. against my shopping. From the next day on not one person ever stepped back into the Palm Court to eat. I guess the lesson learned was you can talk to some people until you are blue in the face and still not get the point across; however, if you show them by example, that might work.

Oh my God, the Plaza had so much history and so many stories. Of course everyone knows the story of "Eloise at the Plaza," written by Kay Thompson, about the little girl who lived in the hotel. Our daughters, Andrea and Christina, kind of lived the Eloise dream, except we kept a closer eye on our children. They could not do some of the funny things that Eloise did in the book.

Paul Hagen, the hotel's Managing Director, was an excellent front man who was very smart and always had some kind of a deal working. He played golf every Saturday in the summer and I was told he even played with Arnold Palmer. Paul had an arrangement where he would take my kids along with his kids to school each morning in a limo. One morning I came down in the elevator and saw Paul. I told him about a story I had just seen on TV about the opening of the Detroit Plaza, the latest Westin addition, adding that I felt it was great coverage to be announced on *Good Morning America*. Paul said sorry, but he missed seeing that story. When we walked into the lobby, Henry Mulligan was there. Paul went up to him and asked him if he had seen *Good Morning America* this morning. He said he had seen the announcement of the opening of our newest hotel in Detroit and it was fantastic. Paul could finesse himself out of any situation and had a habit of making up stories all day long. Although I considered Paul to be very smart, I also knew that he was not the hardest-working person in the world. An excellent politician, he was always at the right place at the right time. It didn't hurt either that he was also very good looking and a real charmer. He wined and dined Henry when he came to New York and Henry thought Paul was the greatest hotel manager. Although I liked Paul very much, I also knew if I wanted to get something done, I'd better do it myself. I met many people like Paul in my career around the world. Because we lived in an artificial world in luxury hotels, some managers could not separate reality from fiction. They believed themselves to be superstars, super politicians, or any other kind of VIP that we catered to. I always lived with the same motto as Grace Kelly, who told her children "don't ever forget that your grandfather was a brick layer." I think this is such great advice — never forget where you came from no matter how successful you become. I used to say when people start to believe their own press releases is when they get themselves in trouble. Another favorite saying is that power corrupts people.

There seems to be no end to Plaza stories. One morning the Chief Engineer came and asked me to come to room 513 as he had found some kind of light shining in the corner of the room. Sure enough, there was light peeking out from the wall itself; it was rather strange. I asked him to get me a sledge hammer and puzzled he asked me why. I told him to knock down the wall with it. He said I couldn't do that and I just told him to watch me. After I knocked down the wall, we found a guestroom with a window and its curtain still hanging in it. It seems that some years ago another manager had decided to build a wall and leave everything as it was.

One day at 3am the night manager called and asked me to come down as we had a dead body on the sidewalk and it was quite a mess. Should I bring Martini to clean up? I joked. He said we would need more than that! Arriving at the scene I found that the body had been cut in half. On one side was the lower part and to the right about 3 feet was the torso. I looked up to the building and saw a window that was open and the light was still on. We went up to the room and a woman was lying in bed with a lamp cord around her neck. At first we thought she had been strangled but later we learned she was only drunk as they had both been drinking heavily. It was obvious he tried to open a window, fell out of the building and landed on a compactor in the street which cut his body in half.

The Plaza was built in 1904, so the guest rooms had beautiful marble fireplaces; however, they could not be used anymore because of fire regulations and had been closed up years ago. One night the night manager called me and said there was a lot of smoke on the 12th floor. I ran up and determined it was coming from one of the suites. I knocked on the door and the guest answered and angrily said he was glad I had come as he could not get the damned fireplace going. He said he was from Texas and used to be a Boy Scout. In his attempt to start a fire he had even ripped up some of the furniture. It was obvious after drinking quite a bit he was trying to impress his lady with how well he could make a fire.

New York had a rule called Rent Control which meant you could not increase the rent to permanent guests. To qualify for rent control a tenant must have been continuously living in an apartment since July 1, 1971. So, the Plaza had several guests who could make use of this rent control system. One was Contessa de la Santa Cruze who I loved along with her little white dog. She would hang around the lobby and practically became a part of the inventory. The problem was that under rent control she only paid us $157 a month, but it actually cost us almost $30 a day just to keep it up.

In all public bathrooms we had attendants. The rooms were staffed by workers from outside the hotel who worked only for the tips they received. There was one attendant who always drove me nuts. Rather than take care of our guests, he would sit in a closet and read dirty books. Many times I spoke to him about his behavior without any success. So one day I walked into the toilette and saw him in his closet reading *Playboy*. Since he did not see me, I snuck in and locked him in the closet then left. He screamed so loudly that a guest called security. He never found out who locked him in, but I also never found him reading books in the closet again either.

Mrs. Ben was a permanent resident of the Plaza who was extremely wealthy due to AT&T money she had inherited. She paid full rates at the hotel. Unfortunately, one evening I received a call she had passed away. I went up to her suite and found her son going through all the doors looking for money or whatever he could find. Since I felt this was disrespectful to her memory, I got furious and kicked him out of the suite. Here was his mother lying dead in the bed and her son did not even care; I even had to pull up her chin to close her mouth and make her look better. His response was he threatened to sue me. I told him to go ahead. Since this is New York, I hear this threat about five times a day from anyone who does not like what you do so the first thing they say is they're going to sue you.

Miss DeLapp was another super rich lady who lived permanently at the Plaza. She paid full rates for the suite for the whole year, even during the summer which she spent at the Claridge Hotel in London. She called us once a week from there to remind us to take care of her plants. She had a fulltime maid, but the maid traveled with her to London. She was a thoroughly fine, worldly lady. Every morning she had the same room service order. One day the Room Service Manager, David Ling, came to me and was all excited. He asked me to guess who he had served dinner to last night, to which I guessed Johnny Cash? Excitedly his reply was no, but he said when he entered the guest room there was Paul Newman, Joanne Woodward, and Liza Minnelli. I told him I hoped he had taken good care of them.

Linda Ronstadt wanted to have dinner in the Edwardian Room, but she was dressed in blue jeans so I asked her to go and change. She looked at me and indicated it was no problem, but she just did not feel like changing clothes tonight. In the most pleasant way she addressed me as "my man" and said she was sure we had room service in this hotel.

One night the Director of Marketing and I had dinner with a strange fellow whom I just did not trust although he was a great talker, extremely smart. He brought each of us an expensive bottle of wine the vintage of the year we were born. He asked a lot of questions; I often gave him the wrong information deliberately while the Director of Marketing kind of spilled his guts. At the end of the night he put his hand in his pocket and I heard a click; he had taped our entire conversation. I told a friend of mine I bet he was doing his homework to purchase the hotel. Years later Donald Trump purchased the hotel when United needed money to keep the airlines going. Still today I wonder what this dinner was all about.

Life at the Plaza could not have been better. The job went well and the hotel started to make money. We had many friends, spent the weekends with them in Westport or Long Island. In the summer we went to Jones Beach and in the winter we went skiing in the Catskills. We visited all the Broadway shows and entertained many of our visitors from headquarters as everyone wanted to come visit the Plaza. Andrea lost lots of weight and was taking painting lessons at the art school. We were really living the good life.

I was ready to become General Manager, but rather than get a new assignment I wanted to stay at the Plaza and of course, I loved New York.

Plus, the direct flights to Switzerland were a nice bonus. That's when Henry Mulligan called me and said he wanted me to fly to Seattle and wanted to talk to me. When we met he explained that we had big problems at the new hotel in Detroit which included management problems, employee morale, and the bad relationship between the owner and the Ford people. In addition, uncontrolled expenses needed to be brought under control—the job sounded overwhelming. He said he wanted me to go there with the Title Manager and report to John Dunken; however, he wanted me to run the hotel. I thought to myself that what he was saying was stupid, just another one of Henry's strange ways of doing business.

When I went back to New York and told Andrea about my conversation with Henry, I hate to admit I cried like a baby. I felt like I was always getting screwed. As I told Andrea, other young managers like me get the plum jobs and I get the shit ones. Time after time I had to prove myself and I thought I deserved a job offer as a General Manager and the opportunity to "smell the roses" for a change. Andrea was supportive but encouraged me to think it over. By the next morning I had turned on my positive attitude. There's a reason for everything in life my mom always said. One of her favorite sayings was "When the good Lord closes one door he opens a window." I called Henry and told him I would accept the job. I had always said I would go anywhere except Detroit—well Detroit here we come! When my new assignment was announced in the company, many of my friends asked me how I could give up the Plaza with its crystal chandeliers, silver, gold, all the glamour, the antiques and the Persian rugs to go work in concrete, cement, glass and plastic. My response was I felt I would learn more in six months in Detroit than I could in two years at the Plaza. Paul and the staff gave us a wonderful goodbye party and off we went to Detroit.

Although Detroit is not New York, the downtown location of the Renaissance Center was an area which was in the planning stages to bring Detroit back. The city was set to go through a tremendous change and revitalization. A consortium of about 50 companies financed the project with Ford Motor Land Company taking the lead in the endeavor. The Renaissance Center was a complex of four office towers with the 73 story Detroit Plaza Hotel, advertised as the tallest hotel in the world, smack dab in the middle.

We found a nice home in the city of Grosse Pointe, a pretty community a few miles from downtown. It was so different from the inner city we had just left behind. With nice schools, parks, a community center, shopping, and churches, I knew it would be a nice place for our family to live.

Once I started working at the hotel it did not take me long to realize there were multiple problems to solve. The hotel suffered from many basic mistakes and the complicated design of this Portman-designed hotel did not make it any easier. The design of the hotel was not very efficient; it was great to look at but failed on its functionality. With its 73 floors, room service and maid service were difficult to properly manage. In the lobby there was a lake with little pods around to be used as cocktail settings. The hotel had 18 exits and entrances and was an absolute nightmare for security. In addition to the physical difficulties at the hotel, many of the department heads had been transferred from the Carlton Hotel in South Africa and for Detroit, which was a "black city," this was a red flag. The locals felt they brought in people from South Africa to handle the blacks. Of course this was not the original plan but their perception became their reality. The person whom I was replacing was a Greek and most people hated him. His supporters were the staff members whom he brought with him from South Africa.

Horror stories circulated about the many incidents that occurred at this hotel. One weekend they offered a special room rate of $25 as the PR people felt the hotel needed some exposure, which it got alright. Just imagine twenty-five bucks for a room in the middle of Detroit; ultimately the hotel was jam-packed full with 4-5 guests in each room. The lobby had been decorated with yellow mums for a lovely ambience; however, on one side of the hotel the customers cut the flowers and on the other side of the hotel they were selling the same flowers for $1 a bunch. Other customers took lamps and other items from their rooms and either sold them in the lobby or simply took them home with them.

In our beige-painted employee locker room, someone had written with black markers derogatory comments such as "screw management" and "to hell with Westin Hotels." That same day I repainted the walls but the very next day more profanity about management was on the wall. This continued for three days until I got smart and painted the walls with a charcoal color so they couldn't write on it. Someone else had an even brighter idea to go over the wet paint with toilet paper. Some of the employees were so destructive and angry rather than being thankful to have a job. I met with some of the ringleaders and begged them to work with us for the good of everyone. Then a big black leader told me they did not want our improvement. He said we had screwed up their business in downtown as they had been happy pushing drugs and hookers. They felt our new morality did nothing to help them. It was quite depressing and hard to hear someone say this so bluntly, but it did not hold me back. We moved forward slowly and day-by-day we made a little progress.

Once, while we had a hotel full of tire dealers the Assistant Manager found me in the Lobby Court and said we have a problem in the lobby. Thinking I had seen them all, I asked what the problem was. He bet me I had not seen this one before. In the lobby we found a man unconscious lying on his back. Some conventioneers had rolled a 600 lb. tractor tire through the lobby and over the man who now had tire marks all over his back (yeah, he was right, I had not seen this one before). Another time a drunk fell from the 8th floor of the hotel down into the lake located on the lobby level. Obviously, he had been leaning over the railing and fell, landing between two steel lights, but luckily it did not kill him. He shook himself off and said he better go dry off.

One night as I made my rounds going through the hotel, three black thugs cornered me in the banquet area and provoked me. In this dark secluded area it's easy to see how I would have felt threatened by them. One called me "honky" and wanted to know what I was doing there. At this point I realized I was outnumbered and I have to admit scared for my life. At about that time I felt a tap on my shoulder; it was two of our Security Officers who asked me if there was a problem. I indicated that I had asked these guys to leave the hotel but apparently they did not want to. One of the security officers told the three black thugs to take a good look at me; this man is God and when God tells you to leave the hotel, you leave the hotel—understood? As if they had been hit by a bolt of lightning, they fled.

On top of the hotel we had a revolving restaurant; it was the only place where you could look south into Canada. It was a continental dining room and during opening it did well, but the novelty wore off fast. My favorite restaurant was the Japanese restaurant Mikado. It was a place that we leased out. We had numerous other restaurants and lounges. Our Banquet Department was also big since we were a convention hotel. The hotel had 1400 rooms and could accommodate 2800 guests at once. We used to say it's not a hotel, it's a convention factory.

John Dunken, our MD was a nice fellow who was getting worn out as it appeared many things became overwhelming for him. Since the hotel was filled with hundreds of living plants, I remember one time someone from Ford Motor Land Company told John about an organization in Minnesota that handled indoor plants. The next day John had someone from our Engineering Department request that they send someone over to study our plants. What information he gleaned from this plant study we will never know as nothing was ever done with the data. Working in an irrational situation like this was not easy; however, I always backed John up since he was the MD and I was the Manager. I looked up to him as if he was the Number 1 and I was the Number 2.

The morale in the hotel was not the greatest as we had many different cliques and that was not particularly good. It led to a political game and the same happened with our owners. The leadership in the Ford Motor Land Company was also a bit shaky. The hotel did not live up to their projections and of course the four office towers did not produce the expected profits. I have seen this before as rosy projections are submitted so a development can be financed with even those in upper management knowing that the numbers are unrealistic. All this combined did not produce a healthy work environment for everyone involved. Naturally, all day long the blame game continued. I was able to make some progress with the Ford people but not nearly as much progress as we needed. I never learned the full story, but the powers that be decided to move John Dunken out and bring in Chris Marker from the Crown Center Hotel in Kansas City. I must say that was one of the better moves Henry Mulligan made. John moved back to Kansas City and worked with the Hallmark Group. They liked him and with Chris Marker we got our new leadership.

Chris was a great fellow whom I liked along with his wife. First time I met them was in Chicago when Chris spent some time with us in an orientation program. Chris brought many new ideas and a good spirit of teamwork to the hotel. He was good in owner relationships as well. I learned a lot that I could use in my later assignments. Also, he hired his old ad agency from Kansas City. They were great and developed a new marketing, advertisement, and PR plan. An employee motivation program was part of their planning. Things began to look up and business increased, which made the numbers start to look better. In the summer we had a program called Renaissance Life which included an outdoor musical concert with up to a thousand or more people attending. Many people were from the surrounding office towers plus the Ford people and it created a platform for bonding strangers together, some of whom had previously had adversarial relationships. It was great to see how everyone got along. There were also attendees from the local business community and this helped to establish the hotel where previously the Renaissance Center had been looked upon as an island to itself, separated from the city. My relationship was very good with Chris and the 18 months I spent in Detroit went by very fast. By now I actually felt that I deserved my own 400-500 room hotel as a General Manager.

7. THE PEACHTREE PLAZA HOTEL

It was a normal workday in October 1979 when Chris Marker asked me to call Henry Mulligan. When I reached him, he wanted to know if I would like to go to Atlanta as the Managing Director of the Peachtree Plaza. My response was a resounding, "Holy Shit, sounds good to me!" Henry continued to say that it was a big job especially since it would be my first Number 1 job. Also, there seemed to be some design problems with the hotel itself, plus the owner relationship was not too good. The hotel had only been open for less than three years and I was going to be the 4th Managing Director. I asked Henry when I could go and he said tomorrow I should fly to Atlanta and plan to meet with John Portman, the builder, then meet with his lawyer, his accountant, and Mickey Steinberg, Mr. Portman's advisor. If the owners approved me, I was to start as soon as possible. My meeting with everybody went well, probably because I was not even nervous and was confident I would pass with flying colors. After the meeting I returned to Detroit, listed the house for sale, finalized a few other details and went right back to Atlanta. I was so glad to move away from Detroit, especially since I had a romantic relationship going on with a married woman and hoped that my move to Atlanta would put an end to that (more details to follow about that subject later).

The first few weeks at the Peachtree Plaza proved to be quite challenging. Everyone had said the hotel was a three-ring circus and they were right; I felt the same thing when I walked in. Although I did not tell anyone about my feelings, I thought to myself, "okay let's run this place like a three-ring circus." I remember my secretary coming into my office and telling me to leave the office through the back door because there was a disgruntled guest who wanted to speak to me. I told her I was not leaving the office but that she should bring the guest into my office so I could hear him out and see if I could be of help to him since that was my job. In disbelief she asked the customer to meet with me. Later I spoke with the secretary again and she explained that the previous manager always asked her to tell him if there was a problem guest so he could leave the office and not have to face the guest. It was hard to believe this behavior and I immediately initiated a new program whereby if any guest asked to speak with the manager, they were to be brought directly to me. If I was not in the office, I wore a pager so I could be there within minutes. Everyone wanted to pass the buck when problems arose and did not want to be problem solvers, just avoiders. Add to this back stabbing between the department heads which was rampant, and you can easily see what I had to deal with.

The manager who ran the hotel before me was asked to leave the Peachtree Plaza. I had the pleasure of working with him for just one day, even though he was supposed to give me a full week of orientation. After listening to him about how bad everything was from the hotel itself, to the owners, the staff, the stupid Southern people, and even the city of Atlanta, I said thanks to him for his help, but that since I knew he had a lot to do to move, I could find myself around. Thus, we had lunch, said our goodbyes and that was the last time I ever saw that gentleman. The previous manager was not involved at all in the community where he should represent the property in the city. Instead he had assigned that job to the Director of Marketing who, along with his wife, became very involved. He was a couple of years older than me and of course it did not sit right with him and his wife to take a back seat to me. All of a sudden, the General Manager would be attending all the functions, parties, as well as TV, radio and newspaper interviews. Within a very short time the business community in Atlanta knew who ran the Peachtree Plaza and who would be the spokesperson. I got involved with the Georgia Hospitality Association, the Atlanta Convention and Visitors Bureau, the Chamber of commerce, Central Atlanta Progress and many, many other organizations. I also asked John Portman to help me get into the Atlanta Rotary Club, which he did, and they invited me to join. Slowly but surely, we made progress at the hotel.

Every three months we had owner's meetings for which I always prepared myself well, but sometimes we sure had fireworks. John Portman's advisor, Mickey Steinberg, could be a challenge to deal with at the meetings. But I loved and admired the man as he definitely knew what he was talking about. In one of the meetings Mickey, who was also a limited partner, told me he had not received a single dollar yet from his investment in the hotel. So I gave Mickey a dollar, and he took it and framed it. Still today whenever I see him he reminds me he still has the first dollar he ever made from his investment. I was told the hotel was built with $50,000 cash and the rest of the cost of building the property was financed with 40 million dollars. Those were the good days of development business.

I remember once Mickey was so mad about something he wanted to fire everyone at the hotel. So I put my arm around him and agreed with him to go fire everyone, then we would not have to worry about the hotel anymore. He replied that we could not do that because if we did we would have to close the hotel. I assured him I was aware of that fact but then all our worries would be over. Needless to say, we both went back to our offices and went back to work.

Sadly, it was around this time Andrea and I divorced. Then I married the lady from Detroit one day after my divorce, but more on that saga later.

My new wife Margot was working in public relations and she was very good in her job and was a great asset to me in representing the hotel. We could walk into a ballroom and she would introduce me to the Governor, the Mayor, or any business executive or VIP in the room. She was a master in her business, so I have to give her credit for that. For me, sometimes I felt she was almost too abrasive. After moving to Atlanta, she got a job as Director of Public Relations with the Atlanta Symphony. Robert Shaw was still the conductor of the orchestra. During the summer the symphony offered a concert series at Chastain Park which was quite an event. When you had a table it enabled you to entertain guests very nicely. The hotel had an excellent table location reserved and did a super job in putting together a menu with the appropriate wines. Usually we entertained convention planners who were either looking at the hotel to book an event or guests who had held a convention and it was our way of thanking them for their business. We served cold food but really did it in style with smoked salmon, seared tuna, roast beef, smoked ham or turkey, deviled eggs, along with different salads like lobster, shrimp or Waldorf salad paired with a mousse or French pastries. It was very elegant with candelabras, tablecloths, and flower arrangements. It was perfectly normal for each table at the event to try and outdo each other. The entertainers were all well-known names such as Manhattan Transfer, Henry Mancini, Roger Whittaker, Marvin Hamlisch, Judy Collins, Bobby Goldsboro, and many, many more. Since my wife was the PR Director, I had the pleasure of meeting many of these stars.

I had several Executive Assistant Managers during my time at the Westin Peachtree Plaza where I was considered a "Trainer of General Managers." One of my execs was Tom Heder, a Hungarian refugee who came with his parents from the East to the West during the riots in Hungary the mid-50s. They later moved to the United States. Tom was a great fellow, a good worker, and a loyal soldier. Whenever I got mad, Tom would calm me down and make me think the situation over. Or if I rattled the staff's cages, he would calm down the troops. Normally the second in command should be the driver and the General Manager should be the one with the father image who would calm down the situation. Tom and I had reversed roles. Tom got a well-deserved promotion to General Manager.

One extraordinary Executive Assistant Manager I trained was a young lady. She was the first female in that job and ultimately became the first female General Manager for Westin. I was so proud of that accomplishment especially since I had two daughters whom I would have liked to see become General Managers. That turned out to be just a dream of mine since they had no interest in the hotel business. But at least I was responsible for producing at least one female General Manager after all.

Another Executive Assistant Manager under my guidance was Jim McKenna. Jim was a very smart young man who was a bit flashy like his dad, who was also an hotelier. Jim and his wife were very nice people and I wanted Jim to become a GM but somehow he did not fit the "Seattle mold," which was too bad. I think Jim could have become a great GM for Westin. Eventually I advised him to relocate to Las Vegas where he worked in one of the major casinos in Sin City. One year on my birthday, at 10am, Jim came to my office with a change of clothes for me which he had previously arranged with Margot. So I changed into the shorts and golf shirt, then he took me down to a limo and drove me to the airport where we boarded a helicopter for a tour of Atlanta flying over my house, Stone Mountain, and the Peachtree Plaza. We landed at Six Flags over Georgia, where Spurgeon Richardson, the General Manager, gave me a tour of the amusement park. In the meantime, the hotel's Executive Committee and some other guests as well as Margot arrived and we enjoyed a southern BBQ dinner. This was a birthday party I will never forget. Only Jim could have planned something like that.

Ray Silvester was the Corporate Director of Rooms in Seattle which he had done for quite some time. However, he had a desire to get out of the corporate system and become a General Manager. So, the powers

that be in Seattle felt he should work in a hotel for a while and it was decided that I would be the right person to take him under my wing. Ray
was with me for about two years and was a newlywed as he had lost his
first wife, a wonderful lady, from cancer. His current wife was a lot like
Margot, what I would call "a lot of hot air." My relationship with Ray
was cordial and we worked together well; however, I must admit I was
always very careful with my actions. I don't know if it was because he was
so Seattle-connected or if there was envy on his side because of my success. Ray got a well-deserved promotion. In my eight years I produced
four General Managers, which was pretty good considering the hotel
had been a total disaster in 1979 when I began there.

The Executive Committee was fantastic. There was Ken Melton in
HR and Bob Taylor in Property Management, both of whom knew
each other from years in the Army. The Rooms Director changed several times during my stay and the same with the F&B Director. The
Executive Chef was Waldo Brun, whom I knew from the Century Plaza
and the Carefree Inn in Arizona. Waldo was one of the finest chefs I
ever worked with and was also a great organizer and leader. He did not
drink and was not one of those temperamental chefs whom I knew all
too well. Waldo was the driving force after whom we conceptualized
our two main restaurants in the hotel. We had the Terrace Room on the
lobby level and the Sun Dial on the top of the building. The Sun Dial
was a revolving restaurant. People would ask us what the difference was
between the two dining rooms and the waiter would say we have continental food, chicken, beef, etc. in the Terrace Room with elegant service,
a piano player and fine dining. In the Sun Dial we have chicken, beef,
continental dining and a spectacular view since it was on the 72nd floor,
plus we have strolling gypsy musicians. Guests would say no since the
only difference between the two restaurants was 72 floors. After I heard
this comment so often, I knew the guests had a point. I had my F&B
Director and Chef Waldo develop two new restaurant concepts. We did

a study of the competition and found out what was available in down-town Atlanta. We looked at steak houses, Mexican restaurants, French cuisine, Italian restaurants, etc., until we had all kinds of ideas. It was clear at this point that we had no good fish restaurants in Atlanta, which is what we needed. So, the Savannah Fish Co. was born and we felt it should be in the Terrace Room. We hired Maurizio Manfredi, the res-taurant manager from Bugatti's, which at that time was the very success-ful Italian restaurant at the Omni Hotel. The restaurant was marketed like it had nothing to do with the hotel. It had its own phone number and the manager had business cards with only the restaurant's logo on it. Nowhere on the menu did it say Peachtree Plaza or Westin Hotels. We had a rule that Westin Hotels had to be identified on all printed ma-terials at the company; however, I figured it is easier to get forgiveness than to get approval. I was really reprimanded for breaking one of the cardinal rules at Westin; however, the restaurant became so successful that my concept was copied in other properties. We created a fish soup and called it the Savannah Fish Stew. It was clear fish broth with a light saffron taste with julienne of celery, carrots and leeks with small diced tomatoes and a few small cut pieces of fish added in the stew. It was then served with butter lettuce with a special dressing. The menu was printed daily similar to a newspaper with a list of the many different fish varie-ties with a price printed. Then it had two spaces where the chef could put a remark such as "available" or "did not bite" so the guest could imagine how fresh the fish was which was delivered fresh daily. As a dessert we offered three little beignets with a choice of chocolate or vanilla sauce. The restaurant took no reservations. The Savannah Fish Co. became a very successful restaurant with lines of guests waiting at the door. We were even contacted by investors wanting to purchase a franchise. Of course, I would have loved to do this, but the powers in Seattle did not like the idea. The concept was duplicated in some other Westin Hotels. Henry, our Chairman at the time, used to say if a guest wants a steak in the Savannah Fish Co. he is entitled to get it because of the room rates he paid. But I argued it was not right since a guest expects a quality product in what we are serving. My example was when a customer goes to a McDonald's he eats what is on the menu and he does not expect spinach or anything he desires. I still remember when I took the oysters off the menu in the Oak Room at the Plaza because of the union negotiations. At that time, I said if a guest wants to have an oyster he can go over to the Oyster Bar and order his oysters and I never had a complaint in New York. Since the Savannah Fish Co. was such a success, I asked my people to come up with a concept for the Sun Dial Restaurant on top of the building, to think about why guests come to dine with us. It was obvious it was because of the fantastic view of Atlanta but that was also why the bloody place was empty when we experienced bad weather. People would make reservations but when the weather turned sour, they cancelled or just did not show up. So, I told Waldo and the F&B staff to come up with something that would make the customer want to come to the restaurant whether it was raining or the sun was shining. We wanted to entice the guest to visit the Sun Dial for the dining experience, not the darn view which was just an extra, I concluded. After many meetings, we were ready to give it a try. The concept was great beef, with a real value for the price you paid. So we changed the table set-ups, also. When the guest sat down we brought them sourdough bread with two different flavored butters, orange and herb butter. Next was a crock of fresh shrimp which the guests had to peel themselves, which we felt was fun and they could have as many shrimps as they desired with a good cocktail sauce as well. Next the customer could order prime rib, different cuts of steaks all seasoned with Waldo's Magic Crystals, a seasoning salt we put in glass jars which guests could purchase. Customers eventually ordered it from all over the country. The dinner concept we developed was great. Our next project was a lunch concept that was built on sandwiches, a business man's luncheon. We guaranteed the customer he could be in and out in 45 minutes or his meal was on us. Lunch had to be different since the dinner concept was much too expensive for lunch. Now that we had two great successes, we gained the respect of the owners and it got much easier to work with them. When we needed for money for capital improvement, the dollars would become available. The greatest handicap we had in the hotel was its functionality. John Portman, whom I absolutely adored as a developer and architect, did not always build functionality in the design of his buildings. Like I said before, I think John is a genius, but he does not take no for an answer. I admire him since he was one of my greatest mentors and just love the man. In the back of the house, it was challenging to operate the hotel with not enough storage space and complicated turnovers for the banquet department. With 72 stories, room service delivery was a piece of work. We outfitted one of the service elevators with a removable kitchen so we could serve continental breakfast faster in the morning during rush hours. Many of the deficiencies we tried to overcome. We had two major design problems in the hotel which had been argued about for weeks between Westin's design team and the Portman designers. We had similar issues at the Detroit Plaza and the Bonaventure Hotel in Los Angeles. These three hotels had been negotiated as one package or we could say one master contract. Each hotel was mortgaged to the roof. I remember talking to Bob Quince who was the Managing Director of the Los Angeles Bonaventure and I asked him if he purchased computers, but he said no, they lease everything except toilet paper. It sounds funny, but it makes it hard to operate a hotel like this.

The two biggest problems we had were also the two biggest achievements of my work at the Peachtree Plaza. I ultimately solved the problems and made the hotel workable. The first problem was the elevators, which stopped in the lobby, stopped at some of the banquet rooms, then went up to the guest rooms, which meant that to go to some of the other banquet rooms, the guests had to use an elevator, then get on an escalator to find their meeting room. At that time, when a guest would come to the lobby and ask a clerk where the banquet room was, the clerk would reply upstairs. The guest would go upstairs and look for the banquet room, then the waiter would have to tell the guest sorry sir your room is downstairs. The guest did not know the only way he could get to this meeting room would be by using the escalators. The confusion and the frustration created for the customers cannot be put on paper. One evening John and I had a drink in the Lobby Pod, since he used to come by and just chat with me as he liked to know what was going on in the hotel. So he asked me what do we have to do to get more business, and I said the first item is to open all the elevators so people can get around by themselves. But John said that was one of his trademarks to force guests to use escalators as it creates movement. I told him I was aware of that, but it also drives customers nuts when they cannot get around by themselves, so I said let me tell you via this recent event. The other day I told him I went up an escalator and this beautiful woman in front of me stamped on the floor and screamed she wished she knew the person who designed this place. I replied that I could not help her there but that I was the idiot who runs this place, and could I help her? John just grinned and ordered another drink. A week later I heard a noise in the lobby and when I investigated I found construction workers sawing out the granite and cement to open the elevators. I could not believe it, but when the project was finished the guests could press the elevator button and get to their desired destination. Man — what an achievement that was!

The second problem we had was the lake in the lobby. We had a 73-story hotel and to go through the hotel to the other side of the property there was just a small, narrow corridor where the bellmen had to bring the luggage through on their carts. When the hotel was full it was a nightmare to get around the lobby because of the lake in the lobby. Again, John and I were having a drink in the lobby and we began talking. As usual he asked me what else needed to be done to get more business. My answer was we needed to get rid of the damned lake so that people could get around in the lobby. And again, John replied that this was another one of his trademarks which we cannot eliminate. To soothe his anger, I put my arm around his shoulder and told him there were only two people in the world who could walk on water—one is you and the other one died over 2000 years ago. He chuckled and ordered another drink. Less than a week later there was no longer any water in the lobby lake and construction workers used their jackhammers to clear out the lobby. A new floor was installed and voila, we could all walk around in the lobby. The improvement was absolutely superb as guests could now move around comfortably without bumping into each other. It just proves that you shouldn't argue about something you cannot win, but instead give an example people can relate to.

It was a few months since Bill Hullet left Westin to take over as President of Stouffer Hotels, a third-class hotel company. Bill wanted to build something himself and realized that he would never become President of Westin. Bill asked me to join him, but I declined.

Alex Post from the famous law firm in Atlanta was the sponsor for me to become a member of the Atlanta Rotary Club. Andy Young, previous Mayor of Atlanta, once said "I don't run Atlanta, it's the Rotary Club who runs the city." We really had an exclusive group of executives in our club. I was asked to give a speech in the club and it went quite well; at least we had a few laughs. Each hotel has a log book where we document the highlights during the day's events. Every morning I would go to the Assistant Manager's desk and read the log book. Following are a few excerpts which I shared with the Rotary Club during my talk.

4:14am—Naked guest was wandering around the 40th floor. He locked himself out of room 4009 when trying to go to the bathroom.

11:15pm—Intoxicated lady jumped in the lobby lake to collect coins. Said she was experiencing a credit problem.

2:32am — Customer in 5903 complained that his "lady of the evening" had robbed him of his wallet. He said he would sue the hotel. The security officer suggested that we call his wife to wire him some money. He declined the offer and dropped the charges.

10:05pm — We lost John Portman's car, so he had to go home in a cab. Mr. Gammeter will probably get a call on this in the morning.

11:19pm — Security officer located illegally parked car. It was determined that it could be Mr. Portman's car. The parking attendant stated when Mr. Portman arrived at 7:30pm we had run out of parking spaces, so the car was placed in the freight elevator.

10:30am — Honeymoon couple on the 70th floor called the Assistant Manager about slow room service. They also advised security that a helicopter had been hovering outside their room for an extended period of time. Guests were advised to pull the drapes closed before proceeding with breakfast.

A book could be written using just the comments from the daily log book. I remember a guest in the hallway in Chicago who was trying to get into a guest room. First I thought he was trying to break into the room and commit a robbery. When I asked him if I could be of assistance to him, he handed me his room key. Unfortunately, it was for the Sheraton Hotel not the Westin Hotel. He was so drunk he ended up in our hotel looking for his room. Another evening, around happy hour time, I heard this loud bang and ran to the lobby where I learned that a woman on the 8th floor was leaning on the edge of the railing, shot herself, and landed on a gentleman having a drink in the lobby. Her fall had broken both of his legs. She was so determined to commit suicide that if the shot had not killed her the fall down into the lobby would. It appears that the atrium style hotels are a magnet for people who consider suicide. In each atrium hotel we operated we kept a green blanket to cover the body if the unfortunate should happen.

Once, when a Japanese guest brought a hooker into the hotel, our security staff cautioned him that she was bad news, but he had no interest in heeding their warning. So he went up and was subsequently asked by the girl to take a shower which was to be followed by oral sex. Of course when he came out of the shower everything was gone: his money, his passport, his suitcase — nothing was left. Sometimes people have to learn the hard way. Speaking of Japanese, Joe Mogush, my Vice President while in Atlanta who was also my boss and mentor, could be very emotional at times. I recall one time he came in from Denver steaming. I asked him what was bothering him and he said he was just in Denver changing planes. His story was that this Japanese guy came up to him and asked him where his gate was. Joe curtly told him "You found Pearl Harbor, you can find your own damned gate." But the best line from Joe Mogush was when I went to Seattle for a meeting. The head office would invite "young chargers," as they called us, to participate as guests in the Senior Management Committee. So the officers were talking about acquiring a new hotel. Joe told them, you fellows can't make a decent deal with a $100 bill and an American Express Card in a whorehouse! Joe Mogush and Joe Callahan were 55 years old when they both resigned to retire. I guess they had enough of some of the incompetence we experienced with the head office. When they left, I lost two fine mentors. Luckily, by now I was an established General Manager myself. A headhunter from New York whom I knew well tried to place me with other companies, but I never had the guts to leave Westin Hotels; today I have to question myself why. The first time, I went to Boston for an interview and they offered me a job as GM in a very large hotel with a big salary increase. Then a few months later I was asked to go to Boca Raton, Florida where I interviewed for the job as Managing Director of a fabulous resort. It was really a great opportunity for me to be king in my kingdom. All went well and Margot wanted me to take the job. Today, looking back, I think the main reason I turned down the job was because I did not want to leave Atlanta. Andrea was only 14 and Christina was 11. Knowing I had left home at 16, I felt I should at least stay with the kids until Christina was 16. When I was at the Annual American Hotel Motel Association Meeting in Chicago, I met with Bill and Penny Hulett; it was great to see them again. Bill asked me to join him and my response was that I could not leave Atlanta until my youngest was 16. Plus, I loved my job at the Peachtree Plaza and the city of Atlanta.

Often I asked myself why we were so successful in Atlanta; coming from San Francisco, Los Angeles, New York, and Chicago, I felt this city was so behind. But I knew it had tremendous potential whose surface had not been touched yet. It only needed inner city living, condos, night clubs, grocery stores, etc. and it could really boom. The locals used to tell me Atlanta was a "black city" and that you would not get people to live in condos downtown; I disagreed and said to look at Chicago, New York and other vibrant cities—they are booming because of in-town living. Today we once again have in-town living and the city is vibrant.

THE ATLANTA WINE FESTIVAL

When I first came to Atlanta, Andrea and I would go out for dinner and when I asked for a glass of Merlot or Chardonnay, the waiters often would say—we have red, white or pink! This used to drive me nuts. In 1979, Atlanta did not have the fine and sophisticated restaurants we have today. I told Andrea that we needed to educate these Southerners about wine. My Beverage Manager, Larry, and I organized a wine festival. He did an outstanding job contacting different wine producers and arranged a weekend in the hotel's ballroom where vintners would have wine degustations. At each table they had sales reps and promotional materials. We had different wine experts involved and also had a judging of the wines following by an awards banquet where we handed out medals to the winners. The next year the wine festival became even bigger and we renamed it The Atlanta International Wine Festival, whose name I protected. A year later it grew so much bigger we had to use different ballrooms in the hotel. We had speakers, seminars, and wine growers from all over featuring wines from Europe, South Africa, Chile, Australia, and even New Zealand. The festival had become very prestigious and generated fantastic publicity for the hotel. Each year the Georgia Hospitality and Travel Association had an annual conference featuring a food exhibit at the Georgia World Congress Center. Since I was the Chairman of the Association for two years, I told Bob King, our President, a paid executive, that I would give the Wine Festival to the Association and it could be held during our annual food show. Needless to say, it was a fantastic addition to the show and was extremely successful. The most famous wine growers in the country attended the show. We had television coverage and numerous newspaper articles throughout the year. In addition, Westin Hotel even started an annual Wine Week during which different guests would go to California and meet at different wineries. This wine program was great. We would try 30 wines before lunch in a blind tasting. Of course, we did not actually drink the wines; we had to spit them out. Our evaluation was judged on aroma, color, taste, price, and value. Following a preset criteria, we would purchase wine for the whole company. It was a very rewarding experience to participate in and I was delighted to be invited for several years. Who in their right mind would not want to participate in California's wine region with all the history and traditions it embodied? Also, the wine estate owners we met were an added benefit and the whole thing was a unique experience. I met Robert Mondavi's wife, Margaret, a Swiss lady who gave me a painting she had created. Another highlight of my Napa

Valley experience was the opportunity to have lunch with Mr. Trefethen, a fine gentleman.

It was so ironic that here I was promoting the enjoyment of wine while the Governor of Georgia, Joe Frank Harris, did not even believe in drinking. I remember participating in the opening of the Habersham Winery and the Governor was the person selected to cut the ribbon. He gave a talk and then said how great it was, how great it was to be here, how great it was to open this new agriculture business in Georgia. He would not even use the word "winery," but instead called it an "agriculture business." Welcome to the South, brother, I said to myself as we all clapped for his great speech.

MARGOT'S CAREER

Margot left the Atlanta Symphony and joined Cotton States Insurance Co. as Vice President. She was in charge of Marketing and Public Relations. She negotiated a good deal and got a company car which was great since we only had one car previously. Call me cheap but it worked. Margot, however, was not as frugal as I; on the contrary, she liked to spend money, often using credit cards. Whenever I found out she had credit card debts and was paying 14-16% interest while I had the money in my checking account earning very little interest, I would bail her out. But six months later we had the same story all over again. We fought a lot over money. Margot was always competing with me and I would tell her she was no competition for me; looking back that was probably not a nice thing to say. She worked hard and did a good job, but I never gave her enough credit for her accomplishments. A fantastic politician, she really knew how to play the corporate game. Coming from humble beginnings, I think she became obsessed with her job and wanted to be someone.

MORE STORIES

One day we had a convention of nurses at the hotel and the Director asked me to welcome the group, which I gladly did. I gave them a nice talk about how important their profession was, etc., and added that the weather forecast for the week was going to be great since I had direct contact with the man upstairs. "You male chauvinist pig!" a woman shouted from the first row. "How do you even know it is a man up there?" I just smiled at her and replied that I would make a deal with her. I told her I promised the next time I needed a weather forecast in Atlanta I would give her a call. The whole room broke up in laughter and everyone started to clap. In our business you have to have thick skin so you can take all the baloney that you are faced with. The guest is not always right, but he has the right to be right — that just goes with the job.

In 1982, I introduced the first concierge in the city of Atlanta. In Europe it is common to have a concierge in a good hotel. They help you to get anything you want as long as it is legal, I used to tell people. It was a big deal to have this service in the early 80s, whereas today you can find concierge service for everything from hotels to hospitals, health clubs, even car dealers. Years later, after coming back from Europe, the Concierge Society of Atlanta awarded me the Silver Plume Award as General Manager of the year.

I was always promotion-minded in my efforts to get recognition for the hotel. My motto was the Peachtree Plaza does not belong to Westin Hotel or any of its investors. The hotel belongs to the people of Atlanta. This philosophy I actually used in any city where I operated a hotel. On July 4th we had the window cleaner of the hotel jump from the top of the building and come down on a rope for 73 floors. It was spectacular! We called it the Jump of Spiderman. For one day our window cleaner was a big star. The kids would sit on the sidewalk and shout for Spiderman to come on down. After landing he would hand out photos of himself and sign autographs. We closed International Blvd. and had police handle the crowds. The media and television coverage were priceless.

Another function we started was the annual Peachtree Plaza Cup, which was a polo tournament organized along with the Atlanta Polo Club. It's well known that people involved with polo are folks with money. We had players from Argentina and Costa Rica who played against our Atlanta club members. The event was with tents and included F&B service, elegant ladies in hats and wearing beautiful summer dresses. It was a classy affair. At the end of the day we had a reception and handed out the Silver Peachtree Plaza Cup. Again, the PR value was super. The profits of the event were given to the homes which provided shelter for battered women. Each year we chose a different charity.

One year, during Westin's Marketing Conference, I was asked to go to Hawaii to participate in a panel discussion about marketing perception by a General Manager for which I came well prepared. Then during a presentation, I received an award as Westin Hotel's Marketing General Manager of the Year. What a nice surprise that was! I was flattered and really happy about this honor. I had no clue when I went to Hawaii; it was a total surprise.

In the hotel's kitchen we had a Chef's Table which I introduced to generate more business. We would invite usually three different types of guests: one who had previously had a convention with us who we invited as a thank you to him for the business, another who was looking at the hotel for a meeting place but had not yet signed a contract, and a third guest who was a potential customer, someone who had no concept of our property but we knew his organization had potential for a large amount of group business for us. The Executive Chef would sit with us, explain the menus, and waiters would serve us with the appropriate wines. This was a great hit and my best salesman was always Waldo Brun. When he was transferred to open the Walt Disney Swan Hotel in Orlando, Gerhard Wind became our Chef. He was very good also and we got along very well. He was from Austria, so we had something in common in addition to the fact that I was a Chef in my younger years. The other key people in attendance were the F&B Directors. We had three while I was at the hotel and one was Karl Riseck, a German who replaced me when I left Singapore. Karl was a good man as long as I was able to hold his hand. Another F&B Director was also a German whom I knew from New York but had never worked with. He proved to be a disappointment and unfortunately I had to release him. Gerhard and Karl both committed suicide a few months after I left the hotel, which I felt so sad about. Many employees said this would never have happened if I had not left, but that was nonsense. The pressure and management problems were the reason for their demise.

A big deal during my stay in Atlanta was the Democratic National Convention in 1988. The parties and festivities during a convention like this are fabulous. It is a fantastic event. Coming from Los Angeles, I was familiar with political conventions plus I had worked with the Republican National Convention while at the Detroit Plaza. Of course, one of the big issues for this type of convention is establishing credit. In our contract all hotels had a paragraph asking for total prepayment of the charges for meetings, parties, room charges, etc. I knew from experience in other cities that a lot of bills would not be settled. The ones whose party loses the election kind of disappear and the hotel is left holding the bag, while the ones who win the elections say we are in power now so watch out. So, beginning three days before the convention, if I did not have the check I would send a telegram to the power-to-be in Washington, DC and tell them if I did not receive a check within 24 hours, all commitments would be cancelled. Then I got a call from Andy Young's office and a bunch of other people to reconsider. I was told I could not do this, that they would run me out of town. My response was, "Fine, just watch me." I sent the second telegram letting them know that either I receive a check by noon tomorrow or all commitments are cancelled. Guess what—I received a check for several hundred thousand dollars, total payment, by noon the next day. In addition, I am happy to say that we were the only hotel in Atlanta who did not have any unpaid bills from the Democratic National Convention.

When I first took over the hotel I brought the ad agency from Kansas City with me because I was so used to working with them and felt I needed their help. We also did an employee motivational program with buttons, t-shirts, a specially-written song, and a whole production that really helped to turn around the morale of the staff. They tried to unionize the hotel but with all the good things happening, we were able to keep the union out of the hotel. Once things got normal in Atlanta, I felt the cost to fly in the people from Kansas City was too high, so I contracted with a local ad agency. We interviewed many ad agencies and settled on Wemmers Communications. Rick Wemmer was the principal of the company and I liked him. He and his staff did a great job for us with new promotional collateral, new ads, and new photography. They did a wonderful job with one exception. We had created a summer promotion with a nasty photo of General Sherman. He looked mean and the tag line said, *"When you make your reservation, tell them Sherman sent you and you have money to burn."* I was against the ad and asked the Portman folks what they thought. They said I was being too sensitive and too serious; loosen up, they said. The OK was given to run the ad. My God did my phone ring! Comments such as "I will never come to the Peachtree Plaza again, my grandfather was killed during the Civil War, how can you print an ad like this!", etc. We immediately stopped the advertisement and a new one starring Scarlett O'Hara in a beautiful dress with the tag line "Tell them Scarlett sent you for a special room rate." This time the phone rang off the hook again, but people told me how wonderful the ad was and how nice it was of us to think about Scarlett. How ironic it is that Rick Wemmer sent the first ad with General Sherman to participate in a national advertisement competition and it won first place! The lesson learned is what is bad for one person might be great for another. You never know what fits.

My almost eleven years at the Peachtree Plaza was a special time. My dream was always to participate in a local community, to be well known, respected, established and recognized in the business community, as well. In Atlanta it was the first time this happened. Before Atlanta I moved an average of every two years, but you cannot really create an aura like that unless you work somewhere for over ten years. They called me Mr. Peachtree Plaza and I loved it. However, all good things must come to an end. I always said if I ever leave Westin Hotels, it will be by the time I am 50 years old. More about my Atlanta time in another chapter.

8. THREE CLANS — THREE MARRIAGES

How blessed I was to have parents who really loved each other and stuck together through good times and bad. I was fortunate to be able to grow up in a family that had rules, values, and a sense of togetherness. I had always hoped to achieve the same style of family and togetherness in which I had grown up. Andrea and I met at the Century Plaza in Los Angeles in 1966 when I had no interest in getting married. My interest in Andrea was triggered because so many of the department heads made comments about what a nice lady Andrea was. Then when I moved to Chicago a few months later, she moved too after I asked her to do so. At the beginning, we had separate apartments. I do have to admit I was very career driven while most of my friends who were on the way up in their careers were already married and had families. So, in 1968, when I was 28, I decided I should get married and start a family. We were legally married in Chicago followed by a beautiful wedding in Switzerland since my parents wanted a real nice wedding in a church setting with all the festivities. We enjoyed an Apero-style bus tour of Switzerland, which is common. Later, the bus was transferred to a boat on Lake Lucerne which took us to an elegant hotel where we enjoyed a wonderful dinner. The dinner menu which follows was designed to honor our parents:

CONSOMMÉ HERMANOS (FOR MY DAD)
  Consommé with cut egg custard, julienne of celery and carrots

FILET OF SOLE ALEXANDER (FOR ANDREA'S DAD)
Poached Filet of sole, sliced mushrooms, diced tomatoes covered with a white wine sauce with chopped parsley

GARDENIA SALAD ANDREA (FOR ANDREA'S MOM)
Fresh Boston lettuce, artichoke hearts, sliced red peppers, chopped eggs and served with a raspberry vinaigrette dressing

STEAK DE BOEUF HELENA (FOR MY MOM)
Filet mignons sautéed with chanterelles and sliced cucumbers, croquette potatoes, Florentine tomatoes, asparagus and beans

KISS IN A CLOUD (FOR ANDREA AND ME)
This was a *baked Alaska served in a container with dry ice. (This created nice clouds)*

On each menu that I personally made we included a 1968 Kennedy silver coin for the year when we got married. The appropriate white and red wines were served with the dinner. There was also a band with lots of dancing, jokes, and contributions presented by the guests followed by stories from Mr. and Mrs. Wyss and many, many other guests.

After the wedding, we went to Frankfurt and picked up a new Mercedes which I had ordered as our wedding gift. Our travels took us to the Italian part of Switzerland where we stayed with Mrs. Bachman, my second mother. Then on to Italy: Venice and Cortina d'Ampezzo, the famous resort where they held the Winter Olympics. From there we went to the area where *The Sound of Music* was filmed and then to Andrea's hometown near Graz. We had a second wedding reception in Austria for Andrea's friends and family who had not joined us in Switzerland. Again it was a super evening of good food, drinks, and lots of laughs where most of Andrea's family and friends were able to meet for the first time.

Andrea's parents were wonderful people whom I grew to love. They were down to earth, good human beings. They had a hard time during World War II and truly appreciated the life they lived now. Their money was tight, but they made the best of what they had. They lived in a rented apartment but had a piece of land with a little garden house. Their cottage had a living room, small kitchen, toilette, and a sofa that could be turned into a bed. Around the house there were many fruit trees including cherry, apple, pear, and plum trees. Of course, there was also a vegetable garden. It was such a lovely place to be in the summer. Later, after Andrea and I had children, they would spend their summers in the garden house, as we called it. The kids called Andrea's parents Opa and Oma. We enjoyed such a nice relationship with them where we were able to sit under the trees with a few beers telling stories—what could have been any nicer! Oma was a great cook and she made all the good Austrian specialties which I could not get in Switzerland. Her Hungarian goulash was the best in the world and today my girls, Andrea and Christina, also make a very good goulash.

Swiss people and Austrians are different, and I hate to admit it but I always liked the Austrians better than the Swiss. Austrians are happy and jolly folks whereas the Swiss are apt to be arrogant and egotistical in general. Swiss people are spoiled because they have it too good; everything is organized and works like a clock. Their standard of living is extremely high, incomes are good, and many people are trying to outdo each other.

After our stay in Austria we went back for a few days and stayed with my parents, then went back to Los Angeles. We worked a few weeks before Andrea got involved with this new church. At first it shocked me because I could not understand it, but I figured it would go away soon; however, it became more fanatical as time went on. Then the call came for us to move to Singapore, so we did not get the opportunity to enjoy our new Mercedes or our new camper very much. Before we left Los

Angeles, Andrea went to Pasadena to be baptized in her new church without any involvement from me.

Once we settled in Singapore we had a good life with so many new things to experience. At night after work we sat on our balcony having a glass of wine waiting for the satay man, a street vendor or hacker as they call them in Singapore and the Far East. The vendors would come by on their bicycles. On the back seat they had installed a charcoal burner on which they cooked the satay sticks or whatever they had to sell. With the cooked satay sticks they served sliced cucumbers and sliced onions. These meat skewers, for which a recipe follows, were an absolutely wonderful dish.

SATAY

- 1 large roasting chicken or 3 lbs. of tender beef or lamb

SPICED MARINADE:

- 1 tsp. coriander seed
- 1 tsp. cumin
- 1 tsp. turmeric
- 1 tsp. aniseed
  (or 1 oz. of good Indian curry powder may be substituted for all the above ingredients)
- 2 oz. light soy sauce4 cloves garlic, finely chopped
- 1 oz. sugar
- 1 oz. finely chopped onion
- 2 oz. peanut oil

Make the spiced marinade by grinding all the spices and mixing with soy sauce, garlic, onions, sugar and oil. Cut meat or chicken into thin slices about 1 inch long and mix well with the spiced marinade. Marinate for at least 6 hours then thread the meat pieces onto 10 inch bamboo skewers.

SAUCE

- 2 tsp. coriander seed
- 2 tsp. cumin
- 1/2 tsp. turmeric powder
- 1 tsp. Conimex Sereh Powder
- 2 cloves garlic
- 1 1/2 oz. chopped onions
- 1 oz. fresh ginger
- 1 tsp. chili powder
- 1 1/2 oz. chopped, roasted peanuts (or crunch peanut butter)
- Lemon Grass
- 2 oz. grated fresh coconut
- 3 cups coconut milk squeezed from fresh of 1 coconut

Add lemon grass, ground pepper and salt to taste

Make the sauce by grinding the garlic, onions and ginger until fine then pound the coriander, cumin, turmeric, lemon grass, peanuts and grated coconut until fine. Mix all sauce ingredients except coconut milk together. Heat the coconut milk gently. Add all ingredients to the warmed coconut milk and simmer for about 15 minutes until the sauce thickens. Do not strain the sauce as it should be gritty.

Cook the satay on a charcoal grill, serve with cucumbers and onions. Dip the meat into the peanut sauce.

Asia has so many different foods and of course so many fine restaurants. However, in my opinion, the best food I found was in the food stalls. Whether it was in Hong Kong, Malaysia, or Singapore—wherever the food hawkers were found each had their own specialty. Many of the hawkers made just one item but whatever it was, you could only describe it as fantastic. The whole atmosphere was very unique and colorful with people shouting. It seemed like a real oasis of happiness.

My favorite Asian dessert is Gula Malacca. Again, you find it in the food stalls or some simple Chinese and Malaysian restaurants.

GULA MALACCA

- 8 oz. sago
- 3 pints of water
- 5 oz. white sugar
- 6 oz. Gula Malacca (date palm sugar) or dark brown sugar
- 1 1/2 to 2 cups thick coconut milk—squeezed from the grated flesh of 2 coconuts
- Pinch of salt

Bring 2 pints of the water to a boil in a large pan. Wash the sago, drain and pour into the boiling water. Simmer for 20-30 minutes, stirring frequently. When every grain of sago is transparent, pour the contents of the pan into a sieve and put under running water. Rinse the sago free of starch until it becomes clear and cool. Put into a rinse mold and chill.

Make a sugar syrup by boiling the Gula Malacca and white sugar in 1 pint of water until the mixture thickens. To serve, unmold the sago and put the coconut milk and sugar syrup in separate jugs. About 3 tablespoon of each should be poured over individual bowls of sago.

The first year we lived in Singapore was one of the best times in my life, at least at the time I felt so. Besides the enormous heat, since Singapore is only 88 miles from the equator, there was another thing that bothered me. It was the fact that Singapore is an island of only about 278 sq. miles and from either end it is only 14 miles long. Having traveled all over the world and being used to miles and miles of highways, I got what the locals call "rock fever." I needed to get out on my days off either by spending time on our speed boat on the ocean or I would drive up to Malaysia and travel through the jungle which I loved to do. I bought a used VW Beetle since cars in Singapore cost about three times what the same car would cost in the US or Europe. Driving on the left side of the road was a very easy adjustment for me. One weekend when Andrea was about 5 months pregnant, we took a trip to Malaysia. Unfortunately we got caught in a monsoon and it rained like it was the end of the world. We got stuck in Segamat, a little town where the car would not make it any further due to the high water level. We had to look for a hotel and I asked a local for a good place to stay and he suggested the Park Hotel; I told Andrea that name sounded good to me. After quite some time looking for this place we found a car repair shop in a garage that had three rooms on top of the building which were available for rent. Since we had no choice, I told the lady who ran the place that we would take a room — man oh man, what an ordeal this was. The room was dark and damp with no a/c. The bed had a white mosquito net that was more black than white because it was dirty. We suffered one night, then the next morning we caught the last train out of Segamat to Singapore. We were very lucky as we learned later on the bridge we had to cross had collapsed because of the rain storm. Ten days later I went back to Segamat to pick up my car which had been in the water. The seats had a growth of over an inch of mold on them, which was just awful. In the garage they were able to get the engine going so I could drive it back to Singapore. I made this trip alone since Andrea was expecting a baby and had enough of our Malaysian trip from the previous week. Since the VW Beetle was finished I bought a Ford Capri, a two-door sports car which was very nice. It came from Europe in a box to be assembled in Singapore since the labor there was much cheaper. Many cars arrived in Singapore in a box since they did not actually build any cars there — they only assembled them. The new car was nice and I felt like a big shot driving it around.

May 12, 1971, the same day as mother Andrea was born, little Andrea came into this world. So, I had two Andreas born May 12th. It was a wonderful feeling to be a papa. We could not go to Europe and show Andrea to the grandparents since we had just opened the hotel and my work kept me busy in Singapore, so I asked my parents to come and visit us; to my surprise they said okay and showed up with my brother Peter. It was a hard trip for them, especially due to the heat, which was a challenge for both my mom and dad. My mother was so European she was wearing the same clothes in Asia as she wore in Switzerland — including undergarments with a corset and undershirt and whatever else a lady would wear. Needless to say, she was constantly sweating but she never complained. I was determined to show my parents more than just Singapore, so I planned a trip to Malaysia. We went with two cars — my brother Peter drove the Ford Capri while mother Andrea rode in the back seat with little Andrea in a basket.

When driving through the Malaysian jungle you can see rubber plantations, a fantastic sight. We saw many trees that had little tin cans attached to them where the white rubber "milk" was collected. It is a sticky white liquid that is used to produce rubber. Rubber trappers would make a very shallow incision into the bark of the tree that would cut through the latex vessels. The dripping latex would then be collected in the tin can attached to the tree. The Malaysian rubber industry has been described as one of the greatest achievements of western colonial enterprises.

While driving, Peter and I lost each other and we had a few hours of panic. My mother asked what happened, where are they, are we ever going to find them again, is little Andrea going to die in the jungle—it went on and on. Peter is an aggressive driver and I was just riding along to enjoy the scenery. Fortunately, Andrea used common sense when they came to a fork in the road, and she told Peter to stop and wait. She knew we had to come that way and she did not want to take the wrong road and continue to miss each other. After a long ride, we happily found the three sitting on the sidewalk and our journey could continue.

Our next destination was Cameran Highlands. The Cameran Highlands is one of Malaysia's most extensive hill stations. The area is at the northwestern tip of Pahang. The resort area is located between Ipho, Kuala Lumpur and Kuentan, the capital of Pahang. The area was discovered by Sir William Cameran in 1885. It is nestled at elevations from 3600 to 5200 feet above sea level. The mean temperature is 64° to 77° F during the day and at night it rarely drops to as low as 46° F and is a beautiful and popular tourist area because of the favorable climate.

We stayed at the Cameran Highlands Smokehouse Hotel and Restaurant. This charming English manor was built in 1937 following the English Mock-Tudor architecture. This nostalgic place remains as original as it was way back then. It has a well-manicured garden with lovely highland flowers. The full-service restaurant serves tea and scones in the afternoon. The rest of the day it is a very fine, three meal dining room. You would think you were in an English castle by the way the waiters pamper you. The eclectic furniture and fittings in this hotel are purely English cottage style. Of course, Malaysia used to be a British colony which is why we find all this British influence. It is just a real jewel of a place.

Our trip back to Singapore was without any major happenings. My parents and Peter really had a good time visiting the local markets plus all the restaurants at the Shangri La Hotel. It was such a treat for me to show my parents the interesting life which Andrea and I enjoyed.

Peter Daetwiler, another Swiss, was our Resident Manager and he was a nut when it came to flying. So, he got me involved in the Singapore Flying Club and I started again to go flying since I had my license in Chicago. Flying in Singapore is something else. You hop around little islands with little grass strips for airports that are very primitive. I remember when we wanted to land we first had to fly over the airstrip to scare the local kids away, since they were playing soccer with coconuts on the landing strip. Thus we had to make sure when we landed we did not run over any of the soccer players. We had a great group of pilots who would meet in the Club Bar each time we landed from a flight and enjoyed our time telling stories.

Andrea and I needed another family member, so we went to look for a dog and found one. It was a little black poodle who we selected out of five dogs. He was quick as could be and he ran up to Andrea and she said this is the one. At the time I was drinking martinis, so we named him Martini. Andrea had great fun with the dog, which she trained and participated in shows with. He never won first place, but he always showed well. By this time Andrea had become more and more involved with the church. Each year she went during the Feast of Tabernacle to a resort where the church met. Sometimes the kids and I visited her, but as far as I was concerned this church was involved with fanaticism with which I could not be bothered.

Our going away party in Singapore was absolutely fantastic with a cocktail reception for about 100 people in the finest style. It was hard to leave Singapore where we had so many nice experiences; however the challenge of my new job in San Francisco was intriguing.

While I was working at the St. Francis, we enjoyed our first home in Marin County, just north of the city. Andrea learned she was pregnant again, so my parents decided to visit us in the USA, which I was very pleased about. We made a trip along the coast of California, visited Carmel, Monterey, and down to Los Angeles. At the Century Plaza they pampered us in every way and Walter Roth made a special Chef's Table dinner for us. I showed my parents as much as I could, including Knots Berry Farm, Sea World, Hollywood, and even Disneyland, but I think I overdid it. I will never forget one evening my dad was in tears and said he did not want to see anymore and he could not cope with all this craziness. He said when he closed his eyes at night he saw nothing but Mickey Mouse, monsters, lights, music—he could not handle it any more. I felt bad because I meant well, but it was just too much for the old man. I guess the lesson learned was that sometimes less is more.

While going back to San Francisco at only six months into her pregnancy, Andrea experienced a miscarriage, a little boy. Of course this put a damper on the remainder of the visit with my parents. Then Andrea learned she was pregnant again but after only four months, she had another miscarriage and again it was a little boy. We were both strong and said there is a reason for everything. The Good Lord must know why this happened to us. At the time we had a new Resident Manager, Larry Magnan, a very nice fellow. When Andrea was in the hospital, his wife Ruth, who also lived in Terra Linda, took care of little Andrea. Still today she talks about how she could not communicate with little Andrea as she only spoke German and Ruth did not understand what she was trying to tell her.

Another unforgettable experience in San Francisco was skiing in Lake Tahoe. What a wonderful area that is! Audrey Smith from Singapore was sent to the US by the company and she visited the St. Francis. While she was there we invited her to our home. Over the weekend we made a trip to Lake Berryessa which is the largest lake in Napa County. If someone would have told me in 1973 that one day she would be my wife and we would live in Germany, Switzerland, and the US I would have said you were nuts and would have wondered what kind of funny cigarettes you were smoking.

Andrea was about seven months pregnant when I got the call asking if I would like to go to Hawaii and be the Executive Assistant Manager at the Ilikai Hotel in Honolulu. Needless to say, I was excited and accepted immediately. At the time Mr. Carlson purchased the Hotel from Chin Ho it was supposed to be a secret, but that did not last long as the Bamboo Telegraph knew that United Airlines bought the hotel. We arrived in Hawaii and two days later Bill Hulett and his wife Penny arrived in Paradise. Penny was also seven months pregnant. As is the custom in Hawaii, the employees started to bet on who would have their baby first—Mrs. Hulett or Mrs. Gammeter. Penny and Andrea got along great as they had the same interests in family and kids and each had a husband who was totally consumed by their jobs. One day Bill invited me to be his guest at the SKAL Club, which is an organization made-up of hospitality people, hoteliers, travel agents, car rental agents, and cruise executives. Bill told me to dress up in a sports coat and tie but when we arrived at the Sheraton Hotel I was the only one with a tie, which they quickly cut off. I was so embarrassed since everyone else was dressed in an Aloha shirt.

We had a horrible occurrence at the hotel. It was a Sunday and Andrea and I had lunch with the Huletts at their home. We received a phone call that there was a fire at the Ilikai Marina Building and the Charthouse Restaurant. We rushed to the hotel and it was quite a mess -- mass confusion and some people had experienced smoke inhalation. We had to evacuate the entire building. Later, we learned the story was that the Polynesian Mafia had taken revenge on the hotel for some dispute they had. A few months later we had another fire, this time in the Canoe Lounge at the Ilikai Hotel, which was an entertainment lounge. The entertainer at the time was Nephi Hannemann, a Polynesian singer and actor. He was a real piece of work, almost seven feet tall, good looking but with a big ego. Each day there were problems with girls and since he was not very dependable, Bill decided to fire him. A few days after that we experienced a mysterious fire in the Canoe Lounge. The story was payback to the Ilikai Management by the Samoan Mafia. After renovating the bar, it reopened with Loyal Garner, a fantastic Hawaiian entertainer. The Canoe House was a delight to visit and became quite successful with very few problems.

Andrea got more and more involved with her church. During the Feast of Tabernacle, she went to Maui with the kids as this was always a very special time. As I look back today, it appears to me this church had a lot of similarities with the Jewish faith — such as no pork, no shellfish, no Christmas, no Easter, and many other restrictions such as the women were not allowed to wear make-up. What bothered me most was that the kids could not have a Christmas tree, but they could receive gifts. All these new customs such as no parties or entertainment after sundown on Friday nights until sundown on Saturday were such a drastic change in our lives. Other than those inconveniences, our life in Hawaii turned out to be one of the best times in our lives. We had so many blessings, the weather, the Hawaiian people — it was such a fantastic time. Often, I think I would pay anything to bring back some of those good times we had.

At the Ilikai we had a Grand Banks yacht which was super. Each Thursday evening, we did a VIP cruise with cocktails and appetizers. We invited guests to thank them for their business or guests who we wanted to book business with us. This was a great way to do sales calls since once we had them on the boat there was no way out for the customers. Normally when you entertain in a ballroom, customers can sneak out, but not on the yacht; they had to stay until the sunset cruise ended.

Once again, the call came to move. Next assignment was the Plaza in New York. What a change from the Aloha spirit to the fast-moving pace of New York City. Andrea was surprised that the change from the Hawaiian muumuus to the elegant fashion of the east coast was relatively easy for her. She lost 20 lbs. and looked fantastic. Since we lived in the hotel she had lots of extra time. While the kids went to school, Andrea took up painting classes at the Art Academy. She became quite a good artist. Weekends we spent with Ruth Schwab on Long Island. Ruth was from the same village as me in Switzerland and actually went to school with my brother Peter. Some weekends we spent with Gretchen Matthers, an old friend of mine who lived in Westport, Connecticut. She had a cozy little country home and the kids loved to spend time with Aunti Gretchen. Sometimes Gretchen stayed with us at the Plaza. Summers we visited Jones Beach, and in the winter went skiing in the Poconos. What a wonderful life we had. We entertained everybody since they wanted to visit the Plaza, thus we entertained our guests at restaurants, Broadway shows, museums, whatever their hearts desired. A special trip was when my parents came from Zurich on a direct flight to New York. To say my parents felt like super VIPs when staying at the Plaza is an understatement. This was really special for them. One night when my dad did not feel like getting out, I took a cab to the Waldorf Astoria, which was an experience my mother never forgot. We gave her a tour and took her to a couple of parties in the banquet rooms. She was so impressed and kept asking how we could do this since we were not invited. I kept telling her not to worry, just to act like we belonged there, which we did. Free dinner, free drinks—what a city this New York is, I told her.

Another visitor we had was Mr. Pauli and his wife. He was the gentleman I made my chef's apprenticeship under many years earlier. He wrote cookbooks and whenever he published a new one, he gave me a copy as a gift. He was so proud of me because he could take the credit for what I had become; in other words, the reason for my success was because he was my mentor when I was training. I even took Eugene Pauli and his wife to the Ringling Bros. Circus which was the first time they had experienced a three-ring circus. Also, we had a visit from Mr. Luethy, my middle school teacher. He was the father of Rolf Luethy, my doctor friend, and they were our neighbors at my parent's home. We really gave him the VIP treatment because we knew he would go back home and brag to my parents and the whole village about his stay with Hermann and his wife.

After lunch I usually did a little walk in Central Park with Frank Finneran. One time a fellow approached me and asked if I would like to purchase some drugs from him. Proudly, I said "Can't you see by the way we are dressed we are businessmen, we don't use drugs?" He just smiled and replied, "What the hell are you talking about, those are my best customers!"

Because of Andrea's church activities I had a few romantic flings, but it did not bring any happiness; on the contrary, my feelings of guilt and shame overtook the temporary happiness. The emotional strain was very high. Also, I felt so bad for little Andrea and Christina even though they were too little to know what was going on. I'm sure mother Andrea knew that something was going on, but she seemed not to be worried.

It was good that the next assignment was our move to Detroit. I used to say I would go anywhere except Detroit. Another lesson learned — never say never. The move was good for us, a new challenge in my career. After living in the hotel for two years, having a home again was nice for Andrea and the kids. Mama did a great job in decorating an English Tudor home in Grosse Point. The marriage went along okay; unfortunately, I met a young lady who also was married. Her name was Margot Archer and she was a Mormon girl. Gregarious, funny, pretty, and full of life, she really screwed up my head fast. We started to date, went out, and planned business trips together. One night we went to see a Broadway show, *Annie*, and when we came out of the theater Margot's husband was waiting for us. He ran to us and hit me hard. I was much fitter and bigger, but because of my guilt feelings, I did not defend myself. We had to go to the hospital and I needed some stitches. The rest of the night we spent at the hotel. There was such turmoil in my life. I knew I was wrong but the affair continued. I guess when you think with something other than your head, you really do stupid things. The behavior became irrational. Andrea went to the feast with her church while Margot and I used the time to go up to Northern Michigan. This is just a very pretty area where we visited Mackinac Island. It's like going back in time with no cars, only horse-drawn carriages. The Grand Hotel is famous for its big porches. It opened in 1886 and is a National Historic Landmark. Many of the employees come from Jamaica and other Caribbean Islands. The Grand is one of the most romantic hotels I have ever visited. In the summer it is a paradise for tourists with many boutique shops, restaurant, taffy places, and just a delightful place to stroll around. Margot and I also went to Toronto and visited the King Tut Exhibit on a Friday night. My brother Peter and his wife Lotti came to spend a vacation in Detroit, so I introduced them to Margot at a Renaissance Life concert. By now Margot and I had an intense relationship and I started to think that I would like to live with her permanently. At the time I felt no one knew about our courting; but looking back, I must admit that surely many friends and business associates must have known what was going on.

The big phone call came when Henry Mulligan asked me to move to Atlanta to take over the Peachtree Plaza. I was excited and glad as I felt that it was the right time to make the break from Margot. I was in Atlanta, and while Andrea was still packing in Detroit Margot came to visit me in the South; the saga continued. I was asked to go to Rio de Janeiro, Brazil and participate in the Annual Meeting of the Steigenberger Hotel Conference. At the time we had about 10 hotels set up with their reservation system. Since Westin had no hotels in Europe, properties such as the Plaza, St. Francis, Chicago and other hotels with a fair amount of international business participated in the Steigenberger System. The conference was great. I loved Rio de Janeiro and the city of Sao Paulo. Othon Hotels was the host of the conference and they did an outstanding job. They really put on the ritz for us with Brazilian Samba dancers, outstanding food, celebrations, and just a fun time of entertainment. New to me were the Brazilian steakhouses. These restaurants grill chicken, beef, and lamb on skewers, then the waiters come to your table and cut the meat in front of you and put it on your plate. The guests have little colored paper markers which say "more" on one side (to indicate you want more meat) and "stop" on the other (to indicate you have had enough). The Brazilian meat service is one of the best meals you can have. You can't be a vegetarian or you would go hungry.

I wrote a long and excellent report of our conference in Brazil with many excellent marketing recommendations. Henry Mulligan was a guest in our hotel at the time, so I gave him a copy of the report. After he checked out of the hotel, I inspected his suite and found my copy of the report in the trash can. I was so mad and disappointed. It once again confirmed to me that Henry was not an international hotelier. He was great in the US, but internationally he was naïve.

When we landed back in the US, I went to call Margot and Andrea seemed to know what was going on. So she looked at me and said she thought it was time to call it quits. I was shocked, but I knew that she was right. Andrea and I decided to get a divorce and I asked her if she needed a lawyer. Her answer was that after living with me for 12 years she knew I was going to take care of the kids and her. So we worked things out with one lawyer, something unheard of. The lawyer we had was a famous Buckhead lawyer and he did not believe we would do it just with him. He kept saying that at the last minute Andrea was going to turn on me, but he was wrong. Since I had the larger income, I gave Andrea a larger amount of alimony payment and less child support for tax purposes. We split our goods fairly and I purchased a brand-new home for Andrea and the girls. I paid cash but had to borrow money from my parents. It was important for me that Andrea and the kids had a secure and safe home. I must admit my finances were pretty low and shaky when our stock split, but I knew my job was secure and future income would be saved and growing. Bill Hulett, who was President of

Stouffer Hotels, gave Andrea the opportunity to go through a management training program. Within a year she was appointed Director of
Housekeeping for the Waverly Hotel in Atlanta. It was a great blessing
for her and a good feeling for me that she had a good job.

Margot was already divorced, and I moved her goods with a budget
travel trailer from Detroit to Atlanta. The day after our divorce was final, Margot and I got married in the Atlanta courthouse. We went to
Switzerland and church for a blessing, then had lunch with my parents
in a castle on Lake Hallwil where I used to go camping as a kid. From
day one our marriage was cursed, and the curse was on me. I did not
tell Margot, but I had tremendous guilt feelings. In so many situations
I felt guilty when I made comparisons of our life and the fact that I left
Andrea and the kids. I believed I had married Julie Andrews from *The
Sound of Music*; however, I married the other lady in the movie, the one
who Christopher Plummer was dating first. It was always an unhappy
situation between my kids and Margot. I must admit many times it was
my mistake. Margot tried to do something nice for the kids and my answer was we don't need this; the kids have a mother. Looking back, this
was stupid on my part. One time I was going to purchase little Andrea
a winter coat. We looked at two, one was $79 and the other was $86,
and Margot said buy the one for $79, she is only going to grow out of
it. I did, but I felt so bad that a few days later I went back to Macy's
and changed it to the more expensive one. Guilty again, because only a
month before I had purchased a $2,000 mink coat for Margot.

We built this fabulous home in Dunwoody where everything was
custom made. I called it "La Chaumiere," a.k.a. French castle or mansion. It had four fireplaces, crystal chandeliers, a library with carved
wood, and in the kitchen, we had hand painted tiles, and the garden had
a beautiful pool with professional landscaping. While it was a very, very
nice house, it was never a home. The family warmth was missing. Since
we had a piano and neither of us played the piano, I felt I needed to take

piano lessons. We used the home for entertainment and each year hosted a big holiday party catered by the Peachtree Plaza. We invited business leaders from the community, Rotary members, and politicians. I felt we had "really arrived." During our marriage, Margot and I went to many parties, any important event, whether it was Save the Zoo or Save the Fox, the Gammeters showed up. Sometimes we attended two or three events a night. The Portman Organization liked my community involvement and the hotel had constant coverage in the newspapers, magazines, even television. The people called me Mr. Peachtree Plaza, which I liked. Margot was in the newspapers many times. One story was that she was one of the five best dressed women of Atlanta. This was a nice honor but also costly. I remember when we were participating in the Steeplechase at Callaway Gardens. She went to Neiman Marcus and purchased an elegant special dress. She was told there was only one dress like this in Atlanta. As we walked into the Ballroom at Callaway Gardens guess what—there danced three ladies in the same blue dress! Steaming, Margot went to ask them where they got their dresses. One lady told her she got it in Birmingham, Alabama. Another lady bought hers on a trip to New York. All three women were steaming. So, I told Margot not to worry as she was the prettiest, had the best figure, and looked stunning in the dress. Then I told her to look around the room, that there were about 150 men wearing the same black tuxedo. It did not help much.

Margot's mother was a strong Mormon and her father was too, except he enjoyed drinking sometimes, which was a no-no. Two of her brothers went on a mission trip, while the third brother for some reason was considered the black sheep of the family. It turned out that he was the one member of her family whom I liked the best. Her younger sister was a strong Mormon too even though she was divorced and living in California. Her older sister lived in Indiana. She was an alcoholic and so was her husband, who ultimately committed suicide. The two of them could really put away the alcohol, mostly vodka, and no one could keep up with them. We would spend all the holidays in Michigan with her family. Although her mother did not like it, Margot's sister, her husband, and admittedly I would openly drink in front of their mother. Sometimes we even took her dad out and got him to drink. Margot, however, did not have a Chardonnay when we were with her mother. My relationship with her family was okay, but not like how it had been between Andrea's parents and me. Our cultural differences were obvious, but you make the best out of it.

Margot's parents and her brother's family visited with us often in Atlanta. They loved to come and enjoy the good life with us in our home, at the hotel and all that went with it. They had never experienced anything like this. At home I did the cooking and we had fun. Margot's dad always said I was the best chef. In the summers we took trips up to upper Michigan each year. The summers there are wonderful, but you can have the winter. I learned I am not a man who enjoys ice fishing. Margot's brother started a business and I loaned him $5,000 which I never got back and that debt eventually became one of the conditions when we divorced. As they say, that's life. We made many trips to Switzerland and visited with our friends like the Holligers, Bachmans, and Zehnders. I was warned over and over that I was spoiling Margot, that someday I would wake up. Even my mother, who did not speak any English and thus whose conversation with my bride was limited, warned me that once Margot found someone who is richer than me she would leave me. My response to her was that she would not do that to me since she was a good Mormon girl! Speaking of Mormons, the members really tried to make a Mormon out of me. We went to church a lot and I liked the people. Our "home teacher" was the leader of the Atlanta church and he and his wife would visit us often. The Mormons have some good principles, one of which was the teaching for women. I gave a class in cooking which was fun, and the ladies loved it. Interestingly enough, one woman came to me and said it was a nice thing I was doing to teach the class but added that she thought I only gave the class to make Margot look good. As far as me becoming a Mormon, that was completely out of the question. I always felt my parents did a good job in bringing me up as a Protestant and that is what I was going to stay.

Margot was successful in her job and so was I, but at the same time we lived in a dream world. She always wanted success and was recognition driven and here I was totally consumed in my own career. I still don't know what happened except I sensed she might be having an affair. This got worse and worse; finally, we even went to marriage counseling for many hours but it did not help. Since she always told me that I was crazy and seeing ghosts, I hired a private investigator and found out she spent time at an apartment of one of her co-workers. It was a horrible time, but I was committed to making our marriage work, especially since it was the reason I left Andrea and the kids. For a short while it got better, then I realized something was wrong. I had a tape recorder installed in the phone at our house. It was horrible for me to come home while she was out and listen to the recorded conversation she had with her new boyfriend. It hurt me so much since she had always said I was crazy and did not know what I was talking about. One time I even went over to Mother Andrea and told her about my problems. She was so nice and tried to console me. Many years later I learned that Andrea had always supported me. When my mother was in a clinic, I found a letter in her home from Andrea. She had written to my mom that she was doing well, that I was taking good care of her and the kids. She even said she was glad I had found someone who gave me something she could not. This touched me so much I had tears in my eyes.

Again, for a short while things got better again between Margot and me although she never knew about the recorded phone conversation. I decided to join Stouffer Hotels as a Vice President and move to Cleveland. I figured this was a good move and perhaps a new beginning for our marriage. We lived in Cleveland for about four months and bought a house on five acres in an exclusive neighborhood. We spent thousands renovating the place because I wanted it to be a place where Margot would be happy. To purchase this home and put so much money into was dumb. In the summer alone it cost me $350 a month to have the grass cut, then in the winter it was over $300 just to clean up the snow. At the same time, I was traveling 3-5 days a week to Hawaii, Mexico, and Canada. It made absolutely no sense to have this property. Sure, it was nice to see deer in the backyard but for what?

Margot was looking for a job but could not find what she wanted and felt Cleveland was a big disappointment, especially after her professional career in Atlanta. I could certainly understand her frustration. Prior to this she had a good job, was the "first lady" at Peachtree Plaza, and now she was a housewife and just a VP's wife. She acted in the community like I was the head of Stouffer Hotels and this created friction with the other Vice Presidents, but for me it was embarrassing. Our Sr. VP told me I should control my wife and he was correct. Before leaving the South, I had purchased a new Mercedes SL, a real dream car. Since I was out of town when it was delivered, I instructed the Controller of the hotel to register it in Margot's name, which came back to haunt me later. When we divorced, her lawyer said the car was a gift to her.

I had a trip planned to Hawaii and we decided that Margot would come over a few days later when we could spend some vacation time together. After I had arrived in Maui, she called and asked if it would be okay to come on the next trip as she did not feel good. Of course, I said, no problem. After my business meetings I decided to go back to Cleveland and Margot was to pick me up at the airport. After getting off the plane there was an announcement notifying me to meet my driver at the baggage area. I met the chauffeur who informed me that Mrs. Gammeter had asked him to pick me up. I did not think too much about it until I got home. There was a nice bouquet of flowers with a card which read *"Hermann, I love you. I will always love you. I went back South.*

Don't try to call me. I will contact you." Immediately I went upstairs and saw that all her clothes were gone along with the new Mercedes. I was totally shocked, so I called Bill Hulett; he and Penny came over to my house. To my surprise, they were totally astonished and dumbfounded.

Needless to say, the next few weeks were awkward for me. I telephoned her parents, who did not know what was going on, nor did her sister in California who I must say acted like a nerd. Before she left Cleveland, Margot had the house professionally decorated. When the interior designer finished her work, she presented me with the huge bill. At my request, she returned and removed some of the decorative items which were way overpriced to start with and made an adjustment to the design bill.

The following weeks and days were some of the hardest times in my life. Whether at work, in the community, or at home alone, it was just terrible. Then I had surgery for polyps and was all alone. To top it all off, my dad passed away, so I had to fly to Switzerland and help my mother get through her hard times. When I returned, I received a phone call from Margot telling me she was living somewhere in Atlanta but she told me not to contact her. A few weeks later she called again and said she would like to meet with me, so we met at Hotel Niko in Buckhead. Over lunch she explained she missed me and the lifestyle. I replied that if she truly missed me, she would be home with her husband where she belonged. I inquired as to how long was this going to go on, and asked if she wanted a divorce. She said no, she just needed more time, which I was willing to give her. I tried everything to save this marriage since I still felt so guilty leaving Andrea and the kids and I sincerely wanted to save our relationship. We agreed that before either of us would file for divorce we would meet again to talk. A month later we met at a McDonald's in Atlanta. I asked her what was going on and was she coming back home. She indicated she needed more time but couldn't answer my question of how much time—a day, a week or a month. So, finally I told her she must be nuts and I was going to file for a divorce.

That's when the fun started. It was almost like the movie *War of the Roses*. The only difference was I did not pee on her fish since she did not cook anyway and she did not drive over my British Morgan sports car since I did not own one. It took almost a year until we had things worked out. She hired a lawyer that one of her girlfriends had suggested and I had a down-to-earth lawyer. We met in front of a judge and got divorced. After it was all done I thanked her lawyer that he had looked out for her as I did not want her to get hurt. I guess I still had some feelings for her after all. On my trip to Atlanta I drove by Cincinnati and brought her some items which we were still fighting over, but it had to be done. I left her and with big tears in my eyes I drove back to Atlanta. Now it was finally over. In no way would I say it was all her fault. My God, I did many stupid things in the 12 years we were married. We all know there are always two sides to every story. What I did not know for a long time is that it was the best thing that happened for both of us. The lesson here is there is a reason for everything that happens to us.

Over the next few months I dated different people, sold the home in Cleveland, and bought a nice condo. I should have rented rather than purchasing another home as a few weeks later the company was sold to an investor from Hong Kong and I was moved to Phoenix, Arizona. This time I was Sr. VP for the West Coast and bought a nice home in the Scottsdale Country Club. It was a gated community and the house was located at the third hole on the golf course. Work went well and so did my private life; as always, I was a survivor. After all I went through the past months it was remarkable how resilient I was even after selling two houses, changing jobs, losing my dad, moving three times, having surgery, and getting divorced. These were some of the most stressful events that occur in a man's life and I did it all in style.

Living in Scottsdale was nice. I was fortunate to have great people to work with like the controller, director of marketing, and my secretary who were a super team. We still had to report to Cleveland, but since the owner lived in Hong Kong I had to make trips to the Far East and report back. In general, things went very well. I even had a girlfriend in Scottsdale when I found the love of my life. I had to visit some properties in Seattle, and after a meeting with the owners, I suggested that we go visit the competition. My associate indicated it had been a long day and he was ready to go to bed. I bugged him further and we finally went to the Sheraton Hotel, a Hilton, and eventually ended up at the Westin. Once in the lobby I was bragging -- look what I did over there and see what I did over here during the Westin General Manager's Meeting the year I was Chairman of the Conference. The hostess in the Palmcourt heard me and came around the corner because she had recognized my voice. It was Audrey Smith, whom I knew from Singapore. I had known her husband before she met him since he was a General Manager with our company and had known her long before she met her husband. She asked me what I was doing in Seattle. I replied I was working but wanted to know what she was doing there. I had assumed she moved back to Singapore after she lost her husband to cancer and then only three months later lost her son. However, she had decided to stay in Seattle and take a fun job, so she was working at the Westin as a hostess. It was nice to see Audrey and we agreed to meet for a drink the next time I came to Seattle. A couple of months later I had another meeting in Seattle, so I called Audrey to go out. She said she could not make it; obviously I was unhappy and thought "women, what can you do?" I went back to my hotel and watched television when the phone rang and Audrey was on the line. She said she did not blame me for being angry with her, but explained she had a flight to Australia the following morning to visit her daughter and had not even begun to pack. Since this sounded reasonable to me we agreed we would meet the next time I returned to Seattle. A few weeks later I had a meeting in San Francisco which ended early. I called her and asked her what she was doing for dinner that night. She said she had no plans, so I jumped on the next flight to Seattle while

Audrey went grocery shopping. She picked me up at the airport, then cooked a great Chinese meal for us. We had such great respect and trust for each other right from the beginning. Maybe that was because we had known each other since 1972—now it was 1992 -- 20 years later. At the time I was still dating the girl in Scottsdale, who usually stayed with me for the weekend. Audrey called me and I told my date I was in love with another woman. Like a hurricane, the girl went through the house, packed up a few things and was gone! I felt so bad; however, I realized how much Audrey meant to me.

Life is interesting to say the least. I can close this chapter of the book since I have so much more to report of my marriage to the love of my life. Audrey is special!

9. MOVING TO OTHER HOTEL COMPANIES

As I indicated earlier, my loyalty to Westin was high. I had several opportunities to move to other companies, however I really never had the guts to do it. I felt I owed it to Westin to stay with the company. I was told that at the time in 1964 John Portman was building this unique hotel in Atlanta. He was looking for a hotel company to manage it. Marriott, Sheraton, Hilton, and Westin looked at the property. The consensus of the experts was this hotel was never going to open due to issues with the local Health Department, fire regulations, and many other issues.

The property was to be an atrium hotel, and this was to make Portman the "father of the atrium style hotel." The head of the Lowes Hotel Company in New York took a chance to take over the management of the hotel, which was named the Regency Hotel. While the lawyers were busy negotiating the deal, Mr. Pritzker from Chicago came to Atlanta and toured the hotel with Mr. Portman. He subsequently decided to take a chance and agreed to purchase the hotel. He told the lawyers they could stop their negotiations. Since Hyatt had only a few hotels at the time, they felt this new hotel could help them create a new brand, so they called it the Hyatt Regency Atlanta Hotel. The rest is history. While still working at the Olympic Hotel I had a chance to join Hyatt but did not. Often I felt I should have because I viewed Hyatt as much more daring than Westin.

In 1968 I made $12,000 a year at the Century Plaza as Director of Restaurants. A fellow who had a chain of restaurants came and offered me $24,000 a year, double what I was currently making. I hardly slept for two nights but then I decided not to take the job; on reflection, it was the correct decision. The lesson learned was that money is not everything. Continuing with Westin was the right decision, especially since just a few weeks later Andrea and I received the chance to move to the Far East. If I had taken the job as the restaurant company's general manager, I would never have had the chance to work in the Far East nor any of the other wonderful places that a career with Westin Hotels offered me. I was very lucky the way my career turned out. I worked in first class hotels like the St. Francis, the Plaza, as well as convention properties like the Detroit Plaza and the Peachtree Plaza. I also had the opportunity to work in re-sort hotels and corporate hotels which catered to the Monday-Friday business travelers. Each type of hotel has its own style and character.

While at the Peachtree Plaza, my head hunter friend from New York convinced me to go to Boston and interview with Sheraton. They offered me the job in a large convention property as General Manager, but with no guts to make the change, I did not take it. The next meeting for a job was with the President of the Boca Raton Resort in Florida. Again they offered me the job but I turned that down too. Next I was asked if I would like to become President of the Callaway Garden Resort in Pine Mountain, Georgia, but again I said no. In early 1980, the President of the Monarch Hotel Company approached me to see if I had any interest in joining him. Since they only had two hotels and Westin was an international hotel chain, I felt there was no way I could make that move. That was probably a major mistake. The developer was going to build the Monarch Plaza Hotel and the Peachtree Monarch Hotel. Shortly before opening the two hotels in Atlanta, the developer made a deal and acquired the name Ritz Carlton. Subsequently he renamed the two ho-tels the Ritz Carlton Buckhead and the Ritz Carlton Atlanta. From this the Ritz Carlton Company was formed. Colgate Holmes left the company and Horst Schultze took over the company. Horst was General

Manager at the Hyatt Dearborn when I was at the Detroit Plaza. Horst was probably one of the finest hoteliers that ever walked the planet. How he developed Ritz Carlton Hotels is an excellent example of how well he knew how to run a quality operation and motivate his staff.

Well, as we all know I finally made the break from Westin Hotels when the company was sold to the Japanese and I know I did not want to work for them. I preferred to work for the Swiss. Stouffer Hotels at the time was owned by Nestlé, the Swiss coffee and chocolate company. Who would have guessed that about four years later I would be working for the Chinese!

My start with Stouffers was great as I loved the company, liked Nestlé and what it stood for. I was sent to Montreux at Lake Geneva where the Nestlé World Headquarters was located. I participated in a seminar and was instantly enthusiastic about Nestlé and Stouffers just as I previously felt about Westin. First, I made a tour of different hotels with Stouffers to familiarize myself with the company. As a new Vice President, I received the red carpet treatment in every hotel I visited. While visiting Valley Forge in Pennsylvania I got a bad ear infection and could not fly. Since I had an important meeting in Cleveland, I decided to travel by Greyhound Bus. It was humorous when going through the dinner line at the next stop the cashier said your meal is free. I asked her why I didn't have to pay. I learned she thought I was the driver since I was the only one well dressed. I chuckled to myself as I admitted to her I was not the driver and I do have to pay for my meal. When we arrived in Cleveland at 1:30 in the morning, the driver did not know where the Greyhound Station was since he was new. It was fortunate that I was able to help him.

First, I took over about half a dozen hotels and my work went well. Three of the hotels, the Rochester Plaza, the Winston Plaza, and the Riverwood Plaza in Mobile, Alabama were managed by Stouffer Hotels and the owner representation was a fellow out of Chicago, Arnold Levi.

He was Jewish, a very smart fellow who I knew from the Century Plaza time. He was demanding but I liked him especially since he knew what he was talking about. Our relationship was almost a friendship because of a common respect.

Living in Cleveland was nice, especially in the summer. This is a city that is totally underrated. It has theaters, a great symphony and a lot of old money, money that can make things happen. I was amazed at all the special events the city hosted. On the weekends I had a chance to go with Bill and Penny to Lake Erie where they owned a nice condo and a large speedboat. It was just super. We had fun and met some of the other Stouffer Executives from the food company. Weekends when I had no plans, I would spend Saturday morning in Chagrin Falls. My standard breakfast was at Yours Truly, a lovely coffee shop. This was an absolutely romantic lovely village. When going there it is like going back in time. The whole area of Cuyahoga County is like living in Connecticut which is why they call it the Western Reserve. The gorgeous white homes with their manicured gardens, green pastures, wild flowers, and trees are just as pretty as can be.

I also did quite a lot of traveling with the company. Then the corporate meetings we had and the long nights when we and the Executive Staff went drinking for hours gave me some stress. My relationship with Margot and all the other happenings such as moving into a new home, personal issues, etc. added to the confusion. We had some reorganization in the company and I was assigned hotels in Hawaii, Arizona, Mexico, California, and Texas. I liked my new assignments and the times in Hawaii and Mexico were great. I always had a soft spot for Hawaii since I used to live there and my daughter Christina was born there. Mexico is so colorful and festive with the music, the good food and all the excitement — how could you not fall in love with this country?

Then out of nowhere the bomb went off — Nestlé decided to sell Beringer Winery, Stouffer Hotels and Resorts, as well as the Stouffer

Restaurants. The hotel company was sold to an investor out of Hong Kong. What a shock this was to all of us in the Executive Offices! First of all we all had to interview with the new President—some of us made it and some did not. Unfortunately, the company brought in their own President, so Bill left the organization. I was very sorry about this, but I guess this happens all over the world when new companies take over. Our new President was a fellow from Germany, a rough manager I would say; smart yes, but in my opinion his people skills were lacking. The company that acquired our organization was Ramada International and the Stouffer Hotels were converted over a period of time into the Renaissance Hotels. First it was Stouffer Renaissance Hotels, then the name Stouffer was dropped. In general, the changeover was done well. Now we had a big reorganization. I was named Sr. VP for the West Coast with hotels in Maui, Hawaii, Vancouver, Edmonton, Winnipeg, Los Angeles, Long Beach, Cyprus, San Francisco, Palm Springs, Scottsdale, Houston, Austin, and Dallas. Now with the new owners out of Hong Kong, the game changed for me. As a Sr. VP, I had the advantage of having operated in Thailand and Singapore previously and I knew the mentality of managers from the Far East is totally different than the American mind. The owners put different advisers in different positions and our American friends looked at them as spies. However, they really were not spies; they just looked out for the interest of the owners. It was a game of intrigue. But you just have to do your job and not worry about all the mystery and everything works out fine. Dealing with the owner and his top advisors was something else. They would visit a resort, play the golf course and bet $2,000-$3,000 on a hole. But I guess when you own the place you can do these things. From the beginning I said the owners look at our hotel company as a quick investment and at the right time they will flip the company and take the profits. It was a new style of doing business. I could feel with all the other investments that they had in the Far East such as hotels, condo buildings, apartment buildings, and jewelry shops, plus many other enterprises, I was convinced Stouffer Hotels was just a Monopoly game for them to play with. At the time the story was that our investor promised Nestlé to pay them $50 million a year for the purchase of the hotel company until they could return to Nestlé $1 billion dollars. So, we heard all day long we have to make the $50 million mark. What a joke that was since the real estate value of the hotels was worth more than a billion dollars, so the hotel company was practically gratis. As they say—time will tell.

Since I was Sr. VP of the West Coast, I was asked to move to Arizona and open a Regional Office with a Director of Marketing, a Regional Controller to watch the finances, and an administrator. The staff was super and I thoroughly enjoyed working with them. I bought a nice home at the third hole of the Scottsdale Country Club. Christina went to school at the University of Arizona, a great academic institution which I jokingly called a Country Club. Often on the weekend she came to visit me since I was single at the time. By now I was dating Audrey, and that relationship was becoming more serious. While in San Francisco and staying at the Stanford Court Hotel, we got engaged. However, there was a hook since I could not drink tea with her father and ask him if I could marry her. So, I called him in Malaysia and he gave us his blessing. A few weeks later Audrey moved to Scottsdale. Our Arizona life did not last for long because I was asked to move to Frankfurt, Germany and establish Renaissance Hotels in Europe. We had an office in Eschborn near Frankfurt. I was happy to move there since it was only five hours by car to visit my mom in Switzerland. We had to organize our moves and decide what came from Audrey in Seattle and what would stay in the home in Arizona since we decided to keep the house and make our move to Europe. In a way I was sorry to move back to Europe because I knew it would be a big challenge since the mentality of people over there is different but as always, I looked at it as a positive move, a new experience, and so we ordered the movers.

10. MOVING AGAIN...NEW OWNERS AGAIN

In the old days I would move about every two years. I used to joke I could not keep a job so they promoted me. Now the moves would be due to re-organization or a change in ownership.

Shortly after Christmas 1996, Audrey and I arrived in Frankfurt, Germany. At first we were living in a hotel until the company learned that a three bedroom apartment they had a long-term rental agreement on was empty. One of the occupants had quit, one had gotten married, and the third was fired. The head of our regional office was delighted to learn we were willing to take over the lease. The apartment was okay although we had to make some changes since it had a tiny living room for entertaining purposes and three bedrooms for just the two of us. Luckily Audrey was superb in making it into a very nice comfortable home for us, especially since we knew it was for a short time. The apartment was in Bad Soden, a very nice residential area in Taunus, a resort area. It was close to Königstein and Bad Homburg, two more lovely resort towns with a casino and concert halls. These were very nice places, especially in the summer time.

Our office was located in Eschborn, a suburb of Frankfurt. The head of the regional office was the fellow who used to be President of Ramada International. Then we had a new president of the company who was staying in Hong Kong and in the USA we had a former Stouffer Executive taking over the company as president. There was a mix of Ramada, Renaissance, Stouffer, and outside executives. At times it created a lot of tension. It was so different from Stouffers and Westin. I was Sr. VP of Renaissance for Europe, the Middle East, and Africa. Kurt Bernt, a German who mostly worked in Germany, was Sr. VP for Ramada Properties. We all had our own team, with Controller, Marketing Person, F&B expert, and other support staff. At the beginning I really liked my job. I was responsible for nine hotels in Germany, two in Austria, one in Switzerland, Belgium, Holland, Moscow, Russia, and Egypt, plus two in Turkey. Then I also had three hotels under construction in Paris, Leipzig, and Chemnitz. The latter two hotels were in what was formerly called East Germany, which presented a real hassle. Everyone went there and wanted to get rich; however, things were complicated and slow. It took me six months just to get a cell phone for the hotel's general manager.

The partners we had in Leipzig and Chemnitz were fairly nice people to deal with. The properties were financed by an investment fund run by Alliance. We had very nice opening festivities in each of those hotels. For East Germany it was all new and exciting, plus I liked the area and the people. My general managers were good people, some I would even call great except for two general managers. The one in Brussels in particular, a Jewish fellow who was a real jerk and a real "know-it-all," whom I had to eventually fire. That hotel had a lot of problems with the owner/developer who ran out of money before the hotel even opened, left town, and disappeared somewhere in Israel; a real con-artist, I decided. The other General Manager thankfully left of his own accord.

I organized a General Manager's Meeting in Heidelberg, which resulted in a real teamwork session. I motivated the managers and we had a great time. The last day our boss from Frankfurt came and I asked him to address the participants. It was horrible! He took the managers apart, told them how bad they were, etc. What I had built up in three days he ruined in 20 minutes. After his talk, I asked him why he did this and he said that the only way the Germans produce results is if they are scared and you give them shit. I argued with him and told him you can catch more flies with honey than with a swat. He said I should learn to forget my American management philosophy and adapt to the European style. In the old European Ramada management organization, the bosses felt when they made a visitation to a hotel if the General Mangers did not have tears in their eyes when the bosses left, it was a lousy visit. I just laughed and figured I would continue with my way of treating people fairly.

My work continued and I had a great time. It was not work for me; even with all the problems I was faced with it was still fun for me. In Egypt the GM was an Italian fellow named Giancarlo whom I learned to love. In 1994 I was very fascinated by the costumes and people in the Middle East. So I went to mosques, as this was my first time to have such great exposure to Moslems. I remember how the guest rooms in Alexandria had signs on the ceiling that would indicate the direction to Mecca so the faithful would know how to pray. When visiting Cairo, Ankara, and Alexandria often I went into the markets, the mosques, and other gathering places. My GM kept warning me I should not do this as it was very dangerous, I could get blown up. Looking back, I must say I was pretty naïve in my behavior. Today I would not visit many cities I used to go to on a regular basis.

Another unusual experience was during Ramadan, a big Moslem holiday; the people don't eat from sun up to sun down; by midday you cannot stand close to them because the odor from their mouths is so strong. I remember riding in a taxi in Cairo; the moment the sun had set, he stopped the car and went into the next coffee shop to eat and drink. The Moslems then celebrate all night and it is a very festive atmosphere.

One time I was on my way to Cairo from Alexandria to catch my plane back to Germany when suddenly all the traffic stopped and we had to wait for nearly two hours. I was furious since I had to catch the plane for an important meeting in Frankfurt. It wasn't until later I learned the traffic was stopped because President Hosni Mubarak's motor coach was in Cairo.

Our owner of the hotel in Alexandria owned a farm and was always telling me about it and invited me to come see it. When I had a couple of days available, I took him up on his offer. He was a gracious host. While visiting his farm, we surveyed some of his fruit trees. I wanted to taste some of the fruit which they bore. He said not to do this as I should wash the fruits first. Oh no, I replied I am a Swiss boy, no problem. Boy was that ever a mistake! I got so sick; I had diarrhea for days. I could not hold anything in my stomach and was so ill when I arrived in Hamburg I ended up in the Tropical Institute which is a special clinic for patients who had to be treated for the same thing I had. They gave me shots and it took almost a week to get back to normal. The lesson is when a local person warns you about something you are unfamiliar with, listen to his advice.

The owner of the hotel in Istanbul was another interesting fellow. He could barely read and write but he had "street smarts"; he was a person hard to get along with. Mr. Polat could not speak any English, so the only way we communicated was with an interpreter. He and I were like best friends. He called me Boxer and I called him Papa. He was a multi-millionaire and made all his money as a brick layer. What a fantastic way to remind your kids where they came from. The manager of the hotel in Antalya also was involved with the Istanbul Hotel. He was a smart Turk, I must say. I would drive with him on the road going 80 km through a red light and when I screamed he replied "Well there was no one coming" or "Yesterday when I passed it, the light was green." He was a real piece of work, very smart, educated in Canada, but in his heart he was a Turk; I liked him very much. Another interesting experience for me was entering Turkey through immigration. There was a large sign which read "Visa charges — French, Germans, Swiss, Holland, etc. $10.00 — Americans $20.00". The Turks felt Americans are all rich — they can afford to pay.

In Frankfurt, we had a press conference to promote our hotels since the name Renaissance was not so well known. It was a good meeting and Erwin, Kurt, and I each made a presentation. Speaking of presentations, every so often we had to go to Hong Kong and make a presentation to the owner of the company. For me it was always an exciting trip. One time, Kurt and I took some extra days and visited our Renaissance Hotel in Seoul, Korea. To make the name Renaissance more well-known in Germany, we organized a golf tournament and called it the Renaissance Cup. The first tournament was held in Heidelberg followed by other tournaments in Cologne, Dusseldorf, Hamburg, Leipzig, as well as other German cities. We held a total of nine tournaments with the final one being held in Heidelberg with a gala dinner and the presentation of the Renaissance Cup to the winner. The entire spectacle was a great success and we received a plethora of press coverage. At each tournament we provided extensive food and beverage presentations to further impress our customers. The time went by so fast I could hardly believe we had spent two years in Europe including visits to Russia, Turkey, and Egypt, all of which thoroughly fascinated me. It was all so different from my previous dealings in Asia and the United States. In Russia I had a bodyguard the whole time since the country was so corrupt. We brought a new Mercedes limo with us from Germany to Moscow and in one day it was gone. I was so upset but our Chief of Security Yuri, who was a former KGB Russian Officer, told me not to worry, that he would get the limo back. One morning shortly thereafter the limo was parked in front of the hotel with the keys in the ignition. I asked Yuri how the hell he did it; he just smiled and said he put a contract out to kill the thief if the limo was not back to the hotel by Wednesday. Russia can be a fascinating country, but it is ruined by the corruption from within.

After being in Europe and constantly traveling, I asked the company to move me back to the United States. I missed the kids, the American lifestyle, and Audrey was not a fan of Germany even though she had lived in Europe previously as she had spent two years in Denmark. The company told me they would not have a job as Sr. Vice President available, which was just fine with me. After spending seven years in an airplane solving problems for the company across Europe, I had finally had enough of the traveling. Also, I figured there were only two good jobs in hotel business, that of President or General Manager. Realizing I could not become President, I asked for a job as General Manager. Within a few weeks they told me they had some opportunities in a hotel in Atlanta and asked me if I would be interested in going back to Atlanta and work as the General Manager of the Waverly Hotel. I was so happy and I accepted their offer immediately. Having spent over ten years in that city previously, I loved Atlanta, had friends there, and my two daughters were living there at the time. It could not have been more perfect for me. Since it was December when I arrived, we hosted a party with the theme of "Hermann Gammeter Came Home for the Holidays." Many of our old friends showed up and it was just great. The *Atlanta Business Chronicle* ran a story and when I Googled my name the other day I could still read the story of my return to the city of Atlanta. I was in Atlanta a few weeks and then the rumor started that our owners in Hong Kong were offering to sell the company to the highest bidder. The speculation and rumors went rampant but at the end, but thank goodness the Marriott Corporation purchased the company. In general, the sale and move went fairly easily and overall it was a good thing we once again had American owners. As in any merger or change of ownership, you have to make adjustments. For me the biggest hurdle was that every time I would make a decision, the Division Head, Dir. of HR, financial Controller, etc. needed to call the head office and check with them first. I had grown up with Westin and Stouffer Hotels and the philosophy was just the opposite. The General Manager made all decisions which was what they were paid to do; if a GM could not make decisions, they did not need them. It was really a change and it often came to the point that if I did something, I felt it was much easier to get forgiveness than approval. I really liked working for Marriott and must say it is a company with fantastic systems in place. Also, the way the people are treated is special. Granted, the politics at times was a bit different from what I was accustomed to, but they have an outstanding organization and thoroughly deserve the success and fine reputation they have.

What I really enjoyed was the fine employee programs the company had. We had many meetings, regional sessions, and general manager meetings. Also, I had the pleasure to participate in the Aspen Institute, which was a one-week meeting to familiarize new managers with the company. This seminar was outstanding and very helpful for me to better understand Marriott values. Our General Manager's meetings were always super affairs. One year it was at the Marriott in New Orleans and one of the special recognition programs was an awards banquet. To my surprise I was named General Manager of the year for all Renaissance Hotels. The prize was a first-class trip to Singapore and Australia. It happened that Audrey's daughter lived in Sydney at the time, so we were able to visit her as well. The trip was fabulous from beginning to end.

Most recognition prize trophies are sent back home via mail. Naturally I was too cheap to do this as I was responsible for paying the postage as that money comes out of my profit and loss statement. So my solution was to put my trophy in the dirty laundry and pack it in my suit case. What a surprise when I arrived back at the hotel. Our Director of Marketing had arranged guests, employees, along with my wife and kids to be present in the lobby of the Waverly Hotel to give me a big welcome home. When everyone wanted to see the trophy, I had to unpack my dirty laundry in the lobby to show off the trophy. Everyone just got a great laugh and said that's just Hermann! A few weeks later, Bill Marriott was in Atlanta and I had the pleasure of giving him a tour of the Waverly. At the end of the tour his comment was he thought it was one of the best tours he had ever had. For me too it was just fantastic to have Mr. Marriott with us.

By now I was over 60 years old, but with the fantastic team at the Waverly I was still having fun working. The hotel was doing well; we produced good numbers and all was great. Then on my 62nd birthday, May 31, 2002, I decided to hang it all up. It was time to retire and maybe smell the roses for the first time in many years. The Executive Committee under the Director of Sales & Marketing's leadership organized a very nice going away party. Music, movie presentation, a gift, many industry and business executive attended. Even some employees from Westin Hotels like Waldo Brun from Orlando came and made a presentation. The whole affair really touched me. In my comments I said a few thank yous to the staff and guests; thanks to Marriott, thanks to America and most of all thanks for what this country had done for me and lastly thanks to my wife and kids.

Now I thought, well work is over or is it? I thought now I can do all the things I never had time for.

11. HERMANN THE DREAMER

I always felt a person should have dreams since what is life without dreaming? It is the essence of our existence — no dreams means no life, I thought. How drab it would be if you could not dream of something, what you would like to be, or have or what you want to achieve in the future, perhaps a journey you would like to make or a country you would like to explore. I often think about my daughters when they say that something is on their "to do list," such as I want to visit Monaco or climb a mountain in Switzerland. When they have accomplished that goal they say they can check it off their list. The feeling of satisfaction is so great and rewarding.

My dad was obviously a dreamer when I recall the illnesses he faced but never gave up. How as a teenage stowaway on a banana freighter he tried to visit his brother in Australia. Or in school when he was only 12 he designed a machine to clean streets with complete plans and drawings of his invention. His teacher told him he was crazy because such a machine could not be invented or built. He was better off studying his books than dreaming of impossible issues. The teacher said that street cleaning was a good job in 1917 and it provided a good income for a person to support a family. What nonsense it was to build a machine that would clean the streets. My dad told me this story over and over and then reminded me that today we have street cleaning machines.

When living in Los Angeles, Mother Andrea and I made many trips with our trailer. We loved the feeling of freedom and after all the hard work we did, we had a ball camping in the great state parks by the beach. Because of our experience I helped obtain a travel trailer for my daughter Christina and her family, too. It is a nice trailer which has a slide-out on the sides and thus can be enlarged for her family. A nice truck to tow it along was all that was needed to transport their home around on wheels. I must say it made me happy to see how much fun they had with their camper trailer. The grand children are in heaven when they can go and live in the outdoors. Today I can afford a beautiful luxurious motor home; however, I don't want it. I'm spoiled; I need a hotel with all the conveniences.

Another dream was to treat myself to a Bentley or a Rolls Royce. My daughter Andrea used to say when she became rich she would buy one for me. Again, I could afford it; however, I have absolutely no interest in driving around in one of those things. A more elegant sport car has my fancy now.

During my youth in Switzerland, I used to sit in a bar and have a couple of beers or red wine and dream about going to America. I imagined that I would go to this new country, work hard, and become successful. I would be recognized for my accomplishments and would be respected. When dreaming like that there was a great feeling of happiness that would overcome my whole body. This went on many times. I could never understand it, but I knew that someday it would happen and thank God, it did.

Another dream I had was to write a book. I would call it *Life...An Emotional Roller Coaster*. The book would be many, many little stories of people; different experiences such as when a baby was born or the death of a family member. Perhaps the thrill of someone winning a lottery ticket or the disappointment when purchasing a new home and the financing fell through. Maybe other experiences such as the struggle a family member might endure when illness occurs or the drug addiction of a child. Other stories could involve the disappointment felt when a relationship does not end happily or the end of a beautiful love story resulting in divorce followed by financial stress. The list goes on and on. The dream of writing this book was there but I never had time to write a book. Hotels were far more important to me.

Some of my biggest dreams have been shared in my conversations with Henry Mulligan the CEO of Westin. There were several meetings where I had the chance to participate and we as the young Turks (as the executives called us) had been asked to come up with new ideas and changes for the future. I always said we should build a hotel underwater because of the cost of land. Today there are several hotels underwater. Another of my dreams was to be the first hotel manager in space. I guess for that one I was ahead of my time, but I am convinced some day we will have hotels in space. In measuring the success of a hotel's performance, the calculation was always average rate and occupancy. I said for years that that wasn't the way it should be calculated; the issue is revenue per available room. Today that is the industry standard. Let's build a hotel with say 500 rooms and 100 condos. Then when we are booked we can rent out a condo. This would help us to maximize occupancy, maximize revenues, and maximize profits. Well, Hermann, you make no sense I was told. Today it happens in our industry.

Two other dreams I had were about restaurant concepts. I would start with one restaurant then expand and ultimately franchise the restaurants. The first was called "Gourmet Soups & Salads." This would be a place that served 5-6 different soups like chili, split pea soup, clam chowder, minestrone, vegetable soup, etc. and would also include an extended salad bar. This was a dream I had in my early career in the restaurant business while still living in Europe. In the early 60s it was unthinkable to have a restaurant that only served soups and salads. I figured it would be great since I would not have to hire high paid chefs and service personnel. I never developed nor started the concept, but it was certainly an idea that had merit. Today there are several chains that operate with this concept. Also, I think this way of eating still has great potential especially with the concerns of health and weight control. The other restaurant dream was to be called the "Gourmet Grotto." This restaurant again had no high paying chefs and would control labor costs. All the cooking would be done in the dining room. The menu would consist of different flambé dishes such as steaks, seafood, crepes, etc. The server would cook in front of the customer, which would be a new sensation. The restaurant would be decorated like an Italian grotto with all the items on sale in a souvenir shop including paintings and the whole inventory. The idea was to generate additional sales like the Cracker Barrel restaurants do. Unfortunately, or maybe fortunately, this concept was halted because of liabilities by the lawyers. I guess it was too dangerous to cook in the dining room with all the gas burners, etc. But it sure was a dream of mine to operate a restaurant like this and then ultimately franchise it. Someone once told me if wishes were fishes we all could have a fish fry.

I used to go to college recruiting for our company where I visited hotel schools all over the country, such as Michigan State, Florida International, schools in Las Vegas, Cornell University, and many, many other famous hospitality schools. I can pride myself in having a retention rate of students of 90% or better. In other words, the people I hired stayed with the company, made a career in the hospitality business and went up the ladder. There are numerous general managers whom I recruited and who continued to be productive. There were few who left, but those who did were more often women who got married and moved with their husbands and left us. Students used to ask me how they could become successful general managers. I told them there are only three simple rules you have to live by and you can make it. With eyes wide open they looked at me and awaited the following answer. The rules are:

Work hard — No matter how good you are you have to continue with hard work; if you start to think you have made it — it is over. You are only as good as your last accomplishments. You have to continue to give your best and work hard.

Honesty—I don't mean not stealing, as that is a given. I mean be an honest, good human being, be fair to all concerned, and remember that a business deal is only good if it is good for everybody.

Be patient—Too many young people move around and have no patience. The grass is always greener on the other side, but remember—it gets cut the very same way. Stay in your job and build your experience and you will advance.

The students used to give me surprised looks, but the ones whom I recognized believed me were the ones I would hire. The main thing I looked for was someone who had ambition and dreams.

It is unreal or weird, but since I have retired I practically dream every single night about things that happened in my work life. Sometimes my dreams are about when I worked as an apprentice, a chef, or when I was general manager having a meeting with the convention bureau. My dream might be about problems or challenges with guests, a confrontation with bankers or investors as a Senior VP dealing with problems regarding the profitability of a hotel. Occasionally it included actions which occurred in conventions, presentations to get a political convention or the Olympics. A recurring dream is about issues with employees or arguments and negotiations with labor unions and other things that have happened in any part of the world. I can't explain, but about 90% of my dreams have to do with my life in hotels. Sometimes when I wake up I'm glad it was just a dream but sometimes I am sorry it was just a dream and not reality. I guess I used to love my job which is why I still have these nightly dreams.

12. FASCINATING ASIA

No doubt every country has its fascination, whether it's their unique costumes, traditions, their way of life or its cultures, rules and issues. Maybe I was so fascinated by Asia because I traveled so much to Singapore, Thailand, Malaysia, India, Pakistan, Korea, Japan, Cambodia, all over China, Vietnam, Indonesia, Bali, and other places. Or perhaps it might be because of my marriage to what I call "my little Asian Princess" when she is nice to me or "my little Asian Hitler" when she gives me a hard time but that title change rarely happens. I used to be so fascinated because Audrey speaks seven different Chinese dialects, plus Malay, English and German. Probably another reason to be an Asian fan is my older daughter Andrea was born in Singapore. But I had to go and denounce Singapore citizenship because I wanted her to be American and Swiss nationality. Asians say we look all the same to them, and the same holds true for us Caucasians, Asian people all look the same to us. Once you know the cultures it is a different story. I can see if a person is Korean, Chinese, Japanese, Vietnamese, etc. The people are so different and I think that Asian women are some of the prettiest human beings there are: the color of their skin, the almond eyes, and the graceful move they make when they walk. When Asians look on us Caucasians whether it is American, German, French, or Greek, they say we all look the same. On the other hand, for us it is also a common assumption that the Asians look all the same. However, after living in Asia sometimes you can easily determine if someone is Chinese, Korean, Vietnamese, etc. Also, the mannerisms are different between the people. A Thai person is probably the most soft and gracious person in the Orient, the Japanese seems very serious and hard to read. Chinese I would compare to Germans; somehow they are rough.

TRADITIONAL CLOTHING IN ASIA

What a wonderful experience it is to see Asians in their traditional clothing so colorful and different especially the women who have gorgeous clothes with many different colors, robes, silk, special shoes and head gear. I remember Balinese ladies with all their hats and colorful silk cloth. There are so many different saris and sarongs. Men have traditional clothes but by far not as nice as the ladies wear. Google "Asian Costumes" and you'll know what I am talking about. Another mystique is the dancing in Asia. It is so different and many of the dances represent a story, similar to Hawaiian dances.

ETIQUETTE IN ASIA

In Asia, paying respect to elders is expected among younger people, and a gesture such as bowing expresses the utmost respect. The elaborate and refined Japanese tea ceremony is also meant to demonstrate respect through grace and good etiquette. Etiquette in Asia varies as much from country to country as it does in any other part of the world, even though certain actions may seem to be in common. No article of rules of etiquette can ever be completed. As the perception of behaviors and actions vary, intercultural competence is essential. However, a lack of knowledge about the customs and expectations of Asia people can make even the best-intentioned person seem rude, foolish or worse.

FOOD — again as different as Greek, Swiss, French or German food is, so too are various Asian foods different from one another. However, I must admit that the real and correct Asian food is absolutely outstanding. There are not many Asian foods I don't like. Chinese of course is my favorite and I should write down some recipes. My absolute favorite food is what is called "stall food." These are meals that are served by hawkers who have a food stand and serve mostly one item. The stalls or food courts as they are called are all over Asia. The absolute best ones are in Singapore and Hong Kong. If someone would say I have only three weeks to live, I would take the next plane and fly to Singapore and eat at a food stall. Besides excellent food, the atmosphere is very unique with people all over, shouting, eating, joking and eating, eating, eating.

When I came to the United States in 1963, my impression was wow, what a country. I did not have this surprising feeling again until I went to China in 2007. Almost 40 years after I arrived in America, now once again it was wow! My eyes opened wide and there were so many new impressions.

We started our China trip in Beijing, a city with a history stretching back three millennia, the capital of China. Even though it is an old city it is known as much for its modern architecture as its ancient sites such as the Grand Forbidden City Complex, the imperial palace during the Ming and Qing dynasties. Nearby the massive Tiananmen Square Plaza is the site of Mao Zedong's Mausoleum and the National Museum of China, displaying a vast collection of cultural relics. Beijing has an estimated population of over 21 million inhabitants and it has grown by half a million a year. Very soon the city will have more people than the whole country of Australia.

The Forbidden City was the Chinese Imperial Palace from 1420 to 1912. It is located in the center of Beijing and now houses the Palace Museum. It previously served as the home of the emperors and their households. It also served as the ceremonial and political center of

Chinese government for almost 500 years. It was built from 1406-1420 and consists of 980 buildings covering 180 acres. The complex is amazing. Next, we visited the Great Wall. Although it was not built by Donald Trump, it is an absolute architectural wonder. The Great Wall of China is a series of fortifications made of stone, brick, wood, and other materials. It was built to protect the Chinese states and empires against the raids and invasions of the various nomadic groups of the Eurasian steppe. Several walls were built and later joined together and made stronger, all of which are now collectively referred to as the Great Wall. The majority of the existing wall is from the Ming Dynasty. Other purposes of the Great Wall have included border control, allowing the imposition of duties on goods transported along the Silk Road as well as the control of immigration and emigration. The Wall measures about 5500 miles. When walking the Great Wall, I must admit I did some huffing and puffing. Needless to say, thousands of tourists are doing the same thing I did. Souvenir shops and snack bars were abundant.

What would Beijing be without Tiananmen Square? It's another symbol of Chinese power and tradition. It is a large square in the center of Beijing named after the Tiananmen Gate of Heavenly Peace located to its north, separating it from the Great Hall of the People. It became infamous worldwide due to the shooting of several hundred (or possibly thousands) of civilians by soldiers there. The demonstrations were broadcast all over the world. Still today the locals are very guarded with their comments. I remember one of the tourist guides telling us when we visited a rice field how much she hates the central government. She could only make this comment because we were all alone in the boondocks.

Another interesting statistic is that in 2007, while we were in China, Beijing had 1,000 McDonald's and 700 Kentucky Fried Chicken outlets. Today there are probably many more. It's quite interesting that the McDonald's use real china in their cafes, not Styrofoam cups or plates. They were also quite colorful, with nice music playing in the background.

The customers were mostly young people in Western clothes with smart phones, etc.

Flying on China airlines, the next leg of our trip was to Xian. This city is located in the northwest of the Peoples Republic of China. It has a population of close to nine million people. While Xian might be a nice and interesting place to visit, the reason most tourists go there is to see the famous Terracotta Warriors. The figures date from approximately the late third century (BCE) and were discovered in 1974 by a local farmer. We had the pleasure of actually seeing him while there. He was sitting on a table covering his head with a fan. "No pictures, no pictures" is all he would say. Like a famous Hollywood star, he was admired by the visitors. The figures vary in height according to their roles, with the tallest being the generals. They include warriors and chariots, as well as their horses. The estimate was that the three pits containing the Terracotta Army held more than 8,000 soldiers, 130 chariots with 520 horses, in addition to 150 cavalry horses. Other terracotta non-military figures were found in other pits, including officials, acrobats, strongmen and musicians. The thought was they would entertain the emperor after death. The Terracotta Army is a collection of terracotta sculptures depicting the armies of Qin Shi Huang, the Emperor or China. It is a form of funerary art buried with the Emperor in 210-209 BCE in an effort to protect the emperor in his afterlife. We felt extremely lucky and privileged to be able to see this and experience this UNESCO World Heritage Site.

Shanghai was our next stop. This is a city with over 24 million people and is the most populous city in China. It is a global financial center and transportation hub with the world's busiest container port. It is located on the Yangtze River delta in Eastern China. For centuries it was considered a major administrative, shipping, and trading town. Shanghai grew due to European recognition of its prime port location on the coast. However, the Communist Party takeover of the mainland in 1949 limited trade to socialist countries and caused a decline in the city's global influence. In the 1990s, Deng Xiaoping introduced some economic reforms which helped redevelop the city and aided in the return of foreign investments and finance to the city. It is now considered a popular tourist destination with historical landmarks such as the Bund, the City God Temple and Yu Garden, as well as numerous museums. Shanghai's breathtaking skyline is fabulous during the day or at night with the multicolored neon signs.

Again utilizing China Airlines, we flew to Guilin. This city is situated on the west bank of the Li River bordering Hunan to the north. Its name means "Forest of Osmanthus" due to the large number of fragrant Sweet Osmanthus (Olive) Trees located in the city. The city has long been renowned for its scenery of karst topography and has become another one of China's most popular tourist destinations. It is the reason we visited Guilin to take a river trip on the Li River and admire the scenery and the karst. The karst topography is a landscape formed from the dissolution of soluble rocks such as limestone, very unusual for a country boy from Switzerland who is used to granite rocks, shale, and other formations. The trip on the Li River was on a Chinese junk boat with cooking done at the back of the ship on a charcoal stove; not exactly first class. However, the food we were served was edible. When going down the river it was like going back in time. It was incredible for us who were used to a different lifestyle to witness what was almost biblical to us. We saw small camp sites, only just a few houses, a couple of shacks, while women washed laundry in the river at the same time as kids played and swam despite the fact that cows were being washed in the same basic area.

The city of Guangzhou beckoned us next. It is historically known as Canton and was nicknamed the City of Flowers and is the third largest Chinese city. It is one of the major birthplaces of China's ancient "Maritime Silk Road" and is located on the Pearl River north of Hong Kong and Macau. The city serves as an important national transportation hub and trading port and is also known as a shopper's paradise. It is best known for the Canton Fair which is a comprehensive trade fair with a long history of exhibit variety and broad list of overseas buyers and turnover in China. While we were visiting there, one of the large fairs took place. Having visited many conventions in my life as a hotelier held in major cities such as New York, Chicago, Las Vegas, and Atlanta, my eyes absolutely popped when I saw what was going on at this city-wide fair.

When traveling to Hong Kong we went by train, but I must note that the Chinese trains cannot be compared to the luxurious wagons we have in Switzerland. Although I had always had a good time in Hong Kong before, this was the first time I had returned since it was taken back by the Chinese. I must say it was quite different than when it was a British colony.

Since I had never traveled to Macau before we decided to include that trip on our agenda, but it was a disappointment. We went by hydrofoil boat, which was fun and unusual. Originally, Macau was founded and run by the Portuguese. It was a rich city and became known as the world's largest gambling center. While there are many casinos like in Las Vegas, these gambling palaces do not have the great entertainment shows that they have in Vegas. Since I do not gamble, I felt our trip to Macau was a waste of time. Although I'm sure it has many interesting points, for some reason it was not my cup of tea.

The trip to China was fabulous and fantastic and included many unusual experiences. Going into a department store or a grocery store in the evening was no fun as it is so crowded with so many people you to begin to feel like an ant—body to body with people. Their street signs and languages can be frustrating, but I was lucky to have Audrey with me who speaks several dialects plus the added fact that she is Chinese made it much easier when we were shopping. The food in mainland China was mediocre as I had enjoyed much better Chinese food in other part of

Asia, even in the United States or Europe. There must be some decent Chinese restaurants there, but we did not find them. Lastly, I must say Asia is fascinating and we will treasure the adventures we experienced.

CONFUCIOUS SAYS...

Eat healthy food, prepared with care

Avoid spoiled items and improperly treated ingredients

Never eat between meals, make sure food is properly shared out and that sauces are in harmony.

Following are some good Asian Recipes which can be enjoyed at home:

CAI TANG (CLEAR VEGETABLE SOUP)

- 4 cups chicken broth
- 7 oz. Chinese leaf vegetables (bok choy or pak choy) sliced to 1 1/2" pieces
- 1 medium carrot, peeled & sliced in 1" pieces
- 1 onion, thick slices
- 3 green scallions sliced into 1 1/2" lengths
- 1 Tbs soy sauce
- Salt & pepper to taste

Bring the chicken broth to a boil, add the vegetables and green onions. Return again to boil. Season with soy sauce, salt & pepper. Stir and serve piping hot. As a variation you can add 8 medium shrimp when the vegetables are half cooked. Some Chinese rice wine or sherry makes it even tastier.

SHU MI TANG (CORN SOUP)

- Ingredients:
- 2 large corn cobs
- 2 egg whites
- 5 Tbs milk
- 3 cups chicken broth
- Salt & pepper to taste
- 2 1/2 Tbs cornstarch mixed with 5 Tbs cold water or chicken broth
- Some fried onion rings or finely chopped fried bacon for garnish

Strip the corn from the cob. Beat egg whites until stiff, add the milk and beat in. Bring the chicken broth to a boil, add the corn, plus salt & pepper to taste. Bring the soup back to a boil stirring constantly and thicken with the cornstarch mixture. Remove pan from the heat and fold the beaten egg whites into the soup. Stir again and serve hot. Garnish with the fried onion rings and/or chopped fried bacon.

XIA MIAN (NOODLE SOUP WITH SHRIMP)

- 3 1/2 Qts of water
- 1 lb. 2 oz. pork ribs, trimmed of fat
- 9 oz pork shoulde
- Salt & pepper to taste
- 1 lb. 5 oz. jumbo shrimp
- 1 garlic clove, peeled & chopped
- 3 Tbs oil
- 2 cups water
- 1 Tbs dark soy sauce
- 1 Tbs sugar

- 1 lb. 12 oz. Fujian Mian (fresh yellow egg noodles)
- 14 oz. bean sprouts
- 9 oz. water spinach, coarsely chopped

GARNISH —

- 2 fresh red chili peppers sliced in rings
- 3 Tbs fried onion rings
- 5 1/2 oz. diced bacon

Bring water to oil in a large sauce pan, add the pork ribs and pork shoulder, salt & pepper to taste. Bring back to boil, reduce the heat and simmer until pork is tender. Remove the shoulder of pork and cut into thin slices. Strain the broth through a cheese cloth. Wash the shrimp, remove the heads. Heat the oil in a sauce pan and add the garlic then the shrimp heads. Cook until they are pink, remove them and pound them coarsely. In a pan bring the water to boil, add the shrimp and simmer until they are done. Remove them (reserving the water) and let them cool, then shell them, devein and slice each shrimp in half. Set aside. Blanch the bean sprouts and the water spinach; quickly plunge the noodles in boiling water. Put noodles, bean sprouts, water spinach, pork and the halved shrimps in small serving bowls. Fill with very hot broth. Garnish. Serve with chili pepper rings and light soy sauce on the side.

GAN BIAN SI JI DOU
(FRIED ASPARAGUS BEAN WITH GROUND PORK)

- 10 1/2 oz. of asparagus beans (not to be taken as asparagus — these are special Chinese vegetables, but regular asparagus can be substituted)

- 3 Tbs oil
- 2 garlic cloves peeled & minced
- 2 slices ginger root, chopped
- 1 1/2 Tbs minced mustard greens
- 1/2 Tbs dried shrimp, rinsed and chopped
- 4 Tbs cooked ground pork or substitute ground beef
- 1 cup water
- 1 Tbs minced scallions

SAUCE —

- 1 1/2 Tbs sugar
- 1 Tbs dark vinegar
- 1 Tbs light soy sauce
- 1/2 dark soy sauce
- Few drops sesame oil

Fry the asparagus beans in a wok until they are lightly browned, remove and reserve. Fry the garlic and ginger. Add the beans, mustard greens, shrimp and ground pork and stir. Add the water and simmer until the liquid has almost totally evaporated. Meanwhile, combine the sauce ingredients. Increase the heat, add the sauce and cook until the aromatic. Serve with green onions.

SUAN LA TANG (HOT & SOUR SOUP)

- 4 dried Shitake Mushrooms 6 ½ oz. canned bamboo shoots
- 2 blocks tofu
- 4 1/2 oz. lean pork
- 3 cups chicken broth

- 2 1/2 Tbs light soy sauce
- 1 Tbs salt to taste
- 5 Tbs vinegar
- 1/4 Tbs pepper
- 5 Tbs cornstarch mixed with 2 1/2 Tbs cold water
- 1 egg lightly beaten
- 1 1/2 Tbs sesame oil
- 1 green onion (scallion) minced.

Rinse the mushrooms and soak for 30 minutes in hot water. Meanwhile drain the bamboo shoots and slice thinly lengthwise. Slice the tofu into narrow strips and finely chop the pork. When the mushrooms are soft, strain them, trim away the hard stems and finely slice the caps. Place the mushrooms, bamboo shoots and pork in a sauce pan, add chicken broth, soy sauce, salt & pepper then gently heat until boiling. Reduce the heat and simmer for 3 minutes. Add tofu, vinegar and pepper. Bring back to a boil, pour in the corn starch mixture and stir until the soup has thickened. Slowly beat in the beaten egg. Ladle the soup into individual bowls, drizzle sesame oil into each bowl and sprinkle with green onions (scallions).

KWEI TEOW GORENG (STIR FRIED RICE NOODLES WITH BEEF)

- 18 oz. fresh rice noodles (kwei teow)
- 8oz. filet of beef, sliced into strips
- 1 cup bean sprouts, roots trimmed
- 8 oz. shrimp, peeled
- 2 cups water spinach, chopped
- 1 1/2 Tbs dark soy cause
- 5 Tbs oil

SPICE PASTE —

- 4 fresh chili peppers, seeds discarded
- 8 dried chili peppers, soaked seeds discarded
- 1 onion peeled & chopped
- 1 garlic clove, peeled & quartered

Mash the chili peppers, onion and garlic in a mortar. Heat the oil in the wok and fry this spicy paste until the flavors are released. Add the beef and stir. Add the soy sauce and shrimp to wok and cook for a few minutes. Add noodles and stir well. Stir fry the water spinach and bean sprouts until the vegetables are cooked through but still a bit crunch.

When stir frying noodles they must be stir fried for 1-2 minutes after the addition of each ingredient.

SAMBAL TERONG (EGGPLANT SAMBAL FOR FISH, POULTRY OR MEAT)

- 7 oz. Chinese eggplant
- 4 fresh green chili peppers, minced, discard seeds
- 1/2 Tbs turmeric
- 3-4 Tbs oil
- 1 onion, peeled & minced
- 1 1/2 Tbs sugar
- 4 Tbs lime juice
- Salt to taste

Wash the eggplant and slice it, not too thin, rub with turmeric, heat the oil and brown the eggplant slices. Combine chili peppers, onion, sugar, salt and lime juice in a bowl, then add the fried eggplant slices.

Since Singapore is my favorite Asian country, we have to have some real Singapore Recipes. By the way, Singapore is also called "The Switzerland of Asia" mostly because of the fact it is clean, has four official languages, different cultures and because of their banking system.

FRIED SINGAPORE NOODLES

- 6 oz. rice noodles
- 1/4 cup vegetable oil
- 1/2 tsp. salt
- 3 oz. shelled cooked shrimp
- 6 oz cooked pork, cut into matchsticks
- 1 green bell pepper, seeded and cut into matchsticks
- 1/2 Tbs sugar
- 2 Tbs curry powder
- 3 oz. Thai fish cakes
- 2 Tbs dark soy sauce

Soak the rice noodles in water for about 10 minutes, drain well, then pat dry with paper towels. Heat the wok, then add half the oil. When oil is hot, add the noodles and half the salt and stir fry for 2 minutes. Move it to a heated serving dish and keep it warm. Heat the remaining oil and add the shrimp, pork, bell pepper, sugar and curry powder and the remaining salt. Stir fry 1-2 minutes, add the noodles to the wok and stir fry with the fish cakes for about 2 minutes. Stir in the soy sauce and serve right away.

When you go to Singapore you should visit the Raffles Hotel, birthplace of the famous cocktail named Singapore Sling. This hotel, one of the most luxurious in SE Asia is named for Sir Stamford Raffles. The hotel opened its doors in 1887 by which time Raffles had already been dead for 61 years. He died at the age of 45 but his presence can still be felt throughout the country. The intense red glow of the Singapore Sling has been served in the Long Bar at Raffles since 1915. The drink was invented by Ngiam Tong Boon, a Taiwanese barkeeper.

SINGAPORE SLING

- 2 Tbs (30 ml) gin
- 1 Tbs (15ml) cherry brandy
- 8 Tbs (120 ml) pineapple juice
- 1 Tbs (15 ml) lime juice
- 1 1/2 Tbs (7.5 ml) Cointreau
- 1 1/2 Tbs (7.5 ml) D.O.M. Benedictine
- 2 Tbs (10 ml) grenadine
- 1 dash Angostura bitters
- 1 Slice pineapple
- 1 cocktail cherry

Put all the liquids into a cocktail shaker with some crushed ice, shake, pour into a glass and garnish with the pineapple and cherry.

13. I LOVED HOTELS

Since I was a small boy, I have loved hotels. Dreaming about those palaces and glorious establishments was a special experience for me. I never could imagine that I would ever stay in those first-class places or even manage them. How could it be possible that my family and I would be living in a place like the Plaza in New York—unthinkable!

Before I write down my thoughts about some of these famous landmark properties where I worked, stayed, or visited, I would like to say a few words about my hotel hero. Unfortunately, I never had an opportunity to meet him since he passed away over 20 years before I came into this world. He was a little Swiss boy, the youngest of 13 children. He was born into a poor peasant family on February 23, 1850. It was in Niederwald, a small village in the District of Goms in the Canton Valais. His nickname came to be "King of Hoteliers and Hotelier of Kings." It is from his name and that of his hotels that the term "ritzy" was derived. Of course, I am speaking of Cesar Ritz. At 15 Cesar Ritz worked as an apprentice wine waiter (sommelier) when his boss told him he would never make anything of himself in the hotel business. His boss felt that it takes a special flair and he thought it was only right to let him know that he did not have what it takes. It reminds me of a time when I was 16 and one of my supervisors said I would never be a good chef. He said I would not become successful and would always be a blue-collar worker. He suggested that maybe I should be a contractor building houses since I was strong and this was probably my destiny. Of course I also recall I read an article once that Glenn Miller was told he would never make a good musician.

In 1867 Ritz went to Paris for five years and in 1873 he moved to Vienna, Austria. In that year his astonishing career in hotel management began at the Grand Hotel in Nice. Max Pfeiffer, the designer of the Grand Hotel National in Lucerne was impressed by the capabilities of Cesar Ritz. Thus in 1878 he became manager of the Grand Hotel National and he held the same position at the Grand Hotel in Monaco until 1888. He was a pioneer in the development of luxury hotels and knew how to entertain wealthy people and customers. Ritz quickly gained a reputation for good taste and elegance. By the mid 1880s, the Grand Hotel National in Lucerne had earned a reputation as the most elegant hotel in Europe at the time. Ritz said the customer is always right. The code he operated by was "see all without looking, hear all without listening, be attentive without being servile, anticipate without being presumptuous." I used to tell my staff that if there is a problem, fix it to the point that the guest is happy. In 1984, the then General Manager of the Grand Hotel National in Lucerne stayed with us at the Westin Peachtree Plaza. I had the pleasure of meeting him when he was in Atlanta to tour our property and the Georgia World Congress Center. After I retired I visited the Grand Hotel National on numerous occasions whenever we spent the summer on Lake Lucerne. It provides me with a great location to make up my Rotary attendance while in Europe. The hotel is still a grand dame of a hotel.

By late 1891, Ritz was an extremely busy man. He had hotel enterprises in Rome, Frankfurt, Palermo, Wiesbaden, Monte Carlo, Madrid, Cairo, Johannesburg, and several other cities. In 1896 he formed the Ritz Hotel Syndicate together with South African millionaire Alfred Beit, who was known as the wealthiest man in the world at the time. Mr. Beit was a bachelor who made his money in the diamond business. Together in 1898 they developed what became to be the Hotel Ritz at the Place

Vendome in Paris. They went on to open the Ritz Hotel in London in 1906, then in 1910 King Alfonso inspired them to open the Madrid Hotel.

Ritz enjoyed a long-lasting partnership with famous French Chef August Escoffier. This relationship lasted until Ritz retired in 1907 due to deteriorating health. Ritz withdrew himself progressively from the affairs of his various companies, finally selling his interest in hotels. By 1912, according to his wife Marie Louise, for all intents and purposes his life was finished. In 1913 he moved to a private clinic in Lausanne and in 1914 he was placed in a clinic in Kuessnacht at Lake Lucerne. On October 26, 1918 he passed away and was buried in the village of his birth. Although from a humble background, Cesar Ritz and his luxurious hotels became legendary. Over the past ten years I have visited Kuessnacht numerous times since we lived just two villages away, oblivious to the fact he had died there until I read his biography, which I highly recommend reading.

I would like to add a few lines regarding historical hotels. When I was a youngster I strongly believed that the only great hotels existed in Switzerland. Nothing could be further from the truth. For instance —

BÜERGENSTOCK ESTATES

The story of the Büergenstock Estates is absolutely fascinating. The Büergenstock is a famous mountain in the middle of Lake Lucerne in Switzerland. The resort can be reached by a private mountain road, then the winding Büergenstock funicular from Lake Lucerne. The place achieved a great reputation during the 20th century from famous actors, artists, politicians, as well as the rich people using it as a retreat and holiday spot. Audrey Hepburn married Mel Ferrer at the Büergenstock Chapel in 1954. Sophia Loren and her husband, Carlo Ponti, along with

Charlie Chaplin, Shirley Maclaine, Yul Brenner, Konrad Adenauer, Jimmy Carter, Henry Kissinger, Kofi Annan, and Golda Meier housed in privates villas or stayed at the hotel. The Kurhaus Hotel, later called the Grand Hotel, opened in the summer of 1873. The next hotel that came on line was the Palace Hotel, which welcomed its first guests in 1904. The complex has several hotels and over 30 buildings. In 1925, Friedrich Frey-Fürst bought the Bűergenstock and had a golf course added in the mountain terrain. He passed away in 1953, at which time his son Fritz took over the reins of the resort. Many structural and infrastructure changes were made. I can remember as a kid reading a story in all the Swiss newspapers about the opening of the "underwater bar." The guests would sip their drinks nearby and look out a window and see the people swimming around. At that time, it was a great sensation. While working in Atlanta I had the pleasure of being host to Fritz when he stayed with us. In 1996 the family sold the Bűergenstock Resort to UBS. It went through a confusing time with management and staff changes, in addition to marketing problems—you name it, they confronted it. An enormous development is currently underway with seven construction cranes on the property. The rumor is that the whole renovation project cost over 500 million dollars. Personally, I cannot wait until next summer when it reopens so Audrey and I can visit the resort to see all the progress.

BAUR AU LAC ZUERICH

This hotel is a luxury establishment on Lake Zurich. It was founded in 1844 by Johannes Baur and it is still held by the Baur family. I visited Baur au lac in early 1980s. It was a treat just walking through the lobby, the hallways, the elegant restaurant, and the bars. This hotel deserves its legendary aura. When you walk into the breakfast room you can see a real power breakfast. You might not know their names, but you realize the big deals that take place when you see the bankers, financiers, sheiks, and other powerful clients. The room rates start at over $500, and a suite can be several thousand dollars. I asked the room clerk for a package deal and he offered me the rate of $492.50 a night. A weekend package which includes a room and breakfast was $538.50. For $732.50 you get one night's accommodations, limousine transfer from and to the Zurich airport. You can stay in this hotel, but you also pay for the style. I was told that the Baur au lac serves an excellent "Zürcher Geschnetzeltes with Roesti," one of the most famous dishes in Switzerland, even more special than Swiss fondue.

ZÜRCHER GESCHNETZELTES WITH ROESTI
SERVES 6 PEOPLE

- 2 lbs. veal cutlets, sliced in ¾ inch strips
- 2 tbs. all-purpose flour
- 2 ounces unsalted butter
- 2 tbs. olive oil
- 1 onion, finely chopped
- 2 garlic cloves, finely chopped
- 7 ounces Cremini mushrooms, thickly sliced
- 1 cup dry white wine
- Sea salt—freshly ground pepper, some finely chopped sage leaves
- 1 dash of Cognac or Brandy
- 1 1/4 cup heavy cream
- Water to thin sauce
- A bit of Fondor or Aromat to make the dish tastier

Sprinkle the flour over the meat and coat well. Heat half of the butter and half of the olive oil in a frying pan. As soon as the butter foams, add the meat and brown it very quickly on all sides—set aside on a plate. Add the rest of the butter and oil to the pan and sauté the onions, garlic and sage for a few minutes, then add the mushrooms. Stir well until the mushrooms start to soften, continue cooking for about 5 minutes longer. Add the wine to deglaze the bottom of the pan using a wooded spoon to scrape away any crust that may have formed. Add the veal and cook, stirring until the wine has evaporated. Turn the heat to low and cook for another 10 minutes. Season with salt, pepper, Aromat or Fondor at the last minute. Add the brandy, and remove from heat. Serve with Swiss Roesti Potatoes.

SWISS ROESTI POTATOES

- 2 1/2 lbs. boiled potatoes
- 3-4 tbs. fat, such as lard, butter or shortening
- Salt to taste

Peel potatoes and shred using a spiral grater called a Roesti shredder. Sprinkle with salt. Heat the fat in a skillet; add the potatoes and cook, stirring occasionally. Then cook the potatoes until golden brown. Push the potatoes with a spatula down and form into a round ring. Then turn the potatoes over so it can be cooked on the other side. Serve on a warm plate.

GSTAAD PALACE HOTEL

My first exposure to Gstaad was through an old army buddy in 1960. His name was Willy Brand, a farm boy from Gstaad. We used to make fun of Willy because of his Bernese Oberland dialect. When he spoke to me I could barely understand 50% of what he said. The Gstaad folks sounded to my people who were from the Unterland like they were singing when they spoke; thus they were very hard to comprehend.

The Bernese Oberland is a beautiful area in the southwest of Switzerland. The homes are all wooden chalets. Gstaad has very strong building codes to preserve the beauty of the picturesque countryside. The village, with a population of about 9,000 locals, is part of the municipality known as Saanen. It is a popular ski resort and a very well-known destination among the high society and the international jet set. During Christmas weeks the population grows to 30,000. The community is about 3,500 feet above sea level. Shopping venues provide a paradise for the most discriminating shoppers. The middle of the village features a picturesque promenade with the finest shops on the planet. Louis Vuitton, Chopard, Hermes, Ralph Lauren, Prada, Moncler, Brunello Cucinelli, Cartier—they all have stores, while many smaller boutiques stock labels such as Dolce & Gabanna, Dior, Chole, Burberry, Oscar de la Renta, MCM, Gucci, and many more. Banks and investment firms are also represented. The finest and most exclusive watch and jewelry stores are also located there. The area is especially famous for its winter activities, but it is also a well-established summer resort with golf, hiking, and horseback riding, as well as transportation that is available via cable cars, gondolas, or horse-drawn carriage tours. The John F. Kennedy International School, which was originally established in 1880 as the Institute le Rosey, is a private boarding school. With a staff of 90 faculty members and student body of 400, the student to teacher ratio is 5:1. The school's annual tuition is currently sfr.108,500, which is at this time equivalent to about $110,670.

A few of the annual events held in Gstaad include the Beach Volleyball SWATCH World Tour, the Swiss Open Tennis Tournament, the Yehudi Menuhin Festival, the Hublot Gold Cup Polo Tournament,

Gstaad Country Night, the Promenade Party, The Christmas Market Circus, the International Week of Hot Air Ballooning, as well as many other annual events.

Famous residents of Gstaad once included actors Sir Roger Moore, Peter Sellers, and Elizabeth Taylor, plus director Roman Polanski, American conservative author and commentator William F. Buckley, violinist Yehudi Menuhin, casino magnate Steve Wynn, and the late playboy and ex-husband of Bridget Bardot, Gunther Sachs. Current famous names include Julie Andrews, Alinghi sailing boss Ernesto Bertarelli, Formula One boss Bernie Ecclestone, and the well-known French actors Jeanne Moreau and Johnny Hallyday.

Name-dropping in Gstaad continues with regular visitors such as Madonna, Prince Charles and his wife Camilla, Duchess of Cornwall, Ghanaian Diplomat Kofi Annan, Indian film actor and producer Saif ali Khan, Bollywood actor Kareena Kapoor Khan, and world famous fashion designer Valentino Garavani, to name just a few.

The jewel of Gstaad is the Palace Hotel, which was established in 1913. With 104 guest rooms and more than 200 staff rooms, the employee count increases from 50 people to over 300 in the December winter season each year. The hotel has been owned for 75 years by the Scherz family, a hotel dynasty. Famous guests have included Elizabeth Taylor, Richard Burton, Sir Roger Moore, Princess Diana, Michael Jackson, Prince Rainier and his wife, Grace Kelly, George Soros and numerous others, including me! The hotel is situated in a park with the resemblance to a fairytale castle. It has numerous restaurants and bars. My first visit to the Gstaad Palace Hotel was in 1986. I had written to the hotel, introduced myself and requested a special rate. My reservation was confirmed at $275 a night since I was affiliated with The Leading Hotels of the World Organization which is comprised of independently owned luxury hotels and resorts. The main goal of this organization is reservations, marketing, and promotion of their member properties. They have strict quality controls and the membership is restricted to only first-class hotels. My first impression of the Palace was their welcome fruit set-up in my guest room. It was not the usual fruit basket but a perfectly arranged assortment of freshly cut exotic fruits on a silver plate with a finger bowl filled with lemon water. At night for turndown service there was a crispy linen napkin placed on each side of the bed with good night chocolates and fresh pralines on a silver dish with a message to enjoy a good life.

Andreas Scherz, the owner of the hotel, invited us for a cocktail in the lobby bar. I asked him about some stories about the hotel which I had heard and asked him which ones were true and which were just rumors. One such story was there is an underground tunnel from the chalets to the hotel itself or the tale that a rich Asian sultan brought his own chef with him to the hotel because he was afraid he would be poisoned. I asked him about the rumor that the Aga Khan supposedly had an orgy with several girls in his suite or the gossip that some guests appear to be more concerned about the cuisine for their puppies than their own food. Mr. Scherz just smiled and said he would never tell. Here was a man who must have met the most famous people in the world, who himself was quite elegant and obviously well-educated, and yet I could still sense the humorous mannerisms of a Swiss Alpine person.

The restaurants at the hotel are super special.

La Fromagerie is an elegant Swiss cheese restaurant, but not for me since I do not eat cheese. People always question me about how I can be Swiss yet not eat cheese. My reply is that I don't yodel either, but I like chocolates and money which qualifies me to be a great Swiss.

Le Grill-Rotisserie is an exclusive grill room. It is the perfect location to enjoy international cuisine combined with on the spot preparation. The chefs prepare personal dinner in the show kitchen. It is rated 16 Gault Millau points and hosts an exquisite wine cellar.

Gildos Restaurant was recommended to me as one that I should not miss before leaving the hotel. In the heart of the Swiss Alps you can savor authentic Italian cuisine prepared by world class chefs. The restaurant is named after the head maitre'd of the hotel who was an integral part of the hotel for many years.

The Spa and Health Club is another exciting part of the hotel. Featuring a steam room and sauna, they also have a pool and offer any kind of massage you desire whether it's oil or stone as well as many health and beauty services — you name it, it is available here.

The last time Audrey and I visited the hotel along with our close friends, George and Jenny. We have made several fun trips with them on river cruises, trips to France, and golf weeks in Austria, in addition to a trip to Bozen and Merano in the South Tyrol. We get along just fine. George is Swiss like me and lived a long time in Asia. His wife Jenny, who is from Hong Kong, is the most giving person I have ever met in my life. I tease Jenny and call her Mother Theresa because she is such a genuine person. It was in 2010 that together we visited the Gstaad Palace. George and I enjoyed a fabulous Cuban cigar in the Smoker's Lounge while Audrey and Jenny had tea and the finest French pastry that money can buy.

What astonishes me is that the hotel with about 100 rooms can employ 300 people during high season. The costs of the operation with so much luxury must be tremendous. But I guess with room rates that start at $750 up to thousands of dollars for suites each night, breakfasts for $45 and a Coca Cola for $12, followed by banquet events with a minimum of $150-$200 per person, it can be done. The Gstaad Palace is a thoroughly magnificent place.

THE BREAKERS HOTEL

In the 1940s and 50s, Pan Am and TWA airlines extended their world routes. However, as they flew to more and more exotic places like Bali,

Katmandu, Tahiti, and other destinations they had no decent accommodations for their customers. So, they had to first build or acquire hotels. This is how Intercontinental Hotels was started. Their first hotel was in Belem, Brazil in 1946. Then TWA acquired Hilton International in 1967 so both these airline companies got into the hotel business. Prior to that, almost a century earlier, someone came up with a similar concept. At that time Henry Flagler, an American industrialist, built first class hotels in Florida to accommodate his customers who traveled the Atlantic coast line of Florida. Mr. Flagler founded what became as the Florida East Coast Railway. Through all his developments Mr. Flagler was known as the father of Miami and Palm Beach. The Breakers Hotel in Palm Beach is an historic hotel and was developed by Henry Flagler. It was first built as the Palm Beach Inn and it opened its doors on January 16, 1896. Later the hotel was renamed The Breakers because the guests began requesting rooms over by the breaking waves of the Atlantic.

After suffering two fires, one in 1903 and another in 1925, the wooden-structured hotel re-emerged more opulent than before. The next reconstruction of The Breakers was awarded to New York City based designers Shultze and Weaver, the same team who would later create many of Manhattan's most coveted hotels such as the Pierre, the Sherry-Netherland, and Park Avenue's Waldorf Astoria. The Breakers reopened in 1926, ushering in a higher degree of European influence and architectural flair. Flagler's newest creation was modeled after the magnificent Villa Medici in Rome. An ambitious effort was made to bring in 75 artisans from Italy to do the beautiful décor of the hotel. Together they completed the intricate paintings, detailed across the ceilings of the 200-foot long main lobby and first floor public rooms, which remain on display today. The Breakers was in a class all its own.

Margot and I went to The Breakers in 1984. We had an invitation from Paul Hagen, who left the Plaza in New York and moved to Palm Beach as the Managing Director of The Breakers. Paul appeared to be the perfect person for this hotel. Needless to say, we got the VIP treatment from Paul, including the grand tour of the property including the front and back of the house. He also included a visit to the golf course, the gardens, the beaches, and the spa. It was just fabulous. The hotel was so large that it seemed like a city within a city. With over 2,000 employees, the staff was an army by itself. They need to fill every thinkable position from mechanical to nurses; just the garden crew is larger than the staff in many hotels. There are numerous restaurants, bars, and banquet facilities. While all the food and beverage outlets are excellent, my favorite one is The Circle, the breakfast room that gives you a thoroughly "Breakers style" breakfast served in old-world elegance. It is an architectural gem and boasts soaring 30-foot ceilings with eight oval murals depicting Renaissance landscapes featuring the Villa Medici near Florence and the Tivoli Gardens south of Rome. Each morning you can enjoy The Circle's elaborate, artfully crafted buffet of hot and cold selections from fresh fruit and pastries to crepes and omelets made to order. Of course, a la carte service is also available.

Our dinner that evening with Paul was a delightful experience. Great food, excellent wines, super company and lots of "old war stories" about the Plaza Hotel. I ordered an Entrecôte Café de Paris which could not have been better. The Café Paris butter or sauce is also an old hotel and restaurant farce. Each chef says he has the best or the original recipe, but this is always debatable. I might write about this later in the book. Our visit to The Breakers was an unforgettable trip to a grand hotel.

THE RITZ IN PARIS

When Andrea was about 14 and Christina was 11, I decided to take them to Paris. We stayed at a lovely hotel and toured the city for several days. Then one afternoon as we strolled down Avenue des Champs-

Elysees, the world-famous street, Andrea had the bright idea that she wanted to discover Paris by herself. My blood pressure went up and I was shocked. Christina took me aside with a recommendation that we would let her go but would secretly follow her. Rather than argue, I said ok. Andrea walked off, but Christina and I always followed her closely. I was nervous as I could be, then we ended up at Place Vendome. Oh my God, I screamed this is where the Ritz Hotel is! I summoned Andrea and told them we're going in to the Ritz and tour the hotel. Please, please be nice and elegant and don't run around when we go on our tour. OK Dad, they promised. We went to the hotel and walked around, then we went to a guest room floor and bingo, we got stopped by a security guard. What are you doing here, are you a guest? he politely asked, and I said no. I told him who I was to let him know that I am a hotel fanatic and just wanted to see his hotel. He said we cannot do it unless we get permission from management and to do this we would have to go to the Executive Offices. He said it in such a way that he thought he would scare me and I would decline. I said OK, let's go to the Executive Office. Slowly we made the walk through the hallways to the Executive Office. As we arrived, the security officer tried to explain to the gentleman in the dark suit that I would like to see the hotel but before he could finish the manager said, "Hermann what are you doing here?" It was Erich Hirzel, a German fellow I knew well from New York. Erich was Resident Manager at the St. Regis Hotel in New York when I was at the Plaza. What a surprise to see you Hermann; let me show you our property, he said. After the tour, we had café and patisserie and I was so happy because the girls lived up to their promise and behaved so well. Now we all know about the Ritz, opened in 1898 by Cesar Ritz and the famous chef August Escoffier. While the place was always fabulous, now it is even more spectacular. The hotel with 159 rooms was closed in 2012 for two years and a projected $200 million renovation was planned; however, the Ritz reopened in June 2016 with the final cost at about $450 million and a two-year delay. The owner of the Ritz is Mohammed Abdel Al-Fayed, an Egyptian billionaire who previously owned Harrod's department store in London and currently resides in Geneva, Switzerland. With all his money I guess you can take a trophy hotel like the Ritz and make it even better. Al-Fayed's eldest son, Dodi, died in a car crash in Paris with Diana, Princess of Wales in 1997.

Before we leave the subject of the Ritz I have to share another anecdote about Erich Hirzel. When Westin Hotels was sold to Mr. Aoki, a Japanese investor, I was asked to go with some other hotel executives to Germany. I spoke the language and knew some of the customs, so I was delighted to go on this trip to look at the Hotel Buehlerhoehe in the Black Forest. Mr. Aoki was interested in purchasing the property. It is known as a Schloss Hotel which means Castle Hotel in German. The place is fabulous and again an absolute trophy hotel. It is known as one of the best hotels in Baden-Baden. When we met the executives to discuss the hotel there was Erich Hirzel, who was the manager. We did not ultimately acquire the hotel, but it was great to see Erich.

THE BEAU-RIVAGE PALACE OUCHY

In 1959, after I had finished my apprenticeship as a chef, I moved to Lausanne and got a job at the Hotel de la Paix in the heart of the city. We had guests who paid the exorbitant amount of $15.00 a night. Never could I have imagined back then that one day I would stay in the Beau-Rivage Palace in a $500.00 a night room. My monthly salary was sfr 275.00 a month plus room and board along with my roommate, a German fellow. Lausanne is a fabulous city on Lake Geneva in the French speaking region of Vaud, Switzerland. It is the home of the International Olympic Committee Headquarters as well as the Olympic Museum and Lakeshore Olympic Park. The hilly city reminds me of San Francisco, with roads constantly going up and then down. But the locals do not ever call the beautiful body of water there Lake Geneva. They call it *Lac Léman*. It divides France and Switzerland. It has a crescent-shaped lakeshore between France and Switzerland and overlooked by the Alps. The city is a diplomatic hub with luxury shops and a cobbled old town. The chic, palm-studded Swiss Riviera stretches from Lausanne to Montreux, where you can find the Montreux Palace Hotel, very similar to the Beau-Rivage. The Beau-Rivage is a hotel in the Belle Epoque architecture style. First opened in 1861, the hotel has 168 rooms, 26 junior suites and eight executive suites. Three lovely restaurants are available for the enjoyment of the guests and there's a bar, numerous conference and banquet rooms, and a wellness facility. This historic hotel is located in Ouchy on the shores of *Lac Léman*. An addition was built in 1908 in the art deco and neo-baroque styles. The Beau-Rivage Palace is owned by the well-known Swiss Sandoz family, founders of Sandoz AG, an excellent pharmaceutical company, today known as Novartis.

In the early 1980s, when the construction of the expansion of the Georgia World Congress Center was in progress, we had numerous international airlines flying into Atlanta. The city and corporate leaders felt we needed a European promotional tour to get the word out about what was happening in Atlanta. A delegation of about 20 VIP's, business leaders, and politicians was formed. I had the pleasure of participating in this endeavor. We visited Munich, Paris, Zurich, Lausanne, and other European cities. We felt we needed the "big guns," which included the then Mayor of Atlanta, Andy Young, as well as Lt. Governor Zell Miller and several other dignitaries who made the trip. In Lausanne at the Beau-Rivage, like in all the other cities, we invited people from the travel industry, convention planners, and travel agents, among others. We hosted an elegant party and got the guests excited about the great city of the South, Atlanta. The mission was accomplished as the city picked up a lot of international business from Europe and I was delighted that I had the pleasure of participating in this promotional trip.

THE CLOISTER RESORT

The Cloister is located at Sea Island, Georgia. I find it interesting that this island has had several names over the years. It is the smallest of the Golden Isles of Georgia and was actually considered a type of resort over 200 years ago. At that time it was known as the Fifth Creek Island and was later renamed as Long Island. Then it was sold for $300,000 in 1926 to a development company named Long Island Beach Properties. The same year it was sold again and Howard E. Coffin then changed the name to Sea Island. The original section of the hotel, to which cottages have been added over the passing years, was designed by the famous Palm Beach architect Addison Mizner. The hotel opened its doors on October 12, 1928 and it was an immediate success. I had the fortunate experience to stay at The Cloister in the 1980s on numerous occasions. Participating in the Georgia Hospitality and Travel Association and as a board member of the Business Council of Georgia, I had the privilege of staying at the resort many times and visited the resort each year. What is absolutely fascinating are the many activities that take place all day long, which included tennis tournaments on the elaborate tennis courts, golf competitions on several lovely golf courses, organized outings, film showings, bridge games in the Spanish lounge, art collections, horseback riding, backgammon, chess in the garden, ping pong, ballroom dancing at the Beach Club, and other activities available for guests. Each owner of one of the "cottages," which are in reality million dollar villas, becomes a member of the Beach Club. John Portman designed and built a "cottage" at the beach which took him several years to complete as he was required to make changes to get their approval. I had the pleasure of visiting the property just prior to its completion and was amazed at what a house it was.

Ted Wright was the General Manager for many years at the Cloister along with his lovely wife Rachel. They were wonderful hosts. Ted eventually retired on Sea Island.

The Cloister was successful for many, many years. The place was owned by the Jones family. By 2003, A. W. "Bill" Jones decided it was time for a complete restoration of the hotel. Over a three-year period the hotel was demolished and replaced with a luxurious structure which retained the look and feel of the original hotel. Just two years after the grand re-opening of the resort the financial panic of 2008 occurred and the following recession hit the Sea Island Company from all sides. Sales declined, development of real estate came to a halt, the revenue from the Cloister dropped by 31% from 2007 to 2009 and staff was reduced by 25%. The loans had to be restructured, but by 2010 the company had to file for Chapter 11 Bankruptcy and was eventually acquired by a financial consortium. In June 2016 the Anschutz family bought out the other investors and became the sole owners of the Sea Island Company. The Cloister is a wonderful resort known for its quality, elegant service, and excellent cuisine. It will be around for many years to come and continue to be a place where one can find oneself. An old Cloister tradition is that before bedtime you get your warm milk and graham crackers. It was my favorite experience before I went to dreamland and began to dream about the next day and all the wonderful experiences I might have.

PENINSULA HOTEL HONG KONG

I never had a reason to stay at the Peninsula in Hong Kong; however, I visited the property several times. Founded by members of the Kadomie family, the Peninsula was built with the idea that it would be the finest hotel east of Suez. It was in December 1928 that the hotel opened in Tsu Sha Tsui, Kowloon Hong Kong located at the junction of Nathan Road and Salisbury Road and directly opposite the quays where ocean liner passengers disembark. Kowloon was also the last stop on the Trans-Siberian Rail, a link that brought travelers from Europe. What an excellent location this was for this fabulous hotel! It was a different time, the mysteriousness and exciting time of the Far East. During World War II the hotel went through some exciting times. On December 25, 1941 the British Colonial officers surrendered to the Japanese on the third floor of the Peninsula. However, the British later regained control of the colonial land and the hotel was brought back as the Peninsula Hotel. The Kadomie (Arabic) family was a wealthy family of Mizrahi Jews from originally from Baghdad. From the 18th century they were established in Bombay, India becoming one of the wealthiest families in Asia, then later moving to Hong Kong and Shanghai, China. The hotel has several outlets including an outstanding gourmet French restaurant called Felix, an outlet named Chesa, which means house in Swiss, where they serve Swiss Cuisine, in addition to the Spring Moon Restaurant serving Japanese and Cantonese delicacies. In the lobby they serve traditional English style afternoon tea reminiscent of Hong Kong's colonial era. A special treat is their fleet of 14 Rolls Royce Phantoms. It was the largest single order of cars that Rolls Royce had ever received. When you see them rolling through the city you know they are the cars from the Peninsula.

When John Portman opened his hotel in San Francisco, the then head of the Peninsula Hotel was a guest and I had the pleasure of meeting him and his wife. It was ironic that I learned he was a Swiss hotelier and came from near where my parents used to live and where I had grown up.

Today the Peninsula Hotel chain has several properties located in Manila, New York, Beverly Hills, Bangkok, Chicago, Tokyo, Shanghai, and Paris. Other hotels are currently being planned.

For many years I was a member of the Swiss Abroad, an organization called the Fifth Parliament. Each country has delegates according to the amount of Swiss people who live in that country. For example, the United States has six delegates representing the continuance in the United States. Annually we have two meetings in Switzerland, one in the spring and again another in the summer. Felix Bigler was the representative for Hong Kong and he was also a member for the Board for the Peninsula Group.

OESTERREICHISCHER HOF SALZBURG

Salzburg, the birthplace of Mozart, is a city in central Austria, relatively close to Germany. I have been there numerous times and Salzburg remains a special place in my heart perhaps because my first wife Andrea was from Austria and our two girls spent many summers there on vacation. How can you not love the gorgeous area in and around Salzburg? *The Sound of Music*, a wonderful musical about the Von Trapp family and what they had to endure during World War II, was filmed here. The story ends with them escaping through the mountains eventually ending up safely in Switzerland.

A great hotel was built in Salzburg between 1863 and 1866 and was called the Oesterreichischer Hof. The hotel is fabulous and has the best location possible. Behind the hotel is the Schlossberg with the Festung Hohensalzburg, which is a baroque castle. Below it is the famous Café Winkler, from which you can get a wonderful view of the city.

I was lucky enough to stay at the Oesterreichischer Hof in the mid 1980s. One of the famous world class hotels built in the 1800s and early 1900s, the Oesterreichischer Hof has an interesting history. The guestrooms are filled with classic antique furniture with exquisite original oil paintings and with magnificent marble bathrooms; the place is a world-class experience. The hotel changed ownership to the famous owners of the Hotel Sacher in Vienna where the famous chocolate cake Sacher Torte was invented by the Austrian Franz Sacher in 1832 for Prince Wenzel von Metternicht. It is one of the most famous pastries in the world. Legend has it the original recipe for the pastry is a well-kept secret; however, we all know it is a chocolate cake flavored with apricots. Following is an adaptation of a Sacher Torte.

This is an Austrian chocolate cake layered with apricot preserves. This version uses the preserves three ways—for moistening the cake layers, as a thick filling between layers and as a glaze to seal the cake before covering it in chocolate. The cake is moist and luscious on its own but it's also delicious served the traditional way, with unsweetened whipped cream.

AUSTRIAN CHOCOLATE LAYERED CAKE

- 6 large eggs, separated
- 1 Cup all-purpose flour
- 1/2 cup almond flour or 2 ounces blanched almonds (3/1 cup) ground
- 1/4 teaspoon salt
- 1 1/2 sticks unsalted butter, softened
- 1 cup sugar
- 5 ounces bittersweet chocolate, melted & cooled slightly
- FILLING & GLAZE
- 1 3/4 cups apricot preserves
- 2/3 cup light corn syrup
- 2 tablespoons rum
- 10 ounces bittersweet chocolate, chopped
- Unsweetened whipped cream for serving (optional)

Preheat the oven to 375°.

Butter a 9 inch spring form pan. Line the bottom of the pan with parchment paper and butter the paper. Dust the pan with flour, tapping out the excess.

1. In a large bowl, using a handheld electric mixer, whip the egg whites at a high speed until soft peaks form.
2. In a small bowl, whisk the all-purpose flour with the almond flour and salt. In another large bowl, beat the butter and sugar until fluffy. Add the yolks one at a time and beat until fluffy. Beat in the chocolate then beat in the flours. Beat in ¼ of the whites then using a spatula, fold in the rest of the whites until no streaks remain.
3. Scrape the batter into the prepared pan and smooth the top. Bake the cake in the center of the oven for 35-40 minutes until a toothpick inserted in the center comes out with a few moist crumbs attached. Let the cake cool on a wire rack for 30 minutes, then remove the ring and let the cake cool completely. Invert the cake onto a plate and peel off the parchment. Turn the cake right side up. Using a long serrated knife, cut the cake horizontally into 3 even layers.
4. In a small microwave safe bowl, whisk ¼ cup plus 2 tablespoons of the apricot preserves with ¼ cup of water and microwave until melted.
5. Set the bottom of the spring form pan on a wire rack and set the rack on a baking sheet. Arrange the top cake layer, cut side up on the spring form pan. Brush the cake with 1/3 of the melted apricot preserves. Spread ½ cup of the un-melted preserves on top. Brush the cut side of the final layer with the remaining melted preserves and set it cut side down on the cake. Using a serrated knife, trim the cake edges if necessary to even them out.
6. In the microwave safe bowl microwave the remaining ¼ cup 2 ta-

blespoons of the apricot preserves until melted, about 30 seconds. Press the preserves through a strainer to remove the solids. Brush the preserves all over the cake until completely coated. Refrigerate for 20 minutes until set.

7. Meanwhile in a medium saucepan, whisk the corn syrup with the rum and 2 tablespoons of water and bring to a boil. Cook until slightly thickened about one minute. Put the chocolate into a heat proof bowl and pour the hot mixture on top. Let stand until melted, then whisk until smooth. If the chocolate glaze is too thick to pour, whisk in another tablespoon of hot water. Let cook to warm.

8. Using an offset spatula, scrape off any excess preserves from the cake so that is it lightly coated. Slowly pour half of the warm chocolate glaze in the center of the cake, allowing it to gently coat the top and spread down the side. Spread the glaze to evenly coat the torte. Microwave the remaining glaze for a few seconds and repeat pouring and spreading. Scrape up any excess glaze. Refrigerate for at least 10 minutes to set the glaze, then cut the torte into wedges and serve with the whipped cream.

9. The torte can be covered and refrigerated for up to two days.

Now back to Salzburg and the famous Oesterreichischer Hof. When I stayed at the hotel one late morning I went down to the lobby. I walked outside and was surprised to see a group of people standing at the sidewalk. I asked a bystander what was going on and he said the Pope is coming but I thought he was just kidding me. Then along came the Mercedes Pope Mobile which drove slowly past us with Pope John Paul II looking at me waving—I could not believe it. Although I am not Catholic, at that very moment a special feeling of peace came over me realizing I was as close as ten feet to His Holiness. What an experience and still today I can experience this feeling once again when I think about this event. What an unusual happening it was. Hotel Oesterreichischer Hof or Hotel Sacher Salzburg, call it whatever you like, my experience in this hotel, the incident with Pope John Paul II and the wonderful time in Salzburg are all unforgettable.

STANFORD COURT SAN FRANCISCO

"I Left My Heart In San Francisco" is a song made famous by Tony Bennett and exactly describes my sentiments about this great city. Whenever I hear it I still get goosebumps as it is my favorite city. Having moved over 30 times and three continents over the past 50-some years, no other city comes close to the charm of San Francisco, not even the beautiful locales in Switzerland. The Stanford Court Hotel could be categorized as a newer hotel, since it only opened in 1972. The hotel was built on the site of the mansion of Leland Stanford, who was a senator and the eighth Governor of California. In the 1906 San Francisco earthquake the mansion was destroyed and was followed in 1912 by an apartment building that was built on the same site. In 1972 the present-day hotel was constructed from the shell of that apartment building. The person who deserves the credit for creating and establishing the 5 Star hotel was James Nassikas, who was President and General Manager of the Stanford Court Hotel when it opened. Jim was previously managing the Pontchartrain Hotel in New Orleans before coming to San Francisco. In the late 1960s he was approached by Edgar Stern, the grandson of the founder of Sears Roebuck. Mr. Stern said he would provide the money for the site of the old Leland Stanford Mansion on Nob Hill and Jim Nassikas would be responsible for creating the finest hotel possible. So often when you are in a city hotel operated by some American hotel management group you have to look out the window to figure out what city you are in, which is exactly what Jim wanted to avoid. He started out to design a different hotel, special in its character, including for example the Tiffany glass roof over the entrance, the guest rooms' design, the design of the banquet facilities and restaurant designs. His motto was the hotel has to be totally San Francisco. One thing that was thoroughly special was the restaurant Fournos Oven, a restaurant on two levels which he designed purposely with an outside entrance and marketed like it had nothing to do with the hotel. In the restaurant's ovens each night were prepared the finest dishes like rack of lamb, roast ducklings, roasted chickens, and roasted filets. I personally loved Fournos Ovens and the many fine meals I had in this establishment. I had the pleasure to serve as Area Vice President when the Stouffer Hotel Company owned and managed the hotel in the 1990s. Chris Steuri, an old friend of mine and fellow Swiss, was the General Manger of this property. Chris and his charming wife, a former Miss Maui, were great hosts and representatives for the Stanford Court. Chris and I worked together in other cities like Hawaii and Vancouver, Canada, plus Chris was also a former employee with Westin Hotels. While working with Chris in San Francisco we went through a period of negotiations for a new union contract with the many different unions. It was not an increase in salaries that was the hang up, but the different work rules that former managers had agreed to which created a lot of difficulties. It was quite an ordeal to work through the negotiations. Our Director of Personnel, Collette Boardley, did an outstanding job. We could write a book about these negotiations, but it was a great experience.

One of my absolute fondest memories of the Stanford Court is when I proposed to Audrey to become my wife. We were having breakfast overlooking the cable cars going by on Powell Street. Audrey said yes she would like to marry me; however, I have to ask her dad and then I would need to have tea with him in the Chinese tradition. My reaction was she would have to forget the tea, but I would be happy to call him in Asia. I picked up the phone and told him who I was and asked him for the hand of his daughter. When I spoke with him he asked if I was a Swiss man to which I confirmed yes, and he ultimately said OK because Swiss people are good people and he liked Swiss people. Audrey's father was a banker and had done a lot of business with the Swiss banks and had been to Switzerland numerous times. Needless to say, the Stanford Court is special to me.

BADRUTTS PALACE ST. MORITZ

The Badrutts are a legendary family of hoteliers in Switzerland. They started in 1815 with Johannes Badrutt from Samedan, just down the road from St. Moritz. Samedan has a small airport where the rich and famous jetsetters land with their private jets and then drive by limos to go to St. Moritz. Johannes built the Hotel La vue de Bernina (view of Bernina Mountain). After his death, his son sold the hotel and moved to St. Moritz. There he built the Pension Faller, which later became the Engadiner Kulm, now known simply as The Kulm. It is still a fabulous hotel. Johannes first was kind of an inventor. He was not happy with running the restaurant, the Cresta Run where bobsled drivers and skeleton drivers find their thrill and excitement. He built a skating rink and started curling in St. Moritz. In 1889 he died and The Kulm was passed on to his son Peter Badrutt, who ran the hotel for 30 years until his death in 1913.

Caspar, the son of Johannes II, built and developed the Palace Hotel. When you are in the middle of Lake St. Moritz and look up at the city, the Palace dominates the skyline of the town like some great gothic castle. The building is thoroughly magnificent and impressive; as a castle, it stands on its own. Caspar Badrutt made sure that the exteriors are extremely grand and elegant, the guest rooms spacious and inviting, while the public rooms are extremely fabulous and grand. His idea was to make sure that he could attract the rich and famous of Europe to come with their families and friends year after year. He certainly achieved his goal. Caspar had a son named Hans and it is his two sons named Hans Juerg and Andrea Badrutt that now owned the hotel. The two boys are also the present owners of the Chesa Velia, the famous restaurant and night club which opened in 1935. I had dinner there once and I must say it deserves the fine reputation it has. It was in 2003 when Audrey and I stayed at the Palace. They had just opened the new spa and swimming pool. I was very impressed to swim through a grotto and the whole fitness center was exquisite. I must admit it was unique the way the whole area was designed and the service that went with it. Our meals were great, and the guestroom was well appointed. The Palace, however, is a bit stiff for me. I am not the Duke of Alba Herrbert van Karian nor Stavros Miarchos, the multibillionaire Greek shipping tycoon. Palace guests have real money. In the winter it's the polo players who stay at the Palace where they play on the frozen lake. They also have horse racing at the lake and the ultimate is when the crazy ones take their Porsche, Ferrari, or Lamborghini and race each other on the frozen lake. It is not unusual when they crash cars worth a few hundred thousand dollars in an afternoon; they think it is fun. We had a good time at the Palace, but the hotel is too stiff and too much "chi chi" for Audrey and me. I guess as we get older we enjoy hotels that are more real. We have nothing to prove anymore. As I said, the service, food, and accommodations were good, but the place is too stiff.

THE GREENBRIER

I cannot imagine any hotel in the world that has more history than the Greenbrier. It is located in the beautiful Allegheny Mountains of West Virginia. The property is located in White Sulphur Springs. The grounds of the resort, the homes, the cottages, and the buildings cover 11,000 acres. There are 710 guest rooms, 33 suites, and numerous banquet and meeting rooms with a total of 20 restaurants and lounges.

Since 1778, visitors have traveled to this part of the country to "take the waters" of the area. A spring of sulphur water is at the center of the resort property. The symbol of the Greenbrier is the green dome with the white columned springhouse. Beginning in 1778, they folowed the Native American tradition of "taking the waters" to relieve chronic rheumatism and for 125 years the resort was known by the name of White Sulphur Springs. In 1858, a large hotel was built, originally known as the Grand Central Hotel, which came to be known by the moniker "The White" and later "The Old White." During the Civil War the hotel changed hands between the Confederate Army and the Union Army. The hotel became a vacation spot. In 1910 the Chesapeake and Ohio Railway purchased the resort property and began building additional amenities, including the bath wing. The current Greenbrier was built in 1913 by the railway company. The British architect Frederick Julius Sterner did the design and it opened September 25, 1913. Just after the beginning of World War II, on December 17, 1941, the hotel began to serve as a relocation center for Axis diplomats who had been interned as enemies of the United States. At first the detainees were joined by Japanese diplomats previously interred at the Homestead in Hot Springs. The hotel served this function until July 8, 1942. By the way, I also visited the Homestead Hotel, another wonderful resort. The hotel briefly reopened for the 1942 season, but it was soon commandeered by the US Army for use as a hospital. The Army paid 3.3 million dollars for the property, which at the time was valued at $5.4 million. They took over control of the property on September 1, 1942 attending many VIPs like the Duke of Windsor with his wife Wallace Simpson. They then converted the hotel in a 2,000 bed hospital. Nearly 2,500 patients had been treated there before the hospital closed in June 1946. Then the property was sold back to the C&O Railroad for just under the $3.3

million they had paid in 1942. Over the years the hotel was open, then closed, then re-opened. It changed hands several times and it had financial challenges, then in 2009 the hotel was placed into bankruptcy. Then the Justice Family Group subsequently bought the property and guaranteed all debts, resulting in a dismissal of the bankruptcy. Justice promised to return the hotel to its former status as a five-star resort. They also introduced "tasteful" gambling as a source of revenue, as well as lectures, to name just a few of the many activities. A total of 26 Presidents have stayed at the Greenbrier. The last US President to stay there during his presidency was Dwight Eisenhower. I don't know if President Obama ever stayed there. In the 1940s, when the hotel underwent an extensive renovation, Dorothy Draper, the renowned interior designer from New York, was hired to do the job. Bringing the hotel back to its former glory was the task, and the official re-opening was scheduled from April 15 to the 18th, 1948. It was a great social event attracting guests such as the Duke of Windsor and his wife Wallis Simpson who spent their first honeymoon with her first husband in 1916 at the Greenbrier. Bing Crosby, Indira Gandhi, Prince Rainier and Princess Grace Kelly of Monaco, and many other national and foreign dignitaries were in attendance. I had the pleasure of staying at the Greenbrier on two occasions. My first visit was with my wife Andrea when we were living in New York. In 1977, we drove by car and passed the Shenandoah Valley. I remember like yesterday how Andrea and I were impressed by the beauty of this area with forests, wide open plains, swift-moving rivers, blue skies, and quaint villages. We kept saying this is as nice as Switzerland. When we drove up to the Greenbrier for the first time our eyes opened wide when we saw the beautiful white structure of the hotel and its thousands of flowers. We came from the Plaza in New York; however, the columns of the Greenbrier and the white building itself were just astonishing. Then the enormous park; the best we had in New York was Central Park, but there was simply no comparison to this. It all made the Plaza seem awfully small. Needless to say, we enjoyed the great experience. We walked around the grounds and saw the cottages that were built some 200 years ago. Some of them were originally sleeping quarters for the slaves or employees but now they are a few hundred dollars a night. We also had a chance to say hello to Sam Snead, the legendary golf pro, who won his first tournament at the Greenbrier. While working at the Greenbrier in 1937, Sam also played in the US Pro Tennis Championship. He was certainly a great athlete and held numerous golf records. Born in 1917, he passed away in May 2002 at the age of 89. He was a great gentleman.

As we started our drive home I told Andrea I would love to come back to this place one day. As I was a big deal in the Atlanta hotel world I was approached by Ted Wright, Managing Director of the Cloister on Sea Island to see if I would be interested in joining a distinguished group of hoteliers. It is by invitation only and I think you are the kind of fellow we would like to have, he said. The group was called Southern Innkeepers and meets three to four times a year, always in a nice resort. We have some education seminars, good fellowship, fascinating functions and just have a great time. Ted said I can make you a member and the next meeting we have is at the Greenbrier. Ted grew up in that place as his father was Truman Wright, for years the President of the Greenbrier prior to his retirement. This is a no-brainer I told him. I said I would be honored to join the Southern Innkeepers, a discriminating group of hoteliers. I went to my first meeting and it was great. We flew to Roanoke, rented a car and drove to White Sulphur Springs. We arrived on Thursday evening and it lasted until Sunday. Since I had stayed there before it was easy for me to get around. The first night we had an elegant reception and dinner, Friday was a work session where Dorothy Draper's Interior Design Group made a presentation about the history of the company which was fascinating. The history and philosophy of the organization keeps going even though Mrs. Draper passed away a long time ago. Dorothy Draper was born to a wealthy privileged family in 1889. Her work was appreciated in different parts of the world, not just in the Greenbrier. Many of Florida's most famous resorts have been done by her, the bright colors of green, orange, red, blue, and stripes are well known designs of hers. When you walk into a place and see you automatically know this is Dorothy Draper; instantly you can see her touch. We also had a financial session on how to increase your personal wealth. We could not just eat and drink and be happy; the IRS would not allow that. Work had to be included to make it a business trip. Saturday night we had a black-tie dinner which was probably one of the most elegant dinners I have ever experienced in my life. Hermann Rush, the Vice President of Food & Beverage, presented the gold service dinner. What a pleasure it was for me to meet Hermann, who I have heard so much about all my life. But it was the first time I could chat with him. He, like me, came as a young lad to the United States from Switzerland and did well. The Greenbrier is in a class by itself.

I have stayed in hundreds of hotels all over the world. There are so many famous places I have visited but did not write about. There are great hotels in Europe, Africa, the Middle East, Dubai, not to "short change" the Marriott World Center in Orlando, or the Raffles in Singapore, Carlton in Cannes, Villa Deste in Italy, Schloss Lauden, Jungfrau Victoria in Interlaken, The Dorchester in London, Imperial Vienna, Pierre in New York, Waldorf Astoria, or the Ritz in Madrid. I stayed in hotels from Tokyo to Tahiti, Copenhagen to Cancun, Singapore to Sidney, Mexico City to Munich, Bangkok to Beijing. There are absolutely thousands of special hotels, inns, and resorts that I love. I chose the few places I wrote about because I had a special affection for them and experiences I do not want to forget.

In school when I had to study history I hated it, and frankly was not very good at it. I could care less who was killed in what war. When it comes to history about hotels, taverns, and cuisine, I could never know enough about it. I just love it and like I have said so often, I LOVE HOTELS.

14. FAMOUS PEOPLE I HAVE MET

For years I had a guestbook which I asked people I'd had interactions with to sign. Also, I have numerous photos with so-called famous people. Some of these photos I did not even ask to have taken; I just received them in the mail. One day Corky, the father-in-law of my daughter, Andrea, came over for dinner and saw my guestbook lying around and noticed some of the famous photos which included Jimmy Carter, George Bush, Arnold Palmer, Margaret Thatcher, Bob Hope, etc. So Corky asked me if I would write down for the grandkids the names of some of these celebrities and how I met them. He felt the kids would love to know about them. Although I have met many celebrities who are famous in Europe, I do not think they are well known in America. However, following are some comments about the people I have had the pleasure to meet over the years.

Karlheinz Boehm—a famous Austrian actor and philanthropist. He starred in many movies of which the most famous were starring alongside Romy Schneider, including *Sissi*, a movie about the Austrian Emperor and his wife. Being a great fan of Boehm, it was an exciting moment when I met him. He was living in Cureggia and Mrs. Bachman, who took care of the yard at his villa, introduced me to him. He was just as charming as he was in the movies.

Hubert Humphrey—38th Vice President of the United States—while working at the Century Plaza in Los Angeles, our Managing Director told me that Mr. Humphrey was having a luncheon in his suite with some VIPs and asked me to personally serve them and take care of them. Boy what a different world it was in 1968 compared to today. They were openly talking about race issues in the US. Mr. Humphrey said several times that we have to take care of these "n....." these "f......" people are ruining our country. The world has changed considerably since then. In my guestbook he wrote *"Hermann, my thanks for your service and kindness. Hubert Humphrey."*

Muhammad Ali—He was in the governor's suite where he was holding a press conference. He went through his circus performance, "I am the greatest, I am the prettiest," etc., waving his hands and shouting when he spoke to the reporters. After the press conference I asked him if he would do me a favor by coming down to our employee cafeteria and speak to his brothers and sisters. His reply was "Sure, let's go." He greeted the staff, shook their hands, gave autographs, and was totally a different person than in the press conference. As we left I thanked him and walked him out to the lobby where a couple of reporters approached him. Here we go again with Ali shouting, waving his hands, and repeating his mantra "I am the greatest" as soon as he saw the newscasters.

Barbara Britten—American film and television actress. She was best known for her western film roles opposite Randolph Scott and Gene Autrey. In addition, she was also a singer and later in the 50s and 60s she entered into our homes daily as the Revlon girl. What a pleasant, lovely lady she was.

Walt Disney—It was at the Century Plaza in 1966 when I had an order for a $6.50 filet mignon for Mr. Disney. I made a little cartoon out of tooth picks and olives to put on the meat. He thanked me by signing a menu for me which said *"Hermann, all the best."* What handwriting he had! The menu has been hanging in my home kitchen everywhere I have lived since then.

Morey Amsterdam—actor and comedian. Well known from *The Dick Van Dyke Show*

Margaret Whiting—singer. She seemed a very kind person. She wrote *"To Hermann Songfully yours, Margaret Whiting."*

Enrico Nicola "Henry" Mancini—American composer, conductor and arranger. Well known for his film and television scores. I met him twice, once in Chicago and later in Atlanta when he played at Chastain Park.

Sandy Koufax— baseball player. I never had a clue about baseball or any interest either. When this famous man was having lunch in the restaurant all my employees told me I needed to say hello to the famous Los Angeles Dodger player, which I did.

Johnny Carson—*Tonight Show* Host. While he was having breakfast with us, I told him how much I loved his show however many times I cannot watch it because I have to get up at 5am to get ready for work. Smiling he said I needed to tell my boss to change my shift to the afternoon.

Art Garfunkel—singer, poet and actor. Well known for his partnership with Paul Simon. *"Thanks for being kind to me,"* he wrote in my book.

Joe Dimaggio—baseball player. Again, I had no idea who "The Yankee Clipper" was; however, when I was told he was the husband of Marilyn Monroe that got my attention fast.

Jack Palance— actor. A man stood at the entrance of our restaurant in Chicago. Our hostess could only say "Oh, oh my God" as he looked over his glasses and requested a table for one. I was a great fan of Jack Palance and his TV show "The Greatest Show on Earth," from which I ultimately learned English. *"Hi Pal, nice to meet you. Jack Palance"* he wrote in my book.

R. Buck Maffei— the giant at the Jack Benny Special. He was close to 500 lbs. and had three orders of ham and eggs, three orders of toast with butter and jam. Obviously, he was not on a diet but a hell of a nice fellow.

Robert Taylor—American actor. I met him in Los Angeles

John Gary—American singer, recording artist, television host and performer on the musical stage.

Gene Autry—actor. I did meet the cowboy and told him how crazy I was about cowboys and Indians. He laughed and commented that today this is just make believe. He was a very nice gentleman.

Dan Curney—Indy-car racer. Andrea and I went to Indianapolis and saw him race in the 500 mile race. Then a week later he stayed at the Continental Plaza in Chicago. He is one of only two drivers in the world who drove Formula One, Indy Cars, NASCAR, Can-AM and Trans-Am series. The other drive is Mario Andretti.

Danny Kay—American actor and comedian. It was in Singapore in 1971 when I had lunch with some of my employees honoring them. In walks Danny Kay, very funny and charming. He tried to make my Chinese guests laugh; however, to no avail. They just looked at him in a stern way. He smiled and told me not to feel bad, it had happened to him before.

Rod Taylor—lead actor in the TV Show "Hotel" along with Connie Sellecca. He told me to watch out as he was an expert in the hotel business. I told him real hotel business was nothing like the TV hotel business. He grinned and agreed that I might be right.

Lys Assia—International singer. It was at the Shangri La in Singapore that I met Lys Assia. She was a very successful Swiss singer, winning the first Eurovision contest. I had dinner with her and her Danish husband and we had a fantastic time together. I tried to drink her under the table, but the situation got reversed and I found myself sick for three days after my drinking with her. I still don't know how she put it away. My mother wrote me a letter full of excitement that she had received a package in the mail with 10 albums from Lys Assia.

Ken Rosewall—Australian tennis player. I met him at the Ilikai in Honolulu when he used it to play and train. The same holds true for Arthur Ashe and Ilie Nastase as they were all often guests with us.

Connie Francis—American singer. Boy was I a fan of hers. She was about my age and I had the pleasure of taking a photo with her in Chicago in 1968. She was born Concetta Rosa Maria Franconero in December 1938. I asked her how she had learned German and she said she didn't speak a word which was hard for me to believe since her German songs were absolutely without an American accent.

Elizabeth Taylor—American actress. I met her at a lunch in the Ritz Carlton when I was fortunate enough to sit at the same table with her. Every second word was "Darling."

Silvia Renate Sommerlath—Queen Silvia of Sweden married to King Carl XVI Gustaf, born in Heidelberg Germany. She was sitting at a table next to us while having dinner at a charity function at the Ritz Carlton in Atlanta.

George Burns — American actor, was a guest in my hotel in Chicago.

Sammy Davis, Jr. — singer, dancer, actor pianist, drummer, and comedian. He did an interview in my office at the Peachtree Plaza Hotel. My PR manager asked him if he would sign my guest book. In a rather stern voice he replied that we could take photos, he would give autographs, whatever we wanted, but let him finish his work first, and he was right. I was surprised that he was such an extremely small fellow.

Roy Clark — country singer. If you ever watched *Hee Haw* then you know Roy Clark, the American country music performer. He wrote in my guestbook "T*o Hermann, my best always, Roy Clark.*" We also took a nice picture together which I had framed.

Dick Van Patten — American actor. My daughters Andrea and Christina were so excited when we took a photo with him in my office. "*We had a great time. Thanks so much. Your friend, Dick Van Patten 8*" he wrote in my guestbook.

Mary Lou Retton — Olympic gymnast. Andrea, Christina and I took a photo with Mary Lou in 1984 after she had won the Gold in Los Angeles. My kids were small at the time, but so was she at only 4'9", 93 lbs.

Tova Borgnine And Ernest Borgnine — American actors. What a delightful couple. She is the founder of Beauty by Tova Cosmetics and he of course and American actor whose career spanned more than six decades. He was noted for his gruff, yet calm voice. They wrote in my guestbook *"To Hermann, Tova Borgnine"* and *"Thank you so much for your generosity. Good luck, Ernest Borgnine"*. They were so nice and charming and easy to talk to.

Thelma "Butterfly" Mcqueen — American actress. She is well-known as Prissy, the maid of Scarlett O'Hara in the movie "Gone with the Wind." She was unable to attend the movies premiere because it was held at a whites-only theater.

Buzz Aldrin — American engineer and astronaut. He participated in the first moon landing on Apollo 11 in 1969. He signed my copy of the book he had written "Encounter with Tiber."

Lee Iacocca — American automobile executive best known for spearheading the development of Ford Mustang and Pinto automobiles. I love his style as a manager — lead or follow or get out of the way. What a philosophy. He signed my book *"To Hermann, with all the best wishes."*

John Tesh — American pianist and composer of popular music. What a nice and friendly fellow. After signing my book, he wrote *"What a great hotel. Thank you."*

Bob Hope — American comedian and actor. What a man! He was at the opening of the Century Plaza Hotel in 1966 and I was fortunate to meet him again at the Peachtree Plaza in Atlanta in the early 1980s. We took a photo together and he signed my guestbook.

Colin Powell — Retired Four Star General, former US Secretary of State. He came to our hotel to give a speech. When he arrived, he had a garment bag over his shoulder with his tuxedo. I welcomed him to our hotel and said I had a suite ready for him with some fruits and soft drinks so he could freshen up. He replied that he didn't need a suite, that he is a soldier. He proceeded directly into the men's room, changed into his tuxedo and within minutes went on stage to give his speech. When he finished speaking, he again headed back into the men's room, changed out of his tuxedo, and left! He is a very "down-to-earth" person.

Bruno Stanek—scientist and TV reporter. My secretary announced there was a Dr. Stanek asking to see me. He brought me a book with a dedication as he had learned that the GM was a Swiss and he wanted me to have a copy of his book. We had a nice conversation. No rocket went into space in the 70s and 80s without Dr. Stanek's report on Swiss Television.

Henry Kissinger—American Diplomat. I was always a fan of Dr. Kissinger, I guess mostly because he had a German accent like me. We had a wonderful photo taken together in my office when I took the opportunity to tell him what a great job he had done for our country. His reply was "*Danke Schoen.*"

John Glenn—American Astronaut and US Senator. He also ran for the 1984 Democratic President Nomination. He held a press conference at top of the world's tallest hotel where he was symbolizing his work as an astronaut and space agent. However, the weather was horrible and when we had our picture taken together in front of one of the windows all you could see was one foot outside because of the thick fog. The entire background was nothing but gray—it was rather humorous.

Bertrand Piccard—Swiss psychiatrist and balloonist. While I was on the Board of the Swiss American Chamber of Commerce, we organized a presentation by Betrand Piccard. He was the first to complete a non-stop balloon flight around the globe. He is also the initiator of the first successful round-the-world solar flight. I have a National Geographic Magazine with him and the balloon photo which he personally signed for me.

Jimmy Carter And Rosalynn Carter—President and First Lady. I can't remember how many times I met the Carters. They are such lovely people. I have several photos together with them. When I was Manager at the Detroit Plaza I gave Mrs. Carter a tour of the hotel. Two weeks later I received a package from the White House with a letter. *"Dear Hermann, I want you to know how much I appreciate the gracious hospitality extended to me during my recent trip to Detroit. I enjoyed my brief visit very much. Thank you also for the lovely flowers, the fruit and the candy. Sincerely, Rosalynn Carter."* The letter and a nice photo of her and me was framed and included in the package.

Franz Beckenbauer And Pelé—soccer players. Franz Beckenbauer is called "der Kaiser" in Germany which means "Emperor" because of his elegant style. Pelé's real name is Edson Arantes do Nascimento. When I was working at the Plaza in New York in 1977, we had a gala dinner in the hotel. Beckenbauer replaced Pelé as a soccer player for the New York Cosmos. I had them both sign the dinner menu for me.

Woody Herman, George Shearing, Ben Vereen— musicians. These are just a few of the many entertainers who I met when I ran a night club in Los Angeles.

Paul Boscuse—famous French Chef. He was at the Wailea Beach Resort in Maui for a food promotion when we brought him in on an outrigger canoe. He was great to work with the way he participated in the food promotion. I took a picture with him and we dined together. He was surprised to learn that I was a Sr. Vice President who had started as a chef.

Ringo Starr — drummer for the Beatles. Our Director of PR asked me to welcome Ringo Starr to the hotel. Since I had no idea what he looked like, she said he is small, has an earring and wears a goatee. The limo pulled up to the hotel and four small fellows got out of hotel, each wearing an earring and a goatee! I welcomed them all to the Westin Peachtree Plaza and asked them who the most important person was; Ringo moved to the forefront and said it must be him. I took him up to the Presidential Suite and he told me to sit down as he wanted to play me a song. He sat at the piano and played a Beatles song for me then signed my guest book. I thought "Man what an experience I just had."

George Bush — 41st President of the United States. I was able to have my picture taken with Mr. and Mrs. Bush and they were very nice; however, I did not ask him for an autograph. About three weeks later I received a package from the White House which included an official photograph of George Bush with a note *"To Hermann Gammeter. "Best Wishes, George Bush."* It was nicely framed so I could hang it in my office.

The Cowsills — musical group from Newport Beach, Rhode Island. They were famous in the 60s. A real nice family group who reminded me of the Von Trapp Family. They stayed with us in Chicago and I still have a post card they sent me following their visit which said *"Dear Hermann, we want to thank you for your kindness to us while we were in Chicago. We hope we meet people as nice as you along the way. Sincerely, The Cowsills."* The group was the inspiration for the 1970s television show *The Partridge Family*.

Margaret Thatcher — Prime Minister of England. I had my picture taken with her; however, she did not give us a smile and I thought she prefers having photos made with international politicians than innkeepers. However, she signed my copy of her book "Margaret Thatcher, The

Collected Speeches." I asked her to sign a dedication to my wife Audrey rather than to me, which she did graciously.

James MacArthur — actor. When I was working at the Ilikai in Honolulu they often filmed at our hotel for the TV show, *Hawaii 5-0*. James MacArthur, who was a very nice fellow, agreed to have his picture taken with me. We learned rather quickly that the wife of the show's star, Jack Lord, was a real pain in the butt.

Jim Nabors — American actor and fantastic singer. I had always enjoyed Jim Nabors in his role as Gomer Pyle and found him quite funny; however, when you meet him he is not the dummy that he plays on the TV show. At the St. Francis, I had dinner with him and his manager. We had a wonderful evening and I was able to have my picture taken with him. About two weeks later, I received a package with ten fantastic albums from him. Prior to that I had no idea that he was such a fabulous singer.

Jacky Icks And Nigal Mansell — Formula One Drivers. While enjoying dinner in the Hotel Bauman in Leoben, Austria. I noticed at the next table the two drivers were having dinner, also, as that weekend was the Austrian Grand Prix. They graciously agreed to give me their autographs.

Linda Ronstadt — American singer. One night the Manager of the Edwardian Room called and said Linda Ronstadt would like to have dinner there; however, because she was wearing blue jeans service had been refused. She requested to see the manager. I met with her and told her unfortunately we do not allow blue jeans in the restaurant. No problem she replied, and since she did not feel like changing she would order room service. With a smile, she walked away.

Barbara Walters—Journalist. In 1971 we had her at the Ilikai in Honolulu as she was there for a week doing the *Today* show.

Peter Charles Archibald Ewart Jennings—News anchor. He was the sole anchor of ABC World News Tonight from 1983 until his death in 2005 from complications of lung cancer. I had the pleasure to have dinner with him and his wife during the Democratic National Convention in Atlanta. They stayed at the hotel for a week.

Buddy Hackettt—American comedian and actor. He stayed with us at the Century Plaza in Los Angeles. I will never forget the car he drove—it was a convertible with steer horns on the hood.

Richard Milhouse Nixon—37th United States President. I was having a drink in Trader Vic's at the Plaza in New York. It was just after he had resigned, so I felt the poor fellow needed a lift, so I went over and told him that I was a fan of his and thought he had been a great President. That is so kind of you, he said and gave me an autograph.

Tom Hanks—American actor, comedian, and filmmaker. When living in Cleveland, Tom gave a VIP one-man performance in a small theater. I was invited to the show and the reception which followed where I had the opportunity to meet him personally. What a nice fellow he seems to be.

Charlton Heston—Hollywood star. I met both Mr. Heston and his son who looks just like him while they were at the Peachtree Plaza in Atlanta and was able to take the occasion to be photographed together.

Aristolelis "Telly" Savalas—American singer, film star, as well as television and character actor. When I told him I was a fan of his *Kojak*

TV show, he said that was good because the pay enabled him to feed his five kids! I was able to have my picture taken with him in front of the Edwardian Room at the Plaza.

Arnold Palmer—American golfer. I met Arnold Palmer at the Westin Peachtree Plaza and was fortunate enough to be photographed alongside him. I told him I was a hacker and just wished I could play golf 10% as well as he did. He said I just needed to practice more.

There are numerous other "famous" people I have met over the years in the United States, as well as Europe and Asia, many who are executives and celebrities, in addition to a few world leaders. I have a wonderful book of personal letters of thanks which I have received over the years. It is a thoroughly wonderful collection of nice, kind comments. It is due to the amazing hotel positions I had the pleasure of holding over the years that I was able to meet such a variety of so many interesting and caring people in this world. It has truly been a blessing.

Unfortunately, many of the famous people I met are now deceased. As my mother always said "*One thing in life is fair. Whether you are rich or poor, famous or unknown, we all go out through the same door and the same way.*"

15. GUARDIAN ANGELS

Yes, guardian angels. I have had them a few times in my life. Quite frankly some of the things I did I must admit were dumb or reckless, or maybe the word should actually be stupid. On the other hand, I guess we have all had times where we were at the wrong place at the wrong time. When kids act out and get hurt, we call it an unfortunate accident, but when the outcome is the opposite and they are unscathed, we say they were lucky. Maybe it was not merely luck; maybe it was their guardian angel watching over them.

For example, when I was about six years old. I was in the car with my mom, and dad was driving. We were crossing the railroad tracks just as the barrier was closed. At that time back in 1940, all railroad barriers were raised and lowered by a human person; they were not automated. All of a sudden, along came a train. Dad reacted extremely quickly, put the car in reverse and the car suddenly jumped back; thank God or we all could have been killed. Dad was going to report the incident, but Mother talked him out of it. She said we all make mistakes and none of us are perfect.

As a kid I made my own bobsled and when we had snow, my friends and I would run the sled for hours on the regular village streets. After World War II there were not many cars, plus gas was scarce for people. One night when the road was really icy, I drove the roads with my six man sled crazy fast and just after the curve in the road, along came a car headed right for us. I was able to maneuver the bobsled between the car and a large tree and hit the open pasture. Was that just a lucky break?

As a youngster I was a great swimmer and always loved to dive into the water, often just to show off and impress the other kids. One day on Lake Hallwil I went up and stood on a tree trunk then jumped head first into the water. It was only later that I learned I had barely missed hitting underwater broken trees. I still get cold chills thinking about what would have happened to me had I hit some of the tree trunks—my face could have been disfigured for life. I will never know for sure why I did not hit those trees.

During World War II, an American bomber made an emergency landing in Lake Zug. A friend of my brother Harry named Mumch and then later nicknamed "Bomber Schaffner" because he was close to 500 pounds, decided to retrieve the bomber plane out of Lake Zug. It was an enormous event in Switzerland. He displayed the plane with all kind of mementos and people came from all over the country to see the display. Of course, my dad wanted to see this spectacle too, so we drove to Zug. After seeing the exhibit, we rented a boat to take a ride on the lake. Lake Zug can become very tricky and unfortunately we got into a horrible storm which was quite dangerous. My mother was crying, "*Oh God help us. I don't mind drowning myself, but I don't want my little seven year old boy Hermann to die!*" Finally, I screamed at my mother and told her to stop the nonsense and be positive. Like a miracle, the lake calmed down, the sun came out, and we were saved. Mother has told me this story a thousand times in my life.

I already wrote earlier about the story when the Mexican came after me with a stiletto and I had to jump out of the window, landing in a garbage can. I survived yet another disastrous situation.

Skiers don't wear helmets because those are for sissies I used to say and was very sarcastic about it. It was just a spectacular, sunny winter day when I went skiing at Mt. Rigi, the Queen of the Mountain. I had enjoyed the winter slopes often in this same area. As a kid I was a wild man, jumping backwards skiing and all the wild and crazy things you can do, well I did it. On this particular day I went down the hill like a mad man, then hit some dirt, stopped, flew back and hit ice and off I went again. During this maneuver I barely missed hitting a wooden structure. If I had hit my head, my skull would have been smashed and undoubtedly some permanent damage would have resulted. The next day I have to admit I purchased a safety helmet and have never skied without one again.

On a flight to Bermuda we hit some rough weather. Rather than calming my scared wife, I was teasing her saying we were in the Bermuda Triangle, that maybe the Martians were going to pick us up. Then we heard a loud bang. It sounded like a bomb had hit us. Later the captain informed us the plane had been hit by lightning. Boy my joking was over; I turned snow white and did not say another word until we landed at our destination.

I was on another scary flight from London to Karachi, Pakistan in 1970. While flying I told Andrea something is wrong with this flight as I felt we were going too slow. I used to fly small planes and certainly was no expert on jets; however, I knew something was not kosher. The Captain then announced that we had a minor problem and needed to return to Heathrow. Later on I found out there was a crack in the window of the cockpit. Just think about it — if the window had broken, we all would have gone down with the plane. We stayed overnight in Britain on the coast and the next day we continued our trip to the Far East.

With three friends we flew in their plane to Phucket in Thailand. Our trip began in Singapore and all went well until we hit a storm. Our friend Peter was a pilot with Cathay Pacific Airways, but because the instruments seemed to have a problem when we hit the storm, Peter said he didn't know what to do. He didn't even know where we were. It was horrible. The plane was shaking and outside nothing but clouds and fog. I was convinced it was all over, especially since we were in an area with mountains, cliffs, and water. Then like a miracle the clouds opened up, the sun shone bright and we could see the runway of Phucket below us. After the landing I took a long walk on the beautiful beaches, enjoyed the blue water and thanked God for keeping us safe yet again.

On one of my first solo flights in Chicago, I was flying while day-dreaming about how great the world was. I continually heard an air traffic controller's voice saying "Would the little private plane please fly lower and get out of the way?" I looked around and like sharks in the sky I saw jet lights around me. Suddenly I realized that I was the culprit the controller was speaking to. I was flying in the landing pattern for the planes that land at O'Hare. Like a madman I made a dive of 500 feet and got out of their way.

Markus, a neighbor's kid, and Christina were playing near my mother's house when Tina came running home crying that Markus came after her with a knife. Unfortunately, I had already consumed a couple of glasses of wine, but my mother kept provoking me to go outside and give Markus a spanking. She really knew which buttons to push to get me angry. So I ran out and hit the kid—what a stupid move that was. Since he ended up red and bruised, his parents took him to a doctor to check him out. Thank God he was okay otherwise I could have gone to jail if his parents had pressed charges or God forbid he had ended up being seriously injured.

In 1964 I was hitchhiking along the coast between Washington State and California when I got picked up by a guy. He was kind of a rough fellow. He was telling me how he had served in both the Korean War and the Vietnam War. "*When you are in the war you have to kill people, my boy*" he said to me. He was really weird and he gave me a very uneasy feeling. He seemed to be driving extremely slowly, which added to my uneasiness. He told me to get his Bible out of the glove box and read it. When retrieving the Bible, I saw a gun hidden under a cloth which really scared the shit out of me. I told him I needed to go to the bathroom if he would stop at the next station, which he did. It was getting darker and darker which seemed to please him. After my bathroom break, I told him I would like some chewing gum, which he offered to get for me. As he went into the station, I grabbed my traveling bag from the car, ran over to the highway, and started hitchhiking in the opposite direction. An old man stopped in a red pick-up and took me along. I told him what happened, and he said there are a lot of crazy people out there. I asked him if he was scared of picking up strangers like me, and he said no, the good Lord knows when it's time for me to go. He let me off in a small village in Oregon, where I found a hotel room. I immediately moved all the furniture against the door later that night before going to sleep, which shows just how scared I still was. The next day I started my trip south again and made it back to my job at the yacht. It was good that it was a 4th of July weekend, otherwise I would never have made it back in time.

While working in Hawaii we had a Grand Banks, which is a very nice yacht, at the hotel. Sometimes on Sundays we could go out cruising. So, on one of these rides we were anchored and enjoying a few beers. I had the great idea of showing off, which when I was young I often wanted to do. I climbed all the way to the top of our boat and got ready to jump into the blue Pacific. Boy what a beautiful sight it was. Then I heard a scream from one of my beer buddies: "*Don't' jump, Hermann. Sharks!*" I looked down and saw five or six good-sized sharks moving around the keel of the boat. Just think if I had jumped that would have been the end of poor Hermann.

In 1954, during our fall vacation my friend Heinz and I got the idea we should make a bicycle trip to the Briesenhouse. This is a nice alpine lodge about 70km from where we lived. We made the ride, which takes several hours, then we had to walk for another three hours to the "Huette" alpine lodge. The next day on a Saturday we went for a wonderful walk in the meadow with the cows, alpine flowers, the trails, and the fabulous wild landscape. It could not have been more beautiful. As we were walking I found a grenade and since we knew some people make flower vases with them, we took it with us. Eventually we decided that maybe we should open it up and see what's inside or we could take it back to the lodge and work on it there. But then we decided if we did that and it exploded, the "Huette" would be a catastrophe. By that time we had gotten scared, so I told Heinz we should throw it away and see what happened. He agreed and tried to throw it far away; however, it slipped out of his hand and flew just behind a big rock near us. "Boom"—it made an awful noise and rocks, stones, metal, etc. flew right over us. It was like the 4th of July fireworks. Neither of us had a scratch, but you talk about being lucky. So we said let's go down to the village and celebrate because we had not been harmed. As we went down the gondola two mountain fellows asked us about the accident that happened in the morning. They said they understood that two boys had been killed and since we came from the Briesenhouse they wanted to know if we knew them. "Funny you should ask" we replied, "because you are looking at them." They told us that there were three grenades, one they found, another one started to roll during the spring when the snow melted and exploded, and the third one was the one we had found.

I guess as kids we are often protected and thus we had been lucky. My friend Willie, who sat next to me in school for four years, had a saying that meant when your time is up, it is up. He was a motorbike racer and his brother was a Swiss champion in racing. Willie's son was also a racer, but he was killed in a race. So Willie told me when his son was killed that the priest told him whenever we are born we all get a candle from God which begins to burn, and that when it burns all the way down, it is over. I guess he has a point when he says when your time is up, it is up.

16. SOME PERSONAL PHILOSPHY

This is a chapter where I would like to share some personal philosophy, i.e. some ideas I have utilized to approach life. Maybe some things which happened to me or to someone I knew such as a friend or family member, may have made an impact on them or perhaps even me. What I would truly like to accomplish with this chapter is to make sure my kids, friends, associates, and especially my grandchildren will know who Hermann Gammeter really was. It is not easy to figure out a human being or a character; however, I hope that some of my personal philosophies will accomplish this. I certainly was no saint, but my intentions were mostly good and I strived to help the underdog and the people who needed support in life. I have discovered that life is definitely a complicated journey. I always felt I had an obligation to help other people at work. One of my usual "preachings" to my department heads was that they had an obligation to help other people to move along, to progress in their field. I always felt it was our obligation to give them a hand; otherwise none of us would have been where we were ourselves without help from someone else.

When I was 22 and dating girls, I would ask them what they liked to do when they worked. They would answer they didn't know as they currently attended college. So I asked what were they studying, what did they plan to do for work when they graduated? Often they said they were going to college to find a husband or perhaps they wanted to study Marine Biology simply because they liked fish. This drove me absolutely crazy because when I was only twelve years old I had already told my mother I was going to be a chef. Once I became a chef, then my next goal was to be a Director of Food & Beverage. After that was achieved, my next objective was to be a General Manager and so on and so forth.

My advice to my kids and grandchildren is to do something that you love then it won't be work. Next do something that makes you money, then you can pay your bills but don't work for the government in a job without a future. Take a job that gives you the opportunity to advance and get promoted, that will increase your income. The best example of that is my son-in-law Sam. He was Assistant Manager in some great hotels but hated his job. So he took some adaptability tests and concluded he would like to be an electrician. God bless my daughter Andrea because even though she had a child, she took different jobs and worked her butt off so that Sam could go to school. In one of her jobs she sold credit card machines, which she hated, partly because she was on commission. Sam studied for four years, was the best in his class with superb grades, and eventually became an electrician. He was promoted several times and today he has several crews working for him. One time I asked Sam if in the winter, when it's cold and rainy and he has to go to a construction site, doesn't he miss his glamorous hotel job, walking around in a nice jacket and tie, warm and dry? His answer was that on his worst day working as an electrician is still better than the best day he ever had in his hotel job. I am so glad he found his niche in life. He enjoys what he is doing, he is taking good care of his family, and I am very proud of his accomplishments.

My daughter Christina has found her dream job too. She is a physical therapist with a doctor's degree and loves what she is doing. She is committed to her family including their three children whom she is home teaching. Her husband Ben works to support them and he and Christina have a wonderful family life. How lucky can you get as a dad!

While living in San Francisco, little Andrea knocked down some food cans in the grocery store. I put them back where they belonged and told her not to do it again. In the next aisle she did it again, so I slapped her with my hand on her butt, not actually spanking her, just to get her attention and let her know I meant business. Some lady came over and said I couldn't spank my child and she was going to report me to the police. My response to her was to go right ahead and do that and you're going to be the next one to get a spanking! She left in a huff, so Andrea and I could continue to do our shopping in peace.

My mom and I had a good relationship and she would do anything for me. Even when I left home at 16 and later when I was 22, she always supported me. Of course her dream was that I would take over my parent's business or operate a restaurant around where they lived. She knew that was not my cup of tea; she knew she had to let me go and spread my wings. But we sure had our differences, too. She was always negative and put herself down. She would say she was nothing; she came from a poor family and would never amount to anything. What a crock of baloney. She did a great job running the shop we had, taking care of her family, educating children from different marriages, etc. She deserved a gold medal for all the fine work she did.

After Audrey and I got married in America, we visited my mom and took her out to dinner. Casually I told her Audrey and I had gotten married. She hardly ate, just sat there and acted like she was in shock. About twenty minutes later she finally said congratulations. I guess maybe she wanted me to stay single for a while.

Having lived in America for so long, I guess I had become Americanized. So on her 75th birthday I arranged a surprise party for her and said let's go to lunch. We went to this fine place where we had about 25 guests, her brothers and sisters, grandkids, cousins, children she has been godmother to, etc. What an absolute disaster this was. She cried and called me a traitor. She asked me why I made fun of her. She would not speak with me anymore. Mama Mia, I thought, we sure do live in different worlds. But again she went back to her old habits; rather than say how nice this was and enjoy a moment of being recognized for everything she had done, she reverted to her philosophy of self-pity. I just ignored it, knowing she wanted me to apologize and acknowledge how poor she was, which I refused to do. The fact is that she was a great mother and was good to all of us and she deserved this recognition. For the last eight years of her life she was in a nursing home and the last five she did not even recognize me anymore. All her life she used to say that she could take anything, but she never wanted to go to a nursing home and have people take care of her and wait on her. For her last years that is just what happened. Every summer whenever I was in Switzerland I used to go and feed her and walk her around the park. It was hard for all of us in the family. She did not deserve this; she was a wonderful woman and took care of all of us. One month short of her 95th birthday she went to the good Lord. I guess this is the cycle of life as I always call it. None of us know what is going to happen to any of us.

Respect your secretary. I had many but am not sure all bosses really appreciate the fine work they do for us. It is not enough to take them to the annual secretary's luncheon. For me they used to be absolutely essential for my success. Granted, I did encounter a few losers over the years, but those disappeared in the sunset. I can't thank the successful ones enough for the fine contributions which they made.

When you manage people, you get to understand that the management style is not "it's my way or the highway." Management is "get the job done through other people." It is a coaching task because it is your team that will bring success. My story to the newly hired used to be — if you serve a guest orange juice that is lukewarm, burn the toast, and the room service table is not properly set-up, the guest will think the General Manager can't be too good. On the other hand, when the orange juice is properly chilled, the toast is perfect, and the table is set-up correctly, the guest will say the General Manager must be good. In any business, whether it is hospitality, manufacturing, service operations, sales, or retail, no matter what, it is the contributions of the individual employee which will ultimately count for the reputation of a business.

One of the simple programs I incorporated in my hotels used to be a program called "Champion of the Week." It was designed to give some recognition to individual staff members and also to have some fun with the job.

CHAMPION OF THE WEEK AWARD

Purpose — To recognize and celebrate our associates at the <u>HOTEL NAME</u> for their outstanding contributions and efforts to our customers, fellow associates and the company.

Eligibility — All fulltime associates are eligible except the General Manager.

Criteria — Any associate can nominate another associate or group of associates for the CHAMPION OF THE WEEK AWARD. Nominations are to be discussed and presented to the General Manager. The recognition should be given to the nominated associate(s) for a kind act or accomplishment that took place in the previous week.

Presentaion Of Award — The nomination associate will make a presentation to the nominated CHAMPION OF THE WEEK at the weekly staff meeting and present the winner with a "traveling trophy." The recipient will keep the trophy until another winner has been chosen. We do not need a weekly champion. It is not quantity that counts but rather the quality of the award.

Summary—Let's have some fun and demonstrate our appreciation by showing recognition and thanks.

BILL MARRIOTT'S 12 RULES FOR SUCCESS

1. Continually challenge your team to do better.
2. Take good care of your employees and they will take good care of your customers, and the customers will come back.
3. Celebrate your people's success not your own.
4. Know what you are good at and mine those competencies for all you are worth.
5. Do it and do it now. Err on the side of taking action.
6. Communicate—listen to your customers, associates and competitors.
7. See and be seen. Get out of your office, walk around, make yourself visible and accessible.
8. Success is in the details.
9. It is more important to hire people with the right qualities than with specific experience.
10. Customer needs may vary, but their bias for quality never does.
11. Eliminate the cause of a mistake. Don't just clean it up.
12. View every problem as an opportunity to grow.

GUIDEPOSTS TO MANAGEMENT

As managers it is important to periodically pause and look back on the principles that the founder J. Willard Marriott used to successfully build his business. These were passed down as guidelines to run the company in a letter from father to son when

J. W. Marriott, Jr. became Executive Vice President in 1964.

1. Keep physically fit, mentally and spiritually strong.
2. Guard your habits—bad one will destroy you
3. Pray about every difficult problem
4. Study and follow professional management principles. Apply them logically and practically to your organization.
5. People are number one—their development, loyalty, interest, team spirit. Develop managers in every area. This is your prime responsibility.
6. Decisions: Men grow making decisions and assuming responsibility for them.
7. Make crystal clear what decisions each manager is responsible for and what decisions you reserve for yourself
8. Have all the facts and counsel necessary—then decide and stick to it.
9. Criticism: Don't criticize people but make a fair appraisal of their qualifications with their supervisor only (or someone assigned to do this). Remember, anything you say about someone may (and usually does) get back to them. There are few secrets.
10. See the good in people and try to develop those qualities.
11. Inefficiency: If it cannot be overcome and an employee is obviously incapable of the job, find a job they can do or terminate now. Don't wait.
12. Manage your time:
13. Short conversations—to the point
14. Make every minute on the job count
15. Work fewer hours—some of us waste half our time
16. Delegate and hold accountable for results.
17. Details:
18. Let your staff take care of them

19. Save your energy for planning, thinking, working with department heads, promoting new ideas
20. Don't do anything someone else can do for you
21. Ideas and competition:
22. Ideas keep the business alive
23. Know what your competitors are doing and planning
24. Encourage all management to think about better ways and give suggestions on anything that will improve business
25. Spend time and money on research and development
26. Don't try to do an employee's job for them—counsel and suggest
27. Think objectively and keep a sense of humor. Make the business fun for you and others.

Teamwork—We will be cooperative, flexible and enthusiastically offer help without being asked.

Integrity—We will conduct business with each other in an honest, sincere and responsible manner at all times.

Courage—We will be creative and fearless in pursuing our goals by taking risks in implementing innovative ideas to maximize the results.

Achievement—We will attain and exceed our business obligations and nurture a culture of high achievers.

Competence—We will strive to be experts at what we do. We will challenge ourselves to learn from each other and seek opportunities for training and development.

Balance—We will foster an environment in which we work hard, play hard, and celebrate life.

I thought it might be fun to write some items that make us laugh—life should not be so serious. In my younger years, when I first came to this country, people used to say "Hermann, don't take yourself so seriously. Loosen up, have some fun and be happy."

YOU MIGHT BE IN THE HOTEL INDUSTRY IF...

1. You sat at the same desk for 4 years and worked for 8 different managers.
2. "Going for cocktails and dinner" is NOT your idea of a nice evening.
3. When someone asks you your exact job profile, you lie.
4. You get really excited about a 2% pay increase.
5. You sit in a cubicle smaller than your bedroom closet.
6. It's dark on your drive to work and from work
7. Communication is something your "group" is having problems with
8. You see a good-looking person and know it's a visitor/guest.
9. Food left over from a banquet/meeting is your main staple.
10. You forget what you look like in anything but a suit.
11. All the work you were hired to do gets done before 9 and after 5.
12. You're already late on the assignment you just received
13. Your boss's favorite lines are:
    - *"When you get a few minutes..."*
    - *"In your spare time..."*
    - *"I have an opportunity for you..."*
14. 50% of the people in your company do not know what you do
15. The other 50% of the people in your company do not care what you do
16. Vacation is something you roll over to next year or a check you get every January.
17. Change is the norm.

18. Nepotism is encouraged
19. You read this entire list and understand it.

"Heaven is where the police are British, the cooks are French, the mechanics are German, the lovers are Italian, and it is all organized by the Swiss. Hell is where the chefs are British, the mechanics are French, the lovers are Swiss, the police are German, and it is all organized by the Italians."

—Anonymous

MIDDLE AGE

- A man knows he's reached middle age when he's cautioned to slow down by his doctor instead of the police.
- Maybe it is true that life begins at 50, but everything else starts to wear out, fall out, or spread out.
- Middle age is when it takes longer to rest than to get tired.
- You're getting old when you think getting lucky means you found your car in the parking lot
- Middle age is having a choice of two temptations...and choosing the one that will get you home early
- At my age, "getting a little action" means I don't need to take a laxative.

THE GIFT OF A CHEERFUL DISPOSITION

- The easiest way to feel good is to extend a kind word to someone. Really it is not that hard to say "Hello" or "Thank you."

- Friends are a very rare jewel and should be treasured. Indeed, they make you smile and encourage you to succeed. They lend an ear, they share a word of praise and they always want to open their hearts to us.

RIMSHOTS...

- A man told his psychiatrist that he suspected that he had a split personality so the doctor charged him double!
- The psychiatrist told his new patient "Since I haven't seen you before, I have no idea what your problem is so just start at the beginning." And the patient said, "Okay, Doc, in the beginning, I created Heaven and Earth..."
- And then there was the cheap counterfeiter. He was so tight he had the first dollar he ever printed.
- Talk about a cheap date! His idea of a royal evening was dinner at Burger King and dessert at the Dairy Queen!
- My insurance salesman set me up with a retirement policy. If I make the payments faithfully for 20 years, he can retire!
- Two fleas are coming out of Sardi's in New York on a brisk autumn evening. One flea takes a deep breath of the bracing night air and says "Well, what do you think? Should we walk or take a dog?"

SERVICE WITH A SNEER

Customer: Waitress, this food isn't fit for a pig!
Waitress: Then let me take it back Sir and I'll get you some that is!

Customer: Waiter, do you serve crabs here?

Waiter: Certainly Sir, have a seat!

Waiter: Sir, I'll have you know we run a very clean restaurant here!
Customer: Must be — all the food tastes like soap!

Customer: Hey Waiter, this plate is wet!
Waitress: That's your soup Sir!

A guy goes home with a black eye and explains to his wife that the waitress slugged him. "Getting fresh again, huh, Henry?" she replied. "No," he said. "I just asked the waitress if she had frog's legs!"

THE JOKE BOOK...

Did you hear about the big accident downtown? A cement mixer collided with a paddy wagon and the convicts escaped. This was this afternoon. Tonight the cops are looking for hardened criminals.

Q: What do you get if you cross the Gulf of Alaska with an Exxon Valdez?
A: About halfway.

My ex-wife and her new husband are a fastidious couple. She's fast and he's hideous!

It's hard to get good help nowadays. The new elevator operator in my building was fired because he couldn't remember the route.

Nurse: Doctor, the Invisible Man is in the waiting room.
Doctor: Tell him I can't see him now.

Patient: Doc — I'm afraid I'm going to die
Doc: Don't worry. That's the last thing you'll do.

Man: Hey, Doc, it hurts when I do this.
Doc: Then don't do that!

Patient: I just don't know what's worse — having my teeth drilled or having a baby!
Dentist: Well, make up your mind lady. I've got to know how to adjust the chair!

Patient: I don't know what's wrong, Doc. My teeth chattered all night.
Doctor: What'd you do?
Patient: Well, I finally had to get up and take them out of the glass!

An old man goes to the doctor and after the examination; the medico says "Mr. Jones, you're healthy as a horse. You'll live to be 90." To which the patient replied, "I AM 90!" And the doctor says, "See, what'd I tell you?"

Doctor: Hmmm, your cough sounds a lot better.
Patient: It should. I practiced all night!

Doctor: What are you worried about? I had the same condition myself once and I recovered fully.
Worried Patient: Yeah, but you didn't have the same doctor!

Doctor: Now remember take this medicine only with meals. That'll be $50.00.
Destitute Patient: But Doc, I haven't eaten for a week!
Doctor: Fine, then the pills will last a lot longer.

Patient: Hey Doc, would you give me something for my head
Doctor: No, but there's a dental college around the corner that might be interested.

A crestfallen man comes home from the doctor. "What wrong, dear?" asks his wife. "The doctor informed me that I've only got 8 hours to live. I'll tell you what—let's go out for the most expensive dinner in town, then we'll dance until dawn." "Oh, that's great for you," the wife replies. "You don't have to get up in the morning."

Patient: Hey Doc, when the bandages come off my hands will I be able to play the piano?
Doctor: Certainly.
Patient: Great. I always wanted to be able to play the piano!

From the Garden of Eden:
Eve: Do you love me, Adam?
Adam: Who else?

A traveling preacher was way out in the sticks one day when his car broke down. The temperature was 95 degrees and he had no water, so he prayed for help and then lifted the hood of his car. After a minute or so of staring blankly at the engine, he heard a voice say, "It's the fuel pump." The preacher looked around and saw an old horse looking over his shoulder. "It's the fuel pump," the horse said once again. "Don't worry though. Old George Buckley comes this way every day around this time. You can hitch a ride with him."

The preacher spent the next few minutes thanking the Lord and the horse for the help and then, sure enough, Buckley's car came bouncing down the deserted road and good old George offered the preacher a ride into town.

Striding into the gas station, the preacher went up to the mechanic and said, "Brother, it's a miracle. I was lost and alone. My car broke down, but my faith didn't. I prayed for help and it came in the form of a talking horse who told me that it was my fuel pump and that someone would come along in a few minutes to pick me up. That horse was a miracle, I tell you!"

Old Clem, the mechanic, spat out his tobacco and wiped the grease from his hands as he drawled, "'Tain't such a miracle, Reverend. That horse talks big but he don't know nothing 'bout engines?"

17. THE EFFECTS OF DRINKING

When I was growing up we did not have much exposure to alcohol. My dad did not drink a lot, just on special occasions, or sometimes he would occasionally enjoy a white wine on Thursday night when he was playing cards with the guys. I must admit now that white wine could make my dad a little aggressive. What he liked best and drank until he was well into his 80s was non-alcoholic beer. My mom never liked alcohol. Even if my dad asked her to try a beer or a taste of wine, she would spit it out and say it tasted terrible. The only person in the family whom I knew liked some wine daily was my maternal grandfather. He had a couple of glasses of red wine practically every day. However, he never really got drunk—he just enjoyed his wine.

Since I was a child my dad used to give me a glass of sugar water which he had colored with a teaspoon of red wine. It was a tradition in Switzerland for most kids to get a taste of wine in their home. The rules used to be very loose regarding who could purchase wine and beer in a restaurant. When I was eight years old, it was considered normal for me to go and get a bottle of beer for dad, but I would never have thought to drink it.

During my apprenticeship, when I was sixteen years old, we would get beer twice a day; however, since I did not like it, I sold it to a fellow employee for a dime. The kitchens are hot when you work which is why we received the beer. While in the Army we had a beer once in a while but nothing to write home about. The same holds true for the time I spent in hotel school. I guess drinking was also too expensive for me. During my time when I came to America I would go into a bar after work and have a beer. It was called a schooner and it was served in a small glass with an interesting shape. It would last me all night and cost only 25 cents.

While I was living in Chicago, Andrea and I would go out for a nightcap two or three times a week; however never more than two drinks. Of course, it is easy to drink when you are in the hotel and restaurant business since drinks are quite often free. As time went on, drinking became more frequent.

After we moved to Hawaii, we would play tennis after work and then end up at Centre Court, which was a bar. Mai Tais, white wine, and wine spritzers were some of the normal drinks we enjoyed. At the Plaza in New York it became a ritual to meet in the Oak Bar or at Trader Vic's after 5:00. Usually the GM, the Controller, and I met there and sometimes we invited some other staff members to show them gratitude.

Drinking in hotels was easy and a nice pastime. After all, we had a lot of stress and did a lot of work. Our motto was "we work hard and play hard." What is interesting to me is that I could drink at the beginning and afterward go out to dinner, drink a glass of milk, and my urge for alcohol was gone. However, as drinking progressed, the world changed, not only for me but also for my friends and for anyone who drinks too much. The effects of alcohol totally change a person's personality. I could write a book about what happens and there are endless stories about people who drink too much. Following are a few reminders:

People start senseless arguments. I was a Republican, but if someone spoke to me about politics and they were a Republican, I would argue as if I was a Democrat. No matter what the subject was, after I had a few glasses of Chardonnay, I would argue about anything. I would have senseless arguments with my kids, especially Christina. So many of my friends who drank too much are like that. You are never happy. First you have a few drinks to calm you down, then you go through "so called happiness" and that ends in confusion, then you fall asleep. Then you become restless, wake up, and it starts all over again. It is like a vicious circle. The urge of drinking is strong and with time it becomes even stronger. You just crave a drink whether you need it or not. Often I did not feel like a drink, but then I figured well just one, then when you have it you get the buzz and you are off to the races.

By the time I was about 35 years old often I asked myself if I thought I drank too much. So I played all kinds of games with myself—I promised myself to drink only three days a week, but after Monday, Tuesday and Wednesday, it continued. Then came the time I would drink only wine and beer, but that too did not last long or if I did stick to only beer and wine I would over-indulge in that, too. Andrea and I even went to the extreme measures of taking anti-booze pills. That is about the dumbest thing you can do, unless of course you do not drink. I took the pills, then I would have beer or a glass of wine. Your heart starts to pound; you sweat, feel lousy, and can hardly breathe. I stopped drinking, but I also stopped taking the pills. Two weeks later I was back to my normal drinking.

Because I felt I might be an alcoholic I took all kinds of tests I found in magazines, newspapers, books, etc. Usually there are roughly 10-12 questions; if you have two to three yes answers you are okay, four or five and you should watch your drinking consumption, six or seven and you might have a problem, eight or more yesses and you are definitely an alcoholic. My results used to be eight or ten yes answers; however, I dismissed the tests because they were just propaganda and didn't really apply to me. What do you know, I thought; I never lost my job, never had a fight, and never had a DUI. How the heck can I be an alcoholic; my mind was set that I was okay. What I totally dismissed was some of the stupid things I did when I was drinking such as the things I said to my bosses, the things I said to people or ladies. Alcohol made me very promiscuous and I would do and say things I would never have done or said were I sober. Because I was drinking I felt some of my behavior was okay which in reality was not. Today looking back, I humbly ask for forgiveness for some of the stupid things I said and did while under the influence of alcohol.

One day an old friend called me and asked if I would come to Chicago and run a hotel he was having some trouble with. Since I was retired and had nothing else to do I said yes. I flew to Chicago and took over a hotel that was in shambles, but within four months we had reorganized it, changed the employee morale, and things were going just great. During that time, the kids visited me; one weekend I invited Andrea and her husband Sam, and another weekend Christina and her girlfriend came to visit. During Christina's visit, the two of us got in a big argument since we both had too much wine and beer to drink. The next morning, I felt so lousy and sad about our argument. So sitting at my desk, I came to the conclusion that I drank too much and I should make a change in my lifestyle so I decided to stop drinking.

I felt I should do some research in the library about what alcohol does to you and how one could get help. It is fascinating to me the amount of information that is available in the library regarding alcoholism. I read about certain programs that are available and learned what alcoholism actually is.

Alcoholism is an illness. Alcoholics cannot control their drinking because they are ill in their bodies and in their minds. If they do not stop drinking, their alcoholism always gets worse and worse. Both the American Medical Association and the British Medical Association, the chief organization of doctors in these countries, also agree that alcoholism is an illness.

SYMPTOMS OF ALCOHOLICS

Not all alcoholics have the same symptoms, but many, at different stages in the illness, show these signs.

They find that only alcohol can make them feel self-confident and at ease with other people, often want "just one more" at the end of a party. They look forward to drinking occasions and think about them a lot, get drunk when there are no plans to, try to control their drinking by changing types of liquor, go on the wagon or taking pledges, sneak drinks, lie about their drinking, hide bottles, drink at work or in school. They drink alone, have blackouts. They might drink to relieve severe hangovers or guilty feelings and fears. They fail to eat properly, get cirrhosis of the liver, shake violently, hallucinate, or have convulsions when withdrawing from liquor.

Following is some information I found in the library about drinking. The excerpts from the Big Book, *Alcoholics Anonymous*, are reprinted with permission of Alcoholics Anonymous Services, Inc.

THE PROMISE

For me this is such a great statement that is fulfilled when you stop drinking

1. If we are painstaking about this phase of our developments, we will be amazed before we are halfway through.
2. We are going to know a new freedom and a new happiness.
3. We will not regret the past nor wish to shut the door on it.
4. We will comprehend the word serenity and we will know peace.
5. No matter how far down the scale we have gone, we will see how our experience can benefit others.

6. The feeling of uselessness and self-pity will disappear.
7. We lose interest in selfish things and gain interest in our fellows.
8. Self-seeking will slip away.
9. Our whole attitude and outlook upon life will change.
10. Fear of people and economic insecurity will leave us.
11. We will intuitively know how to handle situations which used to baffle us.
12. We will suddenly realize that God is doing for us what we could not do for ourselves.

Are these extravagant promises? We think not. They are being fulfilled among us, sometimes slowly. They will always materialize if we work for them.

THE TWELVE STEPS OF ALCOHOLICS ANONYMOUS
THE BIG BOOK, PAGE 59

1. We admitted we were powerless over alcohol—that our lives had become unmanageable.
2. Came to believe that a Power greater than ourselves could restore us to sanity.
3. Made a decision to turn our will and our lives over to the care of God *as we understood Him*.
4. Made a searching and fearless moral inventory of ourselves.
5. Admitted to God, to ourselves and to another human being the exact nature of our wrongs.
6. Were entirely ready to have God remove all these defects of character.
7. Humbly asked Him to remove our shortcomings.

8. Made a list of all persons we had harmed, and became willing to make amends to them all.

9. Made direct amends to such people wherever possible, except when to do so would injure them or others.

10. Continued to take personal inventory and when we were wrong promptly admitted it.

11. Sought through prayer and meditation to improve our conscious contact with God, *as we understood Him*, praying only for knowledge of His will for us and the power to carry that out.

12. Having had a spiritual awakening as the result of these steps, we tried to carry this message to alcoholics and to practice these principles in all our affairs."

THE TWELVE TRADITIONS OF ALCOHOLICS ANONYMOUS THE BIG BOOK, PAGE 562

1. Our common welfare should come first; personal recovery depends upon A.A. unity.

2. For our group purpose there is but one ultimate authority, a loving God as He may express Himself in our group conscience. Our leaders are but trusted servants; they do not govern.

3. The only requirement for A.A. membership is to desire to stop drinking.

4. Each group should be autonomous except in matters affecting other groups or A.A. as a whole.

5. Each group has but one primary purpose, to carry its message to the alcoholic who still suffers.

6. An A.A. group ought never endorse, finance, or lend the A.A. name to any related facility or outside enterprise, lest problems

of money, property and prestige divert us from our primary purpose.

7. Every A.A. group ought to be fully self-supporting, declining outside contributions.

8. Alcoholics Anonymous should remain forever non-professional, but our service centers may employ special workers.

9. A.A. as such, ought never be organized; but we may create service boards or committees directly responsible to those they serve.

10. Alcoholics Anonymous has no opinion on outside issues; hence, the A.A. ought never be drawn into public controversy.

11. Our public relations policy is based on attraction rather than promotion; we need always maintain personal anonymity at the level of press, radio and films.

12. Anonymity is the spiritual foundation of all our traditions, ever reminding us to place principles before personalities.

The excerpts from the Big Book, Alcoholics Anonymous are reprinted with permission of Alcoholics Anonymous Services, Inc.

Over the years, I have experienced many medical problems, including a pacemaker, diabetes, cancer and other health issues. Unfortunately, I take over a dozen pills each day and I am on insulin 24 hours a day, so drinking is out. However, I am so glad and blessed that I decided to stop drinking years ago. My life has been wonderful without alcohol.

18. BITS AND PIECES — PLUS SOME COOKING

In this chapter I would like to write about a few happenings that may have been forgotten. There are also a few excerpts that may be of interest and perhaps a few personal thoughts. In addition, I have also included a few comments regarding cooking which curious chefs may find appealing.

Whenever I hear someone described as "larger than life" I shudder. Although we have all heard it used a thousand times, it is actually complete nonsense. Admittedly some people may have accomplished tremendous feats in their lifetimes, they may have achieved fame or made miraculous inventions or discoveries, or even been extremely successful in business, but no one is larger than life. At the end of the day, as my mother used to say, we all go out the same door.

Be smart about your money and how you spend it. Certainly it's okay to be frugal and get the best deal possible, but you should also enjoy your money. Have a good time and have fun along the way; you earned it and deserve it. I learned a long time ago that the last shirt you will wear has no pockets.

I could never understand the phrase "politically correct." Some years ago, Westin Hotels had a seminar in the mountains of Colorado. It was a gorgeous setting and we had a great time. The whole week was spent on political correctness and how to deal with other cultures, or as they called it "diversity." How do you get along with blacks, Europeans, Indians, Asians, or any persons from other cultures? While the basic idea was good, at the end of the week our President asked me what I had learned that week. I looked him straight in his eyes and replied "not much." Shocked, he asked me "how come?" I replied that I had enjoyed the camaraderie and the interactions with the other attendees; however, the message of the seminar was taught to me by my mother when I was a child. She instructed me to respect and like anybody I met whether they were white, black, yellow or whatever. She insisted that all people are the same and that has been my motto ever since.

Adapt, adapt, adapt is another lesson I have learned in life. And boy did I ever have a learning curve! When I came to America I quickly learned that 350 million people were not going to adapt to me, so I had to be the one to change. Initially I worked with Italians during my apprenticeship, then later in Singapore the work mix was 4% Caucasian and over 65% Chinese plus Malaysians, Indians, Pakistanis and whoever else was around.

All over the world I experienced that people can be prejudiced against other folks. I have seen it over and over again; unfortunately, sometimes it is embarrassing to witness. However, there is one place in the world where your background does not matter and that is Hawaii. It is incredible how the Hawaiians accept the different cultures. You hear them say they are one quarter Portuguese, one third Japanese, and have Chinese and Samoan ancestry as well. It is the greatest mixture of people you can find, and they get along just fine most of the time.

Often when I stayed with Mrs. Bachman I went to deliver flowers to the different flower shops in Lugano. One time I had a beautiful flower arrangement to deliver in a little chapel. I had the name of the deceased person and the room I entered was dark with about six or seven caskets. Suddenly I heard a noise and got so scared I grabbed the flower arrangement and threw it in front of the first casket and ran out of the room. I always wondered if the right person got the arrangement or not.

The Savannah Fish Company was a great seafood restaurant at the

Westin Peachtree Plaza. One night a fellow came by and ordered the Savannah fish stew, a great seafood soup. He said it was for Yul Brynner, the actor who was staying at another hotel. When I heard this, I wrote a little note and asked the gentleman to sign it. It said, "In case Mr. Brynner gets ill from the soup, he has no right to blame the hotel for it." He signed it and thought I was crazy. What he did not know was that Mr. Brynner had a lawsuit going with the Plaza Hotel in New York. I remembered that he said he had gotten food poisoning from the food he was eating in the Oyster Bar. At the time when Mr. Carlson purchased the hotel from Sonesta Hotels, the lawsuit came along with the purchase.

Speaking of Mr. Carlson, he was a really wonderful man who wrote me a very nice letter of thanks that I still have. One night, working at the Continental Plaza, I had a guest who had a little too much to drink and proceeded to give me hell all night long. At the end he said he would get me fired as he was a personal friend of Mr. Carlson and threatened to tell him to fire me. By coincidence Mr. Carlson was having dinner in the same dining room. So I told the guest that Mr. Carlson was in the restaurant sitting at the table right across the room and I suggested that we go over there now. The unruly guest suddenly got quiet, paid his bill, and left the restaurant.

On another night at the Chicago Hotel, a party of four gave me trouble, saying that nothing was right and complaining about everything. I took it well, constantly apologizing until one of the fellows wanted to know if I came from Germany. I said no, I was from Switzerland. It was clear to me they gave me a hard time because they were Jewish and thought I was of German descent. When they left the fellow handed me a large tip for the fine service which I refused and told him it was not necessary as it was my job to make certain that each guest leaves happy. Needless to say, they were quite embarrassed.

One night at the Westin Peachtree Plaza a young man and his girlfriend were riding up in the glass elevator. Since it was late at night and they were alone, halfway up the "brilliant boy" got the grand idea to stop the elevator and proceeded to make love to his lady friend. What a terrible decision since all the guests saw it from their rooms and worse yet, the next day it made it to the local papers, something you certainly do not need.

While working in Lugano, I had an affair with the Mistress of Herbert von Karajan, the famous composer and conductor. Understand that I was 21 at the time while she was 41 and he was 63 — quite a difference in years.

As the old adage goes, you should never argue about religion or politics. Looking back on my life, I find it interesting how the different religions can affect people's thinking. When I met Andrea, she was a Catholic, but we married in a Lutheran Church where we also christened our children. In Los Angeles she became a member of the World Wide Church of God, which changed our whole life. I dated many girls of all kinds of different beliefs, which I found interesting and fascinating. On the other hand, I knew people who had converted to the Jewish or Buddhist faiths even though at the time they had been fully committed to their previous faith. I often asked myself if it was love or money and security that made them change or was it a meal ticket. I just could not understand it but did not believe it was "true faith."

All my life I heard the phrase "circle of life," although I never really knew what it meant until I got older. We are getting older and weaker; the body does not quite move how it used to. Left and right people get sick, pass away, and come to sad ends.

In 1963 I went with Dee to Canada and visited her aunt and uncle. They were the nicest people in the world. Uncle Roy took me to an Indian Reservation. I was excited but also disappointed when I saw that everything was in disarray, dilapidated, and in a mess. I could not wait to get out of there. When we got home I had the pleasure of trying on the famous Royal Canadian Mounted uniform with the red coat and the big red high head piece — I looked fantastic.

Prenuptial agreements — whoever heard of such a crazy idea when you are in love? Having been divorced twice already, I believe strongly in these agreements, but love is one thing and divorce is another; better safe than sorry. Audrey and I have one and each of my girls have one but hopefully they will never need them.

Another of my pet peeves is the waste we have in this world, especially the people who live in the developed world. Whether it is throwing away food, wasting water, gasoline, or electricity, whatever it might be, waste is shameful. In fast food restaurants notice what the customers throw away from the paper napkins to the Styrofoam cups and the plastic utensils, all a waste. When you bring home purchases, pay attention to the way items are packaged; again, lots of waste which just generates more garbage. We have millions of inhabitants on this planet who don't even have clean water, proper shelter, or enough food. They go to bed hungry and yet we waste so much. It is sad how much waste is going on in this world each day.

When my kids or grandkids say they want to become rich or win the lottery, I tell them you have already won the lottery. You are lucky to have been born in a great family, in a terrific country, have good parents and never had to go hungry, plus you have a nice home and all the good things you could ever desire. We are lucky to live in the top 5% of the people on this earth. What else could anyone wish for? We have everything we need and all we can pray for daily is to say thank you to the Lord. The most important thing for us is good health, which is something you cannot buy. We have to work for our existence and that is all we need.

My advice to everyone is to travel, travel, travel, as much and as long as you can. I have visited over 60 countries, lived on three continents, from Singapore to Copenhagen, from Casablanca to Winnipeg; from

Sidney to London; from Auckland to Paris; from Jerusalem to Montreal, from Cairo to Casablanca, from Tahiti to Mexico City and from Saigon to Monte Carlo. The world is just absolutely fantastic. The different people, their culture and beliefs, the food and everything that goes with living is just super. I feel so blessed and lucky that I could experience so much. Of course it is not always rosy and sometimes we have some disappointments, but overall it is just great to see the many, many different cities, countries and cultures.

So you are good in your job, you are successful, and you are the big boss, the ultimate master. That is all good and fine; however, never forget who brought you there. We have an obligation to help other people to become successful and none of us would have made it if we did not have help along the way and guidance in our career. Thus, we have an obligation to help other people get there as well. Most of all we have to thank the ones we had the pleasure to work with. They are the ones who made us look good. I would personally like to thank all the many employees I was associated with over the years, the ones who have done an outstanding job in making me look good. Those folks are the ones who deserve the credit for my accomplishments as it is them who did it, not me. Thanks from the bottom of my heart for all the help I received.

Accidents are something else that I have faced due to the fact that I was such a physical and wild kid. I certainly had my share of unfortunate experiences including a broken leg, broken arm, smashed face, broken ribs and numerous broken teeth. I don't know how many times I got injured but it was usually my fault from skiing, riding a bike, motorcycles, bobsleds, sleighs, or playing hockey like most boys do. In the '80s the doctor from the village where I lived as a boy made a trip to the United States and he and his wife stayed in our hotel. It was a wonderful surprise. He saw my name in the hotel's directory and came to see me in my office. The first thing he said was that I was the only patient he ever had over the past 45 years who required three different casts on one broken arm. Each time I left his office I went right back to playing and breaking the new cast. I remember the third cast was so thick that it was unbreakable.

Illness is another issue I have dealt with but most of the time you can't control it when it happens; however, I do believe strongly that the best cure is a positive attitude. My dad was told when he was 33 that he had five months to live; eventually he did pass away at the old age of 85. Thank the Lord I inherited the same attitude from him. I had tuberculosis, heart palpitations because of arterial fibrillation, diabetes for over 40 years requiring insulin 24/7, a pacemaker for eight years which needs to be changed soon, plus cancer twice requiring two surgeries and 39 radiation treatments. As a joke I used to say if I had been a horse, they would have shot me a long time ago. Having a positive attitude regarding an illness helps you make it. The doctors and nurses in the hospitals where I was treated were fantastic and today's medicine can do a lot also.

Credit cards are another hot button for me. I simply cannot understand why people are so stupid and get in trouble with credit cards. The other day I got an American Express bill and it said "new balance $16,199.27 with the minimum payment due of $311.00. If you make no additional charges it will take you 25 years to pay it off and the total of your payments will be $35,030.00." How can anybody be so crazy and live like this? I think it is criminal what some companies do with credit charges. The idea of "travel now, pay later" is another hot button for me. I can't believe someone could have a good time on a trip or vacation when you know you are going to get a bill at the end. It is just too much for me. The ONLY credit I ever used was to purchase a home and I paid that off as soon as I could. Whenever I had a couple of extra dollars I paid it against the loan. Our motto is if we cannot pay for it, we do not buy it. That policy works just great for us.

Coming to this country I had to join the culinary union; however, I was never a fan of unions. Many years ago, unions were necessary because some employers treated their staff terribly. Today unions can be like a cancer. Members and especially union bosses make decisions on how to keep their jobs, not what is right or wrong for the workers. I remember a union steward in Chicago told me he would not allow what I was instructing my employees to do so I told him to get out of my restaurant. Today I feel that unions are not needed as most employers treat their staff right.

Often when I go to Europe my friends tease me about America. They say America is not what it was in 1963 when you immigrated there and I usually reply that neither is Switzerland the same as it was in 1963. Today the whole world seems to be upside down. Make the best of each situation and the world is just ok.

I don't know if I wrote about the UFO Andrea and I saw in San Francisco. It was a nice summer night in 1972 and we went for an evening walk. Suddenly we saw a UFO, an oval light above us that gyrated in rings like ripples in the water when you throw a stone in a lake or pond. It was really something; we got all excited and scared at the same time. We were hiding behind our house when the spaceship moved away and made an unusual noise like "squish." The next day there was a news story about it as many people called in to report it and stories circulated in the newspapers. I must admit I have always believed in UFO's and personally believe there is life on other planets.

My school sweetheart was the daughter of the mayor of our village. He liked me but his wife, Silvia's mother, was against our relationship. Often Silvia told me that her mother said I was not a good man. One night when we were about 17, I brought Silvia home after a date and her mother was waiting behind the front door; that's when all hell broke loose. I was standing outside under the living room window listening. She said, "This Hermann amounts to nothing, he will never get a decent job, he will never make something out of himself," on and on. Silvia was crying. Right then and there I said to myself, yes, Mrs. Mueller I will show you someday what I can do. Years later when there were stories in Swiss papers about my professional activities, I met her and Silvia and she had to admit that I did quite well for myself. I said I guess I was just lucky. Silvia was married but we stayed friends until she passed away with cancer. Now the old lady can look down from heaven and see that Hermann was ok after all.

Skiing was my absolute favorite thing to do before I got too old to participate, so now hiking or walking are my next favorite pastimes. I love hiking in the Colorado Mountains or anywhere is just great. But the very best are the Swiss mountains because you see the cows feeding in the green pastures and the flowers with all their glorious colors including Alpine roses, which are just beautiful. I feel this is the closest to heaven you can get on earth. You hike and your stress levels are gone and you won't need a psychiatrist. The world will look peaceful and nice once again.

How about diets—haven't we all gone through this? The money we spend, the efforts we put in, the gimmicks that are sold to us, it's all just fabulous. You watch the television ads, the message is 15 seconds and the disclaimer is 45 seconds. On the other hand, it is so easy to get proper nutrition, eat a balanced meal, no junk food, not much sugar, no processed foods, and little fats. When I had cancer I was concerned and asked my oncologist what I should eat and his answer was quite simple "If your grandmother could not make it, don't eat it."

We all should have a hobby; we have to find time for it, especially when you are retired. My mom used to do crossword puzzles until she was 85 and she was great at it. When I retired I started oil painting and playing keyboard. Every week I go to class and try to spend close to an hour on the keyboard. All human beings should continue their education as it is important to keep your mind challenged. Nothing could be worse than being a couch potato. Your mind has to be kept busy and exercised. A body in motion stays in motion. Please force yourself to do it.

My dad used to say, "I can, I will, I must." My philosophy is the same; you have got to do it.

In the fall of 1982 I came home from a business trip. It was a really nice fall evening and Margot had made me a nice dinner by the pool. She had a lovely table set up with flowers, an appetizer, plus chicken with wild rice, a vegetable, and a dessert. She even chose nice white wine. As we were eating I commented that I did not know she could cook such a nice meal. Smiling, she admitted she had not personally prepared it. She had picked it up at the Hyatt Hotel. I asked her how much it was and she said $86.00. But instead of saying thank you or how sweet of you, I scolded her. I fumed about how the hell she could spend that much money for a dinner that I could have made for $15.00. She was crushed! Looking back now I must admit I was an absolute jerk. She meant well and worked hard to prepare it and I did not even acknowledge her efforts. It was really shameful of me.

Another pet peeve of mine is when prisoners are in jail for 20 years or more and then they are executed. Personally, I am for capital punishment but do it when the event occurs, not many years later. Our legal system often is ridiculous. Also, the fact that deals can be made with criminals and often judgments are made based on previous decisions. I feel strongly that the European legal system is much better; there, each case is judged separately and not according to previous judgments.

In 1969 I used to go horseback riding quite a lot in Burbank, California. It was on a nice ranch and I had a good time playing cowboy. On one of my riding escapades I fell off the horse, and then the horse got tangled in some trees. I tried to free it and each time I came close to the horse, it started to kick. To my surprise the horse freed itself and ran away. I had to walk back to the ranch which took over an hour. Nervously I told the rancher I was sorry but I had lost his horse. He laughed and said no problem. The horse had come back an hour ago and was back in his stable safe and sound.

On one of my European vacations I visited an old man in the old folk's home. It was Mr. Lehner, the fellow who used to own the bike shop when I was a kid. He was so pleased that I had come to see him that he called for the nurse to come and bragged about me. "Nurse," he said, "you see this young man? When he was a kid he used to put advertising flyers under the windshield wipers on cars for me. He was the most reliable kid you could have." Three weeks after my visit, my mother wrote me in her weekly letter that Mr. Lehner had passed away. My lesson from my visit to Mr. Lehner was never to forget the people who were good to you.

Audrey and I had dinner in Ticino in a very nice local restaurant. Since Audrey does not like boiled potatoes, she asked if she could have some noodles with her broiled fish. The owner said, "No we don't serve noodles with fish as the proper service is boiled potatoes." It is shocking when you think of it that an owner would give such a response. Only in Switzerland could someone be so arrogant like this. Then I ordered Osso Bucco, braised veal shanks which is served with noodles and I just love it. It is one of my favorite dishes and is also the dish I had to make as my final exam as a chef. So Audrey ate some of my noodles and I ate her boiled potatoes. We called the owner back over and Audrey, smiling at him, told him to look at her plate, "You see, I have my noodles with my fish."

OSSO BUCCO RECIPE
(IT MEANS BONE WITH A HOLE IN ITALIAN) 6 SERVINGS)

- 1 sprig Rosemary, 1 sprig fresh thyme, 1 dry bay leaf, 2 cloves
- 3 whole veal shanks (1 lb. per shank) trimmed
- Sea salt and freshly ground pepper
- All purpose flour

- ½ cup vegetable oil
- 1 small onion, diced in 1/2 inch cubes
- 1 small carrot, diced in 1/2 inch cubes
- 1 stalk celery, diced in 1/2 inch cubes
- 1 tablespoon tomato paste
- 1 cup dry white wine
- 3 cups chicken stock
- 3 tablespoons fresh parsley, chopped
- 1 lemon zest, chopped

Pat dry veal shanks with paper towels to remove excess moisture. The shanks will brown better if they are dry. Season each shank with salt and pepper. Dredge the shanks in flour. In a large Dutch oven heat vegetable oil until smoking. Add the shanks and brown all sides, about 3 minutes per side. Remove browned shanks and reserve.

In the same pot add the onions, carrots, celery, rosemary, thyme, bay leaf, cloves, and season with salt & pepper. Sauté about 8 minutes. Add the tomato paste and mix well. Add browned shanks to the pan and add the white wine. Reduce liquid by half about 5 minutes, add 2 cups of chicken stock and bring to a boil. Reduce heat to low, cover pan and simmer for 1½ hours until meat is falling off the bone, check every 15 minutes, and add more chicken stock as needed. Add the chopped parsley. Carefully remove the cooked shanks from the pot and place in a decorative serving platter. Pour all the juices and sauce from the pot over the shanks. Garnish with chopped parsley and lemon zest. Normally served with Risotto, Polenta or Pasta.

Ever wonder how many types of people there are in this world? There's a simple answer: there are three types of people:

There are people who make things happen

There are people who see things happen

Lastly there are people who wonder what the hell ever happened

Naturally we should be the type of people who make things happen!

Lee Iacocca was one of the best industrial managers we ever had in this country. I loved his motto — Lead, follow, or get out of the way. We need more people like this in our business world.

In 1982 we built our dream home. It was beautiful with marble floors, a piano, a great pool and gardens plus a kitchen that had hand painted tiles. We had four fire places, an oak library, exquisite carpets, and nothing but the best throughout. Unfortunately, it ended up as a very nice house but not a home. The soul was missing from it. This is a great lesson for everyone. Don't judge your home by its appointments but ask yourself is it a home, does it have a soul? I am happy to say that every place I have lived in with Audrey has always been a home, not just a nice house. This is so important to me and I am so thankful that we have this.

An old friend called me and said he wanted to join me for lunch. I was concerned and asked him if he needed advice because he was getting a divorce. No, he said, his marital problem had been solved. I was delighted as I was afraid he wanted my advice on the subject. I went through it myself and my advice is whenever possible do not get a divorce. It is not worth it. The grass is always greener on the other side, but it gets cut the same way.

When we opened the Shangri La Hotel in Singapore I invented a new dish, Filet of Sole Shangri La which was fantastic — fish and veal mixed. At first I thought it was crazy to put a fish and a meat on the same plate; during my apprenticeship my boss, the chef, would have kicked me in the butt if I had done that. On the other hand, I figured why not; we serve Surf & Turf in the USA, Lobster and Steak, so we might as well serve Veal and Sole together.

FILET OF SOLE SHANGRI LA

- 1 1/2 oz Veal farce
- 2-3oz filet of sole-stuffed with veal farce folded into paupiettes or just flip over
- 2 chopped shallots
- 1/4 pine white wine
- 1/4 pine fish stock, salt, pepper, lemon juice
- 1 oz diced mushrooms
- 1 oz. diced cucumbers
- 1 slice truffle
- 1/2 roasted almonds
- 2 tbsp. fish Velouté
- 1 oz. butter
- 1/4 cup fresh cream

Butter the bottom of a stainless steel pan intended for the sole, and sprinkle with chopped shallots. Lay in the filet of sole moisten it and add the white wine and some fish stock then poach it gently, basting from time to time. When the sole is poached, drain off the cooking liquid into a pan and reduce it quickly in half by cooking it. Thicken it with the fish Velouté and fresh cream and finish the same with butter (monte).

Garnish: Sauté diced mushrooms and cucumbers separately.

Serve: Coat the sole with this sauce and place garnish on top mushrooms, cucumber, truffle, roasted almonds. Serve with broiled tomatoes, steamed potatoes, parsley and lemon wedge.

How can you pay thousands of dollars for a sporting event ticket on the black market, i.e. Kentucky Derby, Masters, Wimbledon, Super Bowl, etc. Wouldn't it be so much nicer to send the money to a charity and watch it on TV without the hassle? The overpayment of sports athletes is crazy. Although I realize some work hard at perfecting their sporting abilities, a $2,000,000 payday for a weekend golf game or multimillion dollar contracts to ball players whether it is football, soccer or baseball is ludicrous. It has gotten out of hand. I think some of the sacrifices families make just so they can go and see a sporting event are ridiculous. Man-o-man, how have we become so obsessed with sports.

This chapter is not meant to be a synopsis of complaints but an avenue to share some of my feelings and to remind my children and grandkids what life is all about, what is important and what is not. As you get older, everything seems to change 180 degrees. What used to be important is not important anymore and on the other hand what was meaningless or unimportant now becomes important. My first saying each morning is "another day in paradise." I thank the Lord each day for what we have and not what we would like to have.

Long before I was a Sr. Vice President in charge of many hotels I was a foodie, so I think it is appropriate to share some comments I wrote in my training manuals when opening new hotels and getting the staff ready to take care of our guests. I was trained in classical cooking so following are some comments in explaining the classical dishes that I had to learn and some of the background of some of the dishes.

BEVERAGES

Spirits— A spirit is a potable alcoholic beverage obtained by distilling off the essence of an alcohol containing liquid. Spirits mature and improve as long as they are stored in porous containers, usually wood, where the action of the oxygen in the air and the wood of the cask mellow the spirit. However, some spirits do not require aging and are ready for consumption at once, for example: gin, aquavit, vodka, and white fruit brandies like Kirshwasser, Framboise, Mirabelle, etc.

The principal classifications of spirits are: Whiskies, brandies, rums, gins, liqueurs, specialties, and bitters.

Whiskies — are distilled from a fermented mash of grain (usually corn, rye, barley, or wheat) and then aged in oak barrels.

Rums — are distilled from a fermented juice of sugar cane, cane syrup and molasses. It is aged in uncharred barrels where it picks up very little coloring. Dark rums often have caramel added to them for color.

Gins — are distilled from grain and receive their flavor and aroma from juniper berries and other botanicals (every gin producer has his own special recipe).

Vodka — one of the most versatile of all alcoholic beverage, is a highly refined and filtered liquor distilled from any material at or above 190 proof, bottled at no less than 80 or more than 110 proof. It was originally made in Russia from potatoes but in the United States, vodka is usually distilled from grain, primarily corn and wheat.

Liqueurs (Cordials) — The words cordial and liqueur are synonymous, describing liquors made by mixing or redistilling neutral spirits with fruits, flowers, herbs, seeds, roots, plants, or juices which are sweet and colorful, with highly concentrated dessert-like flavor. The following list gives you the name and flavor of the most well-known cordials:

Absinth — Anis seed flavor; contains wormwood
Amer Picon — Biter, orange-flavored, made from quinine & spices

Anisette — Anise seed

Apricot — Apricots

Benedictine — Secret herby formula first produced by Benedictine monks

Blackberry — Blackberries

Cherry — Cherries

Chartreuse — Yellow & green herb liqueurs developed by Carthusian monks

Crème d'Ananas — Pineapple

Crème de bananas — Bananas

Crème de Cacao — From cocoa, vanilla

Crème de Cassis — Black Currant

Crème de Fraise — Strawberry

Crème de Framboise — Raspberry

Crème de Menthe — From mint, peppermint

Crème de Noyaus — From bitter almonds

Crème de Roses — From roses

Crème de Vanille — From vanilla

Crème de Violettes — From violets

Curacao — Orange flavored, made of dried orange peel

Dubonnet — French aperitif wine from aromatics, slight quinine taste

Grenadine — Made from pomegranates, used for flavoring

Kummel — Caraway and anise seeds and other herby flavors

Mandarine — Made from tangerines

Maraschino — Liqueur made from cherries grown in Dalmatia, Yugoslavia

Parfait Amour — Made from violets

Pernod — Anise flavored

Peach — From peaches

Prunelle — From plums

Sloe Gin — A liqueur made from sloe berries from the blackthorn bush

Swedish Punch — Scandinavian liqueur Batavia Arak rum, tea, lemon & spices

Tequila — Aged colorless Mexican liquor from Mescal plant

Triple Sec — Colorless Curacao, but less sweet

Grand Marnière — Finest orange Curaçao liqueur

Cordial Medoc — From brandy, Curacao and Crème de Cacao

Drambuie — Scotch whisky flavored with honey

Tia Maria — Original coffee liqueur

Strega — Spicy aromatic copying the magic witches brew of Benevento

Kahlua — Mexican coffee liqueur

Irish Mist — Spicy whisky & honey liqueur from lost secret formula

Cointreau — Accepted as an outstanding Triple Sec

Galliano — — A fine spicy aromatic liqueur from Livorno Italy named after Major Giuseppe Galliano, a hero defending Fort Enda Jesus near Mekele, which is shown on its label.

BEER

Beer is a brewed and fermented beverage made from water, malted barley, and other starchy cereals, flavored with hops. Beer is a generic term embracing all malt beverages. It should be served cold and you can drink beer with almost any food.

COCKTAILS

The following list tells you the ingredients of the most popular cocktails. It is important to know the basic ingredients of cocktails which are served.

MOST COMMON COCKTAIL INGREDIENTS:

Alexander — Crème de Cocoa, brandy or gin & fresh cream

Americano — Campari, Sweet Vermouth

Amer Picon — Grenadine, Amer Picon

Bacardi Cocktail — Bacardi Rum, Grenadine, fresh lemon juice

Black Russian — Vodka, Kahlua

Bloody Mary — Vodka, Worcestershire Sauce, tomato juice, salt & pepper lemon juice

Blue Hawaii — Rum, pineapple juice, Curacao, sweet & sour mix

Bull Shot — Vodka, cash of Lea & Perrins, cold consommé

Champagne Cocktail — Angostura bitters, sugar cubes, chilled Champagne

Cuba Libre — Lemon wedge, rum, Coca Cola

Daiquiri — Rum, rock candy syrup, fresh lemon juice

Egg Nog — Brandy, bourbon or rum, rock candy syrup, milk, egg, vanilla

Gibson — Gin, vermouth, onions

Gimlet — Vodka, roses sweetened lime juice

Gin Fizz — Gin, lemon juice, rock candy syrup, sparkling water

Gin & Tonic — Gin, fresh lime, tonic water

Golden Cadillac — Galliano, white Crème de Cacao, fresh cream

Grasshopper — Crème de Cacao, green Crème de Menthe, fresh cream

Irish Coffee — Sugar cubes, hot coffee, Irish whiskey, whipped cream

John Collins — Blended whiskey, lemon juice, rock candy syrup

Mai Tai — Rum, Curaçao, orange syrup, lime juice

Kim Royal — Crème de Cassis, Champagne

Martini — Dry gin, vodka, dry vermouth

Moscow Mule — Vodka, lime juice, ginger beer

Old Fashioned — Sugar cubes, angostura bitters, water, blended whiskey

Perfect Manhattan — Blended whiskey or scotch, French vermouth, sweet — Vermouth Angostura bitters

Rob Roy—Blended whiskey or scotch, French vermouth, sweet—Vermouth Angostura bitters

Pink Lady—Dry Gin, lemon juice, grenadine syrup, fresh cream

Pisco Sour—Pisco, lemon juice, rock candy syrup, fresh cream

Planters Punch—Lime juice, orange juice, rock candy syrup, grenadine syrup, Bacardi Amber, Myers Jamaican Rum

Royal Gin Fizz—Dry gin, lemon juice, rock candy syrup, cream, whole egg

Rusty Nail—Scotch, Drambuie

Sangria—Red wine, sugar lemon juice, club soda, fruit garnish

Screw Driver—Vodka, orange juice

Side Car—Brandy, Cointreau, lime juice

Singapore Sling—Gin, sloe gin, cherry herring, grenadine, lemon juice, soda

Silver Fizz—Dry Gin, lemon juice, candy syrup, egg white, cream

Stinger—Brandy, white Crème de Menthe

Tom Collins—Dry gin, lemon juice, rock candy syrup, fresh line

Whiskey Sour—Blended whiskey, lemon juice, rock candy syrup, or sour mix, and maraschino cherry

The above-mentioned ingredients for the cocktails are standard recipes which you can order anywhere in the world and they would taste the same. If any explanations tend to confuse you, rest assured that tasting will amaze you.

A Little Cooking History

Albufera — Duckling with Financiere sauce, truffles, mushrooms

Amiral — Fish dishes, mussels, oysters, crayfish, truffles, mushrooms

Andelouse — Tomatoes (eggs, soup rice)

Anglaise — Carrots, cauliflower, green beans

Bechamel — White sauce, milk, flour, butter

Bonne-Femme — White wine sauce with mushrooms

Bordelaise — Brown sauce with bone marrow

Bourgeoise — Carrots, onions, bacon

Careme — Marie Antoine, French Chef 1784-1833

Cassata — Neapolitan ice cream

Chantilly — Denotes fresh cream beaten to consistency, invented on a farm outside Paris

Chasseur — Mushrooms, brown sauce, shallots

Choron — Artichokes, peas, tomato spiked béarnaise sauce

Curry — Mixture of spices

Chateaubriand — Preparing of beef filet, 1768-1848 Diplomat, Ambassador

Clamart — With peas, tomatoes, artichokes

Dauphinoise — A method of preparing potatoes

Dijon — Capital of Burgundy, mustard

Dubarry (1743-1793) — With cauliflower — Countess, Mistress to Louis XV executed during French Revolution

Duchesse — Garnished with duchesse potatoes

Escoffier Auguste — Famous French Chef 1847-1935

Excelsior — Lettuce braised. Fondantes potatoes

Fines Herbs — Mixture of herbs

Fermiere — Carrots, celery, onions, turnips

Florentine — With spinach

Forestiere — Mushrooms, bacon

Flamande — Brown sauce, vegetables, bacon braised cabbage

Gaspacho — Soup/salad, Spanish, tomatoes, cucumbers, onions

Gnocchi — Semolina dish

Grand-Duc — Asparagus, gray fish, truffles

Henry IV — Chicken Pot — 1553-1610 French King wanted to give a chicken pot each Sunday to all the people

Hongroise — Hungarian style, paprika

Helden — Sauce béarnaise, tomatoes

Indenne — With curry

Jardiniere — Carrots, beans, peas, cauliflower

Judic — Tomatoes farci, lettuce braised, château potatoes

Kebob — Turkish cookery, skewered

Lucullus — Truffles, kidneys, brown sauce, Roman General (110-56 BC)

Lyonnais — Sautéed in butter, onions

Madrilène — Cold soups and broth

Maison — House specialty

Milanese — Tongue, ham, mushrooms, Madeira sauce, cheese

Mirabeau — Anchovies, olives

Montmorency — Cherries — Family name from French nobility

Marengo — Garlic tomatoes, crayfish, brown sauce. Napoleon in 1800 defeated the Austrians

Massena — Artichoke hearts filled with Béarnaise sauce, garnish to meat cuts strips of poached beef bone marrow.

Meuniere — Method of cooking, seasoned. Lightly floured, fried in butter, lemon juice, herbs, etc.

Mimosa — Coarsely chopped hard boiled eggs

Nicoise — Dishes with tomatoes and garlic

Normande — Fish in white wine sauce

Olla-Podrida — Spanish national soup, meats, vegetables

Orly — dipped in batter, fried, lemons, tomato sauce

Oscar — Asparagus, crab legs, béarnaise

Parmentier—Method of various preparation of potatoes (Antoine-Auguste 1737-1817)

Paysanne—Carrots, turnips, onions, celery, lean bacon, potatoes

Peach Melba—Vanilla ice cream, peaches, raspberry puree, whipped cream. (1861-1931) Australian Singer Nellie Melba

Princesse—Asparagus tips

Printanier—Mixture of vegetables

Provencale—Tomato and garlic mixed

Renaissance—Various new vegetables arranged in little neaps used as garnish for roasts

Rossini—With goose liver truffle sauce, truffle slices (1792-1868) Italian Composer

Sicilienne—Filled tomatoes as garnish

Terrine—Earthenware dish in which meat, game and fish are cooked

Tyrolienne—Fried onions, tomatoes Concassees

Vichy—with carrot's vichy

Zingara—Ham, ox tongue, champignons, brown sauce, estragon.

Beef Wellington—Beef with pate fois gras and Duxelle puff pastry

Wellington, Arthur—Duke 1769-1852, English General who was the victor over Napoleon at Waterloo.

19. RETIREMENT

What a lucky fellow I am. How could I be so blessed? Many of my friends and acquaintances worked all of their lives while looking forward to their pensions and they've gotten sick, had health problems, or even worse yet, they've passed away too early. I worked all my life without "working" because I loved my jobs so much. Yes, I worked many long hours and had some ups and downs in my life, but in general it was fun and I always felt as though I was having a great time. For nearly 50 years I was affiliated with cooking, whether in restaurants or in hotels. No challenge was too much because it was fun and a part of the game.

On May 31, 2002, which was my 62nd birthday, my retirement party was held at the Waverly Hotel in Atlanta. My boss from Washington DC sent me a nice telegram of thanks and congratulations. Local business leaders from Atlanta and friends from all over, as well as the wonderful staff of the Waverly, were in attendance. The most important person in my life, my wife Audrey, was there plus my kids and family members. We heard many nice speeches and comments and my Director of Marketing, Al Luciano, presented a movie that was very entertaining. Then Waldo Brun, the retired Executive Chef from Orlando, made a nice presentation. I knew Waldo from Arizona, Los Angeles, and Atlanta. We have been friends since 1966 and it was my pleasure to see him and his wife again. I used to go camping with him and his family in a tent. At one time, the *Atlanta Journal Constitution* wrote a story about the man who could stay at the Presidential Suite at the Westin Peachtree Plaza and the next week could be found roughing it in the woods at Lake Hartwell. Like always at the end of such a celebration, the honoree has to say a few words. The basic theme of my comments was a big thank you to all the people attending and the folks who helped me over the almost 40 years since I had arrived in America. A big thanks to the Waverly staff and to Marriott for the years I had the pleasure to work for them. Then thanks to my kids and my wife Audrey who had helped me so much. The last big thank you was to America, which has been so good to me all these years. I owe America a lot. This country has been fantastic to me. The party was nice, but now the fun of retirement started.

I was out of a job and scared; actually, I was more than scared. All my life it was work, work, work, go, go, go. Now what was I going to do? I asked myself. Was I going to be bored? Well it worked out just fine. I was busy with oil painting, babysitting the grandkids, traveling, and learning to play the keyboard. I kept busy with hotel consulting work, the Rotary Club, planning my next adventure, buying and selling homes, playing the stock market, etc. Soon after my retirement I asked myself how the hell did I ever have time to work before? My life became so fulfilled. On top of it all I had several hospital visits, including surgeries. Retired life definitely was not boring.

I had barely stopped working when an old friend who had been an associate many years ago called me and asked if I would go to Chicago and run a 500 room Holiday Inn for him. Since I liked the fellow, I accepted immediately. Coming from Westin, Stouffer, Renaissance, and Marriott Hotels I think it is fair to say the hotel was a disaster and really needed some TLC (Tender Loving Care). But that was okay and was thus the reason I was there to help get the place back in shape and re-organized.

Holiday Inn is owned by Intercontinental Hotels and since I had never worked for either one of these companies before, I had to learn a lot about their philosophy, procedures, and operating standards. I must admit I was intrigued and had fun doing it. I stayed there for about four months and had a blast. Chicago in the summer is just fabulous. During this time, Sam and Andrea came up for a weekend and then another time I sent Christina airline tickets for her and a friend to visit. Later, Audrey visited for another great weekend. Arnold Levy, the fellow who represented the ownership of the hotel and whom I had known for many, many years, invited us to his house for dinner at his country club. We hired a new General Manager and the hotel was back in proper operating order, so I left, and we took a trip to Europe in the later summer of 2002. Although we owned a condo in Weggis at Lake Lucerne, we could not stay there since we rented it out. We had purchased the home in 1995 and the lady who occupied it at the time feared that we would tell her to move out immediately. She was relieved to learn that we would give her at least six months notice before we wanted to move in. Unfortunately, my honesty and kindness did not work out. I ultimately gave her a one- year notice that we would like to move in. The whole situation ended up in a law suit before we were finally able to move there in 2003. In the meantime, we rented a condo in another complex. We had a second larger place in the same building, but I was so disgusted with the whole scenario that I sold both homes and started to build a new home, which worked out just great. Actually, we wanted to purchase a certain unit in a new development that was the top unit with a fantastic view, but it was already sold. Audrey and I were at the St. Francis Hotel in San Francisco for a Westin Hotel Reunion when she told me that we had a message from the real estate agent letting us know that the unit we wanted was now available. I had missed the message and thanks to Audrey's alertness we were able to message the agent back that we would take the unit. We were fortunate this time since the unit was originally to be purchased by a German businessman, but he had encountered problems with the income tax commission so he had left the country. His troubles became a lucky break for us.

It was during a horrible storm in 2005 that we were able to move into our new home. It was really beautiful with a fantastic view over Lake Lucerne and the Swiss Alps. In the springtime, with the snow-covered peaks, it was just gorgeous. Our summer life was so changed from the winter life in the U.S. We usually moved to Europe in April and came back to the U. S. in October. There is so much to do in the summer time such as playing golf, traveling, numerous lake activities, and especially hiking. When the weather was good we were somewhere on a mountain. The walking trails are absolutely fantastic in Switzerland with everything clearly marked with signage, plus the opportunity for tours is endless. There are numerous restaurants and lodges where you can refresh yourself. The first few years it was also nice to visit with my mother every week; unfortunately, later on it became a sad story. She was able to drive until she was 85, then everything went to hell in a hand basket. She could not take care of herself anymore. Her house and garden were neglected; sadly, we had to put her in a nursing home. That was a story all by itself. It hurts so much and you really suffer with the individual who has to be taken care of. It was especially hard with Mom since she was so stubborn and fought with everything. She did not want to be put in a nursing home where she would have to be cared for. All her life she used to say that being cared for in a nursing home was the last thing she ever wanted to happen to her. She used to think her sister Aunt Heidi was confused and stubborn, but now she was in the same boat. At the beginning it was okay, and I think she finally realized she really needed the help. Later, when she was wheelchair bound and it was nice weather, during my visit I was able to take her out in the garden for a walk and my brother Peter with his wife Lotti did the same thing. She did not say much anymore, but we could talk to her. She was well liked in the nursing home because she never complained and appreciated the help she received. But for a woman who had worked so hard all her life, first as a child on her parent's farm, then later when she was married, where she took care of so many of us, it was not easy for her to be catered to. She loved her independence in her earlier life and had such a nature of giving and helping others but now she felt so helpless. I must say she had a nice room and the nursing home was really well managed. They took care of their patients but at over $10,000 a month, they had to. Her room was nice and I painted her a picture of flowers so she has "permanent" flowers. Also, I displayed some nice family photographs for her. The nursing home had all kinds of activities and one time on my visit there was a keyboard entertainer whom I really liked because of the type of music he played. So, during his lunch break I talked to him and said I was 70 years old, but would I still be able learn to play the keyboard? He said you can learn at any age, as long as you are interested. He gave me the address of Peter Dennler in the Italian part of Switzerland who has a music school. So in my "old age" I courageously contacted him. He told me that he had a free spot in a couple of months, so I signed up. What a nice addition this became to my retirement life. For the past few years each summer I make the trip to Riva San Vitale at Lake Lugano, a village of about 2610 inhabitants. It is first mentioned in 774 as Primo Sobenno and subsequently in 1115 it was known as Ripa Santi Vitalis. Because of many Roman era finds, it appears that there was a significant Roman settlement here. The place has a lot of history as well as famous churches. The parish church of St. Vital is first mentioned in 962-966; however, it likely dates back to the Christianization of the southern foothills of the Alps. It is the oldest church in Switzerland although I think there are other churches much prettier. I visit the parish church of St. Vitale each summer and light candles for Oma and Opa, my parents, as well as Mother Andrea, and Parker, Audrey's former husband, and her son who were killed in a plane crash.

Now let's talk about the music school, which is located in a house that is over 500 years old. Peter Dennler was able to purchase the house because he was committed to operate a music school. It was stipulated in the testament from the former owner who happened to be a famous conductor and musician that it must remain a music house. Needless to say, with a 500-year old home you have some electrical, water, etc. challenges. Of course, the home had no air conditioning and in the summer it can get quite hot. It has three guest rooms and the students must share one small toilette and shower. So, we all have to agree who takes a shower when. For me it is easy since most students like to sleep in; however, I go for a walk at 6am due to my diabetes so I am always the first one to take a shower. Breakfast is included in the room rate and it is rather good. From muesli to eggs, a croissant, bread and butter, granola bars, and fruit choices, breakfast is as good as many hotels. At 9am the first lecture starts, then at 10am Peter gives a talk, then back to practice and later we enjoy a coffee break. At noon we go to lunch on our own. I usually take a 15-minute nap followed by more playing and a lecture, then an afternoon coffee break. At 5pm we stop and meet for a drink. Peter and his wife prefer beer while others enjoy wine. We are on our own; however, three times a week Peter invites us for a round. For me it is always Diet Coke since I don't drink alcohol. After this break, the students go for dinner together. Some of them are good drinkers but a few of the students were not able to make it for the morning session; I guess that is just part of growing up. We have students in their early 20s all the way up to their 80s. There are Swiss, Germans, Austrians, and Americans; a really funny, mixed up group of folks from beginners to professional musicians. Peter is a real genius when it comes to music. He studied at the conservatorium and had been a bandleader in a well-known Swiss circus. His wife Este is also a musician; together they do a great job of hosting the weekly classes. There are 4 to 5 students per week, so Peter really has time to coach his students. For me the music week is therapy and I really have a great time. It gives me time to relax and learn something, plus I always loved being in Ticino, the Italian part of Switzerland. I have many, many fond memories from the army when I lived there. Also, it gives me an opportunity to see Verena and her husband Rene and Freddy, brother of Verena and an old army buddy of mine. I hope I can go many more years to participate in this program.

One thing is different in retirement; I don't look out for the "fastest gun" anymore. As I said before, when I was a kid I loved cowboys, cowboy movies and stories. In the early years it was always the same theme—a stage coach robbery, a bank robbery, or a train robbery and at the end of the movie there was the final shootout between the good fellow and the bad guy with exciting music, many people around, and lots of drama and commotion. Then the final shot and the person with the fastest gun survived. So, all my life I have adopted this stupid philosophy to look out for the "fastest gun," so to speak. When working with fellow managers, bosses, clients, vendors, and other hoteliers I always felt in competition to be faster, smarter, etc. It might sound crazy, but thank God this sense of competition is over. Life is more relaxed and fun. I don't have to compete anymore. Today it is happy-go-lucky, which is a pleasant and rewarding feeling and a nice life style.

It was the spring of 2003 when my friend Arnold Levy called me and asked if I would run the 800 room Marriott Airport Hotel for him. With similar problems to the hotel in Chicago, I said yes since I needed some pocket spending money to go to Switzerland. For four months I was in Orlando and while we did have our challenges, it was by far not as bad as it was in Chicago; different problems but manageable. The company who was supposed to operate the hotel was a group of hotels and the management person for this company was a fellow who worked for me at the Plaza in New York, as well as at the Detroit Plaza Hotel where we got along well. Arnold was a tough and demanding Jewish boy who was not easy to please, but he was smart and knew what he wanted. So my longtime relationship with him helped to smooth things over between the management company and the owner group represented by Arnold. The best thing about the assignment was the weekly meeting in the Rotary

Club at the Bay Hill Country Club and admiring the flight attendants from Virgin Airlines. They stayed with us and since they came from London, they spend most of their time in bikinis down at the pool. Although we had multiple problems, I had fun running the hotel. I was also able to make some side trips to Naples, Captiva Island. Best of all I had the opportunity to enjoy dinner with Waldo and his lovely wife, who at the time were retired and living in Orlando. Yes, hotel business is fun when you have a nice property, interesting owners and lovely associates with whom to work.

I asked Audrey to plan a trip to Greece where I figured after we spent the summer in Switzerland, we would fly Andrea and her husband, plus Christina who was still single, and Audrey's daughter from Australia to meet us in Switzerland. We would spend a few days together and then have a vacation in Greece. Needless to say, the kids were all excited and expected to spend all their time at the beach. However, the old man, me, felt they could always be on the beach in Australia and America. We planned a culture trip with many old ruins, historic sites, museums, and Olympic sites where the Olympic Games had taken place.

Greece, even with all its disorganization and money problems, is a fascinating country. Its history is certainly unique. Greece is in southeastern Europe with thousands of islands through the Aegean and Ionian Seas. Influential since ancient times, it is often called the cradle of Western civilization. It is also officially known as the Hellenic republic. The population of Greece is close to 11 million. It has the longest coast line in the Mediterranean basin and the 11th longest coast line in the world at 8,498 miles in length, featuring a vast number of islands of which 227 are inhabited. 80% of Greece is mountainous, with Mount Olympus being the highest peak at 9,572 feet.

We also spent time in Athens, which was absolutely upside down since it was 8 weeks prior to the Athens Olympics. Everybody said they will not be ready, but of course they were prepared and all went well. It is like opening a new hotel three days before opening and everyone says, they can't open; then like magic, everything falls into place. We planned our trip with Kuoni, a famous Swiss travel agency who did a great job. Audrey and I have taken several other trips with them to Dubai and other places. Our Travel Guide was a German fellow who spoke excellent English, which was important to everyone but me. We had a nice bus and a great driver. Our vacation started in Athens where we saw different sites, especially old historic buildings and venues related to the upcoming Olympics.

One night we spent at Plaka, which is an old historical neighborhood of Athens. It is clustered around the slopes of the Acropolis. Plaka is built on top of the residential areas of the ancient town of Athens. It is known as "the neighborhood of the Gods." Plaka is visited each year by hundreds of thousands of tourists. It is a real fun place with numerous restaurants, bars, night clubs, shops and boutiques and is a "must see" when visiting Athens, a very special place. We spent a great evening at a lovely Greek diner and enjoyed lots of wine. The "Ouzo N nia Seink" helped us to generate some excitement, especially for Sam who loved the anis flavored aperitif which is widely consumed in Greece and around the Mediterranean. It is similar to pernod, sambuca, arak, and raki. What an unforgettable evening we all had with laughter and fun. No visit to Greece is complete without a visit to the Acropolis in Athens, an ancient citadel located on an extremely rocky outcrop above the city. It contains the remains of several ancient buildings of great architectural and historic significance. We learned that it is designated an UNESCO Heritage Site with evidence that it was inhabited way back to the fourth millennium BC. We also were informed that it was Pericles, a prominent influential statesman, who coordinated the construction of the sites of the buildings in 495-423 BC in the fifth century BC. He subsequently died in 429.

We spent most of our trip in Peloponnese which is a peninsula in

Southern Greece. It is the location of the city of Olympia, which hosted the first Olympic Games in 776 BC. Our "Historic Greek Tour," which we did instead of the expected 10 days on the beach, had come to an end. It was a fabulous trip, and the drive through the country and all the many things we had seen and experienced were memories no one will ever forget. Even the kids by this time were convinced that it was better than just laying around on the beach.

After flying back to Switzerland, the kids spent a few days with us then had to go home. I told Audrey, "Schatzi" (which means little sweetheart in Swiss), "now we are alone and will enjoy the summer and have a real restful vacation." Well that lasted only three days, then I received an e-mail from an old friend of mine, wanting to know where I was. He said he had tried to contact me in Atlanta for several days but got no answer and the answering machine said my mail box was full. I gave him a call in Paris, where he was living at the time while working for Dolce Hotels as Vice President. They had a property in Bad Nauheim near Frankfurt which was owned by George Soros. According to Andy, they had to fire the General Manager and the hotel was in disarray. He asked me since I had lived in Germany and knew the European mentality, plus spoke the language, if I could help run the hotel, get it stabilized and find him a new General Manager. I said I would be happy to and inquired as to when he needed my help. His response was he needed me the next day so off I went.

The hotel was a conference center in Bad Nauheim called Park Hotel. It was located in a beautiful park setting and the address was One Elvis Presley Drive. During his Army time in Germany, Elvis Presley lived in Bad Nauheim and had quite an influence on his German fans. Even today each year they have an Elvis Presley Festival. Bad Nauheim is a world-famous resort noted for its salt springs, which are used to treat heart and nerve diseases. It is famous for its Bathhouse Row. The city is located 22 miles north of Frankfurt am Main on the east edge of the Taunus Mountain range. It has many hotels, bathhouses, clinics, restaurants, shops and boutiques. The walking trails are very unique and when you move around Ban Nauheim there is a feeling of serenity, with a healthy spa atmosphere and an overall sense of healing and well-being.

The Park Hotel had large and well-appointed rooms with nice conference and restaurant facilities. We had a Department Head Meeting and it did not take me long to find out that there were a lot of unhappy employees. There were two camps: one party was glad that the General Manager was gone and the other party complained about his release. I sensed that a Mrs. Rohde, supposedly a very influential lady in the community, was angry at the owners and the management company. Everyone referred to Mrs. Rohde as the "mayor's wife." She was real "poison" if you believed only half of what the people said about her. I figured the only way I could get to the bottom of this story was to meet with Mrs. Rohde myself at the so-called mayor's office, so I asked her if she would have lunch with me. The next day a lady returned my call and agreed to meet with me in the Plantation Room at the hotel. A nice-looking woman showed up, well dressed and elegant, and introduced herself as Mrs. Rohde. We had a delightful conversation where we spoke about the hotel, my background, what I wanted to do with the hotel and its employees. I just could not understand how people could have the audacity to call this woman an absolute bitch. Then she looked at me and said "I think you have the wrong Mrs. Rohde." Surprised by her response, I asked her what she meant by that. Still smiling, she replied that although she had been married to the mayor for 10 years, I should probably be speaking with his former wife. It turned out she was right; however, in the future she and her husband, the mayor, became very close with Audrey and me and grew to become a delightful relationship. My next mission was to schedule a meeting with the other Mrs. Rohde which turned out to be an angry and hostile meeting. Thank God I did a Dale Carnegie training course many years ago and read his book

"How to Win Friends and Influence People" and learn about the idea I never met a person I did not like. At the beginning of our lunch this lady was very, very nasty, talking about how bad Dolce Hotels was, and how bad the hotel's management company was. She thought the former General Manager was a Dutch fellow who could do no wrong. She said he looked like a Greek god and was absolutely wonderful and was highly respected in the city. Boy, what an earful I got. I just listened and said yes and let her talk. A few days later I invited her for cocktails and our conversation was a bit more civil. A month went by and I had a much better understanding of the hotel, its status in the city, and what was going on in general. Then there was a big concert put on by a famous Italian singer named Albano Carrisi. I invited Mrs. Rhode, the troublemaker, to come to the concert with me since we were one of the sponsors. All went well. Mrs. Rohde, the troublemaker, introduced me to several of her friends as the General Manager of the hotel. Of course the pleasant Mrs. Rohde was there too with her husband, the mayor. She just smiled and said she was happy to see I was making progress. Today, looking back, I can only say it was funny and fun at the same time.

We had fun all that summer. The owners paid for one employee but they got the work of two. Audrey was with me in Bad Nauheim and she got very involved. She gave training classes to the housekeeping department. We had lots and lots of geraniums around the terrace. Each day she worked several hours cutting the flowers and by the end of the summer we had the most beautiful geraniums in the city of Bad Nauheim. I will never forget a dinner Audrey and I had with the Director of Housekeeping and her supervisors. These poor employees were continuously beaten up by the management, harassed about labor costs and the cost of guestroom supplies. Audrey broke bread with them and thanked them for a job well done. These employees dressed up and were so appreciative for the nice evening my Schatzi gave them.

One day I went to the old storerooms and found an absolute priceless menu from the hotel's opening. What a great find it was. Items on it were listed such as Beefsteak Tartar $2.20; Italian Salad $.90, Consommé $.40, Oxtail Soup $.60, Poached Salmon $3.00, Grilled Sole $2.50, Scrambled Eggs $1.20, Lamb Chops with Beans $2.00, Veal Brain $1.80, Rump steak $2.00, Veal Liver with Bacon, $1.80, Green Salad $.40, Peach Melba $1.20, Omelet Surprise $1.60 — all these prices were in D Marks, 1 DM was about 50 cents US at the time. One of our major customers in Frankfurt cancelled all future meetings with us because of bad service in the past. It was no fun, but I had several sessions with the customers from this accounting firm. We finally convinced them to come back and have their seminars with us. It was not all just work. We had some good times with Andy and his family when they visited us from Paris. Also, Audrey and I made some trips to Weggis to check on our apartment. Then the best trip we had was a weekend in Holland. We visited one of our sister hotels which was a castle and turned out to be one of the best hotels stays I ever enjoyed. It was so romantic and the food was fantastic. The summer went by fast, but our Bad Nauheim time came to an end. We hired a new General Manager and they all gave Audrey and me a very nice going away party. We returned to Switzerland for a few days to close up our summer home when we went back to Atlanta for the winter.

We decided to take a golf trip to Austria where Audrey and I went alone the first time. We enjoyed a nice trip through the Tyrolean Alps which brought us to Elmau. It is in the District of Kufstein and is a winter and summer resort town. Elmau is in a very picturesque alpine countryside famed for its proximity to the Wilder Kaiser Mountains and the steep wooded and meadow hills to the south. The village is a very popular spot for winter and summer activities. In the summer it is a golf paradise with nice courses. We purchased a package deal at the Föhrenhof Hotel, a delightfully charming place. It is a family operated hotel with the rooms decked out in Austrian décor, featuring a cozy restaurant with warm, friendly service and outstanding food. The Chef is the owner of the hotel and "Mama" as I called her is the heart of the operation. We had a super time there on our first trip. Then the year after we made the same tour and golf package with Jenny and George Mummenthalers, our close friends from Heuneburg. George took a different route than Audrey and I had, and we went through the Swiss National Park. I must admit I had never been there before. It is located in the Western Rhaetian Alps and is within the Canton of Graubuenden in the Engadin Valley on the border with Italy. It is part of the worldwide UNESCO Biosphere Reserve. In the park, one is not allowed to leave marked paths, make fire, or sleep outside or do camping. It is also forbidden to disturb the animals or the plants, or to take home anything found in the park. Dogs are not allowed, not even on a leash. It is really a unique piece of real estate. Our stay in Elmau and the Föhrenhof Hotel was outstanding like before. The family was extra nice and accommodating to us since we were repeat guests. The golf was not the greatest since none of us were great golfers but just walking through the beautiful course with the background of the Wilder Kaiser Mountains was breathtaking.

Another super trip we made with the Mummenthalers was a vacation to the South Tyrol, a province of North Italy, set in a valley amid hilly vineyards. It is the gateway to the Dolomite Mountain Range in the Italian Alps. In the medieval city center, the South Tyrol Museum of Archaeology features a Neolithic mummy called Oetzi, the Iceman. We visited Oetzi where he lived around 3300 BCE and the experts think he died between 3239 and 3105 BCE. The mummy was found in September 1991 in the Oeztal Alps. He is Europe's oldest known preserved human body. I must say looking at him was worse than looking at Ho Chi Minh in Vietnam and believe me when I say that was no pleasure to see him in his coffin. We stayed in Merano during this trip. Again, it was just a very charming city where we stayed in a nice hotel. While we were there, since I had no smartphone, Jenny showed me how to use her smartphone and she got me hooked.

Unusual about the area are the number of apple orchards. There are thousands and thousands of apple trees. You can go to farms and try different types of apples; I had no idea there were so many different of apples. We just had a ball and lots of fun. In addition to the apples, Merano is also known for its spa resorts. It is located in a basin, surrounded by mountains standing up to 10,942 feet. The whole area of South Tyrol is in Italy but it is much cleaner than Italy. The people are very friendly and courteous however most of them speak German rather than Italian.

Since we are talking about trips we made with George and Jenny Mummentaler, I have to write about our river cruise in France. We went by train from Zurich to Geneva, where we met them. By bus we went on to Lyon, France which is located in the historical Rhone-Alps Region. It sits at the junction of the Rhone and Saone Rivers. It is the third largest city in France with about half a million population. It is right after Marseille and Paris. The city is famous for its cuisine and gastronomy as well as historical and architectural landmarks. It is another of the UNESCO World Heritage Sites. In Lyon we boarded a riverboat operated by a Swiss company. The boat was elegant and held about 120 passengers. The rooms were tastefully decorated with private balconies. Service and food were very good with no complaints from us. River cruises are so different from the large ocean cruises where you have thousands of guests. We started our trip at night and floated on the Rhone River toward the junction of the Saone River. Then it took us north toward Macon and Beaune. These two cities are world famous wine cities in the well-known wine regions. I have visited this area earlier in my life when I was enjoying wine at its finest. We then went back south into the Rhone River. While we experienced a lot of nice landscaping and villages, the best were the following three cities that absolutely fascinated us—Châteauneuf-du-Pape, Avignon, and Arles have so much history and are so well known all over the world.

Châteauneuf-du-Pape—A commune in the Provence-Alpes cote d'Azure Region. A medieval ruin of a castle sits above the village and dominates the landscape to the south. It was built in the 14th century for Pope John XXII, who was the second of the popes to reside in Avignon. Almost all of the cultivatable land is planted with grapevines. The community is famous for the production of red wines; also, some white wines are produced in the region as well. The wines are classified as Châteauneuf-du-Pape Appellation D'origine Controlee which is produced from grapes grown in the commune of Châteauneuf-du-Pape and in portions of four adjoining communes. The village as I call it has a population of less than 2300 people, a relatively small town, but it has a tremendous history and is important in the wine production of France. We visited a wine estate that was just fabulous. At a local romantical yet historical building they hosted tasting rooms, a wine shop and hundreds of barrels filled with red wine. Even though I do not drink alcohol, I went to the tasting to see all the production, to listen to the talk and to enjoy the atmosphere. It definitely was an unforgettable experience. We enjoyed our experience driving through thousands of acres of planted grapes and seeing how they are carefully tendered to by the vintners; it was just unique seeing nature at its best. You have the opportunity to witness dedicated workers in their fantastic landscapes and know there is a God who oversees all this beauty.

Avignon—Eight miles south of Châteauneuf-du-Pape is the lovely city of Avignon. Who has not heard the romantic melody written by Giovanni Paolo Martini "Plaisir D'Amour"? Even I play this song sometimes with my keyboard. When we were in Avignon it was a sunny day with a blue sky and the tour guide made an announcement that the captain had a surprise for us. Our ship was in front of the Pont Saint-Benezet, also known as the Pont D'Avignon. This is a famous medieval bridge in the town of Avignon in southern France. Then the music started playing "Plaisir D'Amour" and the ship started a slow 380-degree turn. What a wonderful site it was! Avignon has a population of over 90,000 inhabitants with about 12,000 of those living in the ancient town center enclosed by its medieval ramparts. Between 1309 and 1377 during the Avignon Papacy, seven successive popes resided in Avignon and in 1348 Pope Clement VI bought the town from Joanna I of Naples. Papal control persisted until 1791, when during the French Revolution it became part of France. Needless to say, when I learned all this, it was a big surprise to me as I was under the assumption that all Popes always lived in the Vatican in Rome. I had no idea about this piece of history. The historic center, which includes the Palais des Papes, the cathedral, and the Pont D'Avignon, became a UNESCO World Heritage Site in 1995. The medieval monuments and the annual Festival D'Avignon have helped to make town a major center for tourism. The Palais des Papes, a historical palace in Avignon, is one of the largest and most important medieval gothic buildings in Europe. After the popes left it went through several changes and a multitude of historical happenings. The Palais is today a palace of culture and primarily a tourist attraction. It is attracting around 650,000 visitors per year putting it regularly in the top ten most visited attractions in France. With all the historical hoopla of Avignon I must write down that my favorite French singer was Mireille Mathieu, who was born in Avignon. She was the eldest daughter of a family of 14 children. The Mathieu family lived in poverty; however, all that changed with Mireille's success in singing. She has recorded over 1,200 songs in eleven languages, with more than 150 million albums sold worldwide. I have seen the "Spatz of Avignon," as we call her in Germany, in many performances; Spatz, which is German, means sparrow in English. Each time I am fascinated by her performance and talent.

Arles — Our trip continued in Arles which is located close to Marseille and the Mediterranean Sea. Once again it is a city of magnificent buildings, great architectural beauty, and features parks containing magnificent gardens with a population of about 52,000 inhabitants. Arles has been historically and economically important since Roman times. In the modern era, Arles remained economically important for many years as a major port on the Rhone. In the 19th century, the arrival of the railway diminished river trade, which brought a big change to the city and caused the town to become something of a backwater. This made it an attractive destination for the painter Vincent van Gogh who arrived in Arles on February 21, 1888. He was fascinated by the Provencal landscapes, producing over 300 paintings and drawings during his time in the city. Many of his most famous paintings were completed in Arles including *The Night Cafe*, *The Yellow Room*, *The Starry Night,* and others. It was Paul Gauguin who visited van Gogh in Arles. However, van Gogh's mental health deteriorated and he became alarmingly eccentric, culminating in the ear-severing in December 1888 which resulted in two stays in the Old Hospital of Arles. The concerned citizens circulated a petition the following February demanding that van Gogh be confined in a home, just like Cesar Ritz was. However, van Gogh took the hint and left Arles for Saint Paul Asylum at nearby Saint-Remy de Provence. As an "amateur" painter, I was always fascinated by van Gogh. In the short visit to Arles I saw as much as I could about van Gogh. Just think, he sold only one painting in his life, and that was to his brother. Today his paintings bring in hundreds of millions of dollars at auction. Such is life I guess.

After Arles we moved back up to the Rhone River toward Lyon and then back home to Switzerland. This trip with Jenny and George Mummentaler was just an outstanding experience that left us with more great memories.

Each summer we somehow tried to take a special trip somewhere like hiking in the mountains or taking painting classes for a change of scenery. It turned out I was usually the only fellow in a class with a dozen women which was okay. My painting classes in Switzerland were good but I did not learn as much as in my winter classes. In Europe we could do whatever our hearts desired whether it was pencil, oil, watercolor, charcoal, or gouache. The subject matter was also up to us to decide. We had a fun group where the classes were held from 2-5 pm Thursday afternoons with a coffee break. Most of the time of the ladies brought cookies or homemade baked goods. Also, at times we painted outside, weather permitting. One time we visited a mountain resort where one of the participants had a vacation home. Terry, our instructor, was a very nice lady who in her younger years had spent a few months in the USA with her husband. However, I must say that our winter classes with Chris di Domizio were more educational since there we had a strict program. You had to do what you were told. With Chris you had to obey. Chris is an outstanding painter and kept telling us of all his studies in Italy, how good he is and that he is one of the best painters in the world. I think he is the kind of instructor where you have to be able to take some of his nonsense or you will not make it. I must say over the years I have come to really enjoy the classes. I think for me it is a certain therapy going to art school. I don't have to do it to make a living, so the classes can be fun for me, plus as I mentioned before I like Chris and his wife JoDette. One spring, Audrey and I went with Chris's group to Italy where we stayed in Bellagio and Venice. We held classes in the morning then enjoyed a great dinner each evening. We joined the group from Switzerland since we spent the summer there and had our own car.

One year, during our summer outing in Europe, we took a trip with Twerenbold Travel Agency and went to Corsica and Sardinia. Twerenbold has fantastic buses with beverage service and toilettes and they are very luxurious. The trips are very comfortable, with stops every 2-3 hours to visit a local café. We started in Lucerne and went through the Gotthard Tunnel and on to Italy to Livorno, an Italian port city on the west coast of Tuscany. We boarded a ship with our bus, enjoyed dinner, and went to our cabin to sleep. After an overnight cruise, we landed in Sardinia. This is a large Italian island in the Mediterranean Sea. It has 2,000 km of coastline with sandy beaches and a mountainous interior crossed with hiking trails. Its rugged landscape is dotted with thousands of "Nuraghi," mysterious Bronze Age stone ruins shaped like beehives.

I was absolutely fascinated by the fact that in earlier times the land in the area of the Costa Smeralda in Sardinia was divided by the families. The men in the family took the land in the inner portion of the island since it was worth much more than the coastal land. They could use it to develop farms and industrial projects. The girls in the family would get the worthless rugged coastland. Then in 1961 development started and was financed by a consortium of companies led by the Prince Karim Aga Khan. With the development of tourism, the "worthless land" became a very expensive commodity overnight. Today Costa Smeralda is the most expensive location in Europe. Home prices reach up to $392,200 per square meter. Each September the Sardinian Cup sailing regatta is held off the coast. Polo matches are held between April and October, along with other attractions which include a film festival and vintage car rallies.

We next moved south of Sardinia to Cagliari, the capital of the island of Sardinia, which has a population of about 155,000. Cagliari is an ancient city with a long history which has seen a rule of several civilizations. Today, however, the city is a regional, cultural, educational, political, and artistic center known for diverse Art Nouveau architecture and several monuments. It is Sardinia's economic and industrial hub, having one of the biggest ports in the Mediterranean Sea, an international airport, and a high per capita income. After driving through the beautiful landscape, we reached Alghero in the northwest of the island. This town of more than 44,000 is in the Italian insular province of Sassari. Many of the inhabitants descend from Catalan conquerors from the end of the

Middle Ages when Sardinia was part of the Crown of Aragon. This is why the Catalan language is the co-official language in the city, unique in Italy, taking the name of the Algueres dialect.

After an overnight stay our bus moved eastward to Olbia, the most northern city of Sardinia. Olbia is very ancient and was possibly founded by the Greeks. It is the economic center of this part of the island and is very close to the famous Costa Smeralda tourist area. It is a dynamic city which presents itself as a tourist destination due to the beautiful seas, beaches, and for the large number of places of cultural interest to visit. In Olbia we loaded our bus on a boat and floated north to Corsica where we landed in Bonificio. Of course Corsica is an island that belongs to France. A single chain of mountains makes up two thirds of the island. Napoleon was born in 1769 in the Corsican capital of Ajaccio. His ancestor's home, Maison Bonaparte is today used as a museum. The baroque 16th century Notre Dame Cathedral, where Napoleon was baptized, contains paintings by Delacroix and Tintoretto. In Aljaccio you can also find the Aljaccio Napoleon Bonaparte Airport, which is the main base of the regional airline Air Corsica. Bonifacio is located at the southern part of the Island of Corsica. It has a lovely harbor and is the French leg of the Red Bull Cliff Diving World Series. The unique charm and proximity to idyllic beaches makes it a popular tourist destination in the summer, predominately for residents of mainland France.

Calvi was our next stop, a town on the northwest coast of Corsica. The city is well known for its great beaches and its crescent shaped bay. A large medieval citadel overlooks the gorgeous blue marina. Lovely restaurants and cafes line the harbor on the quai. According to legends, Christopher Columbus supposedly came from Calvi, which at the time was part of the Genoese Empire; however, this has not been proven.

Our last stop in Corsica was Bastia. It is located in the northeast of the island. Bastia is the principal port of Corsica and is its principal commercial town, famous for its wines, with about 10% of the population being immigrants. Unfortunately, the commune persistently has one of the highest unemployment rates in France. The city is located 22 miles away from the northern tip of the Cape Corse, 31 miles west from Elba, an Italian island where Napoleon was imprisoned and 56 miles away from the continental Italy, which can be seen a few days per year when visibility is excellent. Once again, we loaded our bus on a boat and made the short trip to the mainland. Through northern Italy we went back to Lucerne. It was an excellent trip and Twerenbold Travel did a great job and we want to plan another journey with them. Next time we will visit Croatia, we decided.

Being a bit more familiar with Twerenbold by this time, we again met in Lucerne behind the main station. Our bus took off on a beautiful day under a warm blue Swiss sky; it could not have been more perfect. The same route we took toward Italy, a last café stop, and then over the border in the direction of Bergamo, Udine, and the country of Slovenia. As we got into Slovenia, I felt this is not the richest country. I am sure there are wonderful places, but we basically just hit the highway toward Croatia. The Republic of Slovenia today is independent, but of course for many years it was under Yugoslavia together with many other countries which today are independent. President Josip Broz Tito ran Yugoslavia with an iron hand after the revolution from 1940 until his death in 1980. As a teenager I remember well of the great power of Tito. I give him credit that he had the ability to keep the country together for many years. Slovenia is a very mountainous country with great ski resorts. It is surrounded by Italy, Austria, Hungary, and Croatia to the south. We stopped in Umag, where we stayed several nights and then took day trips to different destinations. Umag is a city in Croatia's Istrian Peninsula. It is a coastal city and is quite pretty and known as a tourist destination. The city has a population of about 13,000 and is certainly multi-ethnic. Croats comprise a majority of the population at 59.6%, Italians 18.3%, Serbs 3.8%, Bosnians 1.7%, with Albanians and Istrians making up the rest. The Republic of Croatia is a sovereign state with its capital being Zagreb. Croatia's Adriatic Sea coast contains more than a thousand islands. Beside tourism, the country has a great agriculture business well-known for its' olive plantations. One day we had an outing to an olive farm, which was fabulous. Acres of land, as far as the eye can see, leaves you fascinated by the olive trees or bushes. I had no idea there were so many different types of olives. Of course a big part of the olive is in the pressing of olive oils. That is a science all by itself. Sometimes I think it is partially a marketing idea to get more money for their products. Naturally we had tastings of olives and olive oils. It was quite an interesting and a colorful festive experience.

Visiting the Brijuni Islands of Croatia was definitely the highlight of our trip to Croatia. These are a group of fourteen small islands in the Croatian part of the northern Adriatic Sea. They are separated from the west coast of the Istrian Peninsula. The history of the islands is fascinating. The islands had some ancient Roman settlements and used to belong to Venice from the Middle Ages. Then they were part of the Illyrian Provinces after Napoleon's brief annexation. In 1815 the island became part of the Austrian Empire, which later became Austria-Hungary. After World War I ended in 1918, Brijuni became part of Italy. After World War II, the Brijuni islands became part of Yugoslavia and President Marshall Josip Broz Tito made the main Brijuni island his personal State Summer Residence. This part of the island's history is what I find so fascinating and it is the reason I enjoyed my visit so much. Tito asked Slovenian architect Joze Plecnik to design a pavilion for him which ultimately became Tito's home and palace. Almost one hundred foreign heads of state visited Tito on his island home along with many stars who came to visit Tito in Brijuni including Elizabeth Taylor, Richard Burton, Sophia Loren, Carlo Ponti, Gina Lollobrigida, and many more. Tito died in 1980, and by 1983 the islands were declared a National Park of Yugoslavia.

In 1991, Croatia gained independence and made the Brijuni Islands an International Conference Center with several hotels and a safari park. The majority of the flora in Brijuni has the typical Mediterranean characteristics. There is also much vegetation that Tito received from foreign dignitaries. He received gifts from Indira Gandhi, Jawaharlal Nehru, Gamal Abdel Nasser from Egypt, and Sukarno of Indonesia, to name just a few. The many exhibits in Tito's palace are extremely interesting, including his exhibition of cars plus the photographs of the numerous important guests whom he hosted. The entire experience is beyond special. While we visited some other nice places in Croatia, it was time to say goodbye.

Once again we drove back through Slovenia, then on to Italy where I was able to smuggle 12 bottles of good red wine back into Switzerland. I put the bottles between my legs and when the customs officer came by I told him how much I loved their country and how beautiful the scenery was.

As you get older, you continue to have birthdays, but with age sometimes you get to enjoy special birthday celebrations. So, since it was summer and we were going to be in Switzerland, my 70th birthday did not look like it was going to be special seeing as how the children were back in America and we had previously celebrated my 70th birthday with them by taking them all on a cruise. On my real birthday, May 31, 2010, Audrey and I planned to celebrate by going out to a nice hotel or restaurant for dinner. Audrey put out my clothes to get dressed and suggested we go to the Gerbi Hotel, which is a nice hotel with a pleasant restaurant on Lake Lucerne in Hertenstein next to Weggis. As we arrived, Audrey led me to a private room and boy was I ever surprised. Our closest friends, about 20 guests, were there. Needless to say, I was totally shocked to see them all. My really close friends who lived in Weggis, Roland and Sandra Eggli, Juerg and Ingrid Spross, my Rotary friend Ilene and Otto Kuenzel, Jenny and George Mummenthalers, in addition to our neighbors Lisbeth and Kary Keusch, the senior boss of Gerbi Hotels, and Hans and Verena Hassler who are owners of three hotels themselves. Hans and I went to the same hotel school many years ago. Berni was there, but unfortunately his wife was sick. Urs and Salome Buechler were in attendance. Urs is the real estate tycoon of Weggis who sold us most of our homes. Audrey organized the party, but Sandra Eggli is the one who did all the special details. She even produced a book of the evening with many, many gorgeous photos. The whole party could not have been nicer. As an invitation they had a photo of me as a baby in a stroller. The invitation read — *ssshhh, ssshhh a Surprise Party is being given by Audrey for Hermann's 70th birthday. It would be a pleasure if you could join in celebrating this special occasion.*

WHEN: Sunday — May 30, 2010
WHERE: Gerbi Hotel Weggis
TIME: 18:00 hours, sharp
Attire: Jacket, no ties please
RSVP: sandraeggli@gmail.com, on or before May 3rd

First, we had a reception with lots of goodies and laughter, plus photo ops, etc. The menu included a buffet of appetizers, featuring seafood, salads, Westphalian ham, salami, grilled vegetables, cauliflower, poularde, and bresaola. The main course was braised beef with red wine sauce, polenta and risotto, and six different vegetables. The dessert buffet had tiramisu panna cotta, cassata, as well as seasonal fruits. Beverages included white and red wines, coffee, liquors and champagne for a toast.

Audrey had ordered all the items that I like, and I must say the meal was fantastic -- plus the flower decorations, the printed menus, and the candles made it an extremely festive occasion. The absolute hit of the evening was a presentation organized by Sandra and the wives of George, Roland, Urs and Otto.

ALOHA...with love from
Ms. Hong Kong, Ms. Malaysia, Ms. Cebu and Ms. Manila

The above listed ladies were dressed in Hawaiian outfits with flower leis, flower head bands, and looked absolutely lovely. They started to dance to Hawaiian tunes such as "Pearly Shells," "Blue Hawaii," etc. Then they started to sing the following song they had composed:

My Hermi from Georgia Atlanta
The land of the Diet Cola
With Audrey they found paradise in Riedsort over the lake
Weggis, Weggis a beautiful home with a view, it is
Weggis, Weggis, a wonderful place to be
While Audrey is off to the Rigi
My Hermi waits patiently
In Kaltbad with pipe and a coffee
My Hermi sits on his bankli
Rigi, Rigi a challenge for Audrey, Audrey,
Audrey life is always fun with Hermi
An hour of walking is plenty
He'd rather go painting Thursday
And Rotary always on Monday
My Hermi is busy all day
Hermi, Schatzi
How nice of you to be here, my dear
Hermi, Schatzi
We wish you a very good year.

The ladies did a superb job and I could not thank them enough. Many of the guests were telling stories or reading poems they had created. I must say my 70th birthday in Weggis was just a fabulous party with wonderful friends whom I will cherish as these people are really special to me.

My other 70th birthday celebration was actually before my birthday, which is considered bad luck in Switzerland. However, since we were planning to spend the summer in Switzerland we would not be in Atlanta. We decided to take a trip with the kids during their spring break. So, with Christina and Andrea's two vans, which had been nicely decorated with *"Swiss Pa's 70th Birthday,"* we started our trip south. We stopped in Lakeland, Florida which is located east of Tampa. We stayed overnight in a nice hotel since we had to arrive in Cape Canaveral early the following morning to board our cruise ship. Cape Canaveral was dis-covered by the Spanish conquistador Juan Ponce de Leon in 1513. Today it is part of a region known as the Space Coast and is the site of the Cape Canaveral Air Force Station.

After parking our car at the dock, our check-in to the Carnival cruise ship was easy and very efficient. I'm always amazed when I go on a cruise at how well organized they are and how efficiently everything goes. The ship had a capacity of 3,500 guests and 1,500 staff members, but everything seemed to work like a Swiss clock. The activities on an ocean liner are fabulous with lectures, movies, casino, demonstrations, even meetings where I learned I could make-up my missed Rotary meet-ing for the week. They have theater and entertainment performances, exercise classes, even swimming; you name it, they have it. Of course the food is absolutely fabulous with different buffets, numerous restaurants, bars and lounges. Audrey had Indian food almost every day for lunch. The kids loved their hot dogs and hamburgers and Hermann of course ate whatever was available. The first thing we had to do after check-in was to participate in a fire drill that went off like clockwork. Our cabin was very nice and practically appointed. We had a balcony which was nice, and where I could smoke my pipe in peace.

Our first stop was to be Rotan Island in Honduras. It is one of the Honduras Caribbean Bay islands. Unfortunately, the bad weather stopped us from visiting this place, so we just kept cruising. The captain tried to convince us that it was "safety first." Too bad we did not see the reefs, whales, and sharks as promised. Then we visited Cozumel, Mexico. This was a place I was very familiar with because I used to go there when I was involved with our hotels in Mexico. Cozumel is a real tourist destination. My friend Alberto Andradi and I used to treat ourselves to crazy trips, each of us on a wave runner. After work this was our outlet for relaxation and we called it "Chips on Patrol." Boy was this ever fun, two grown men acting like kids. Cozumel is well known for its national park. It is a popular stop for the cruise ships with wonderful beaches and water, a real paradise. To top this all off, they had Mexican dancers and mariachi musicians perform for us. I was very excited about going to Belize, but somehow I was disappointed. Belize today is an independent country and used to be known as British Honduras. It borders Mexico on the north while the south and west borders on Guatemala. It has the lowest population density in Central America. Belize has a very diverse society, composed of many cultures and languages which reflect its rich history. Belize is a commonwealth realm with Queen Elizabeth II as its monarch and head of state. It has many banks and it is said a lot of money laundering goes on in Belize. It also has petroleum exports and is well recognized for its sugar cane export.

Our next stop was in Costa Maya, a small tourist region in the municipality of Othon P. Blanco in the state of Quintana Roo, Mexico. It borders on Belize with the area generally undeveloped. It has been growing quickly and rapidly after construction of a large pier to accommodate cruise ships. Costa Maya has a new and modern tourist shopping mall. The center has a central plaza with sculpture, pools, and swim-up floating bars. There are several jewelry shops and souvenir stores selling "Mexican Art" -- more like a tourist trap than shopping mall. It is actually only open when the cruise ships are in; otherwise it is closed.

We cruised back to Cape Canaveral where our check-out was just as efficient as anything else on the cruise. We got our vans and started our return trip to Atlanta, which we made in one day. We all came home with many great memories of Swiss Pa's 70th Birthday. What a blessing it was that everything went so well. Personally, I thoroughly enjoy it when we are all together as a family with daughters, their kids, and their husbands.

Schatzi (Audrey)'s 70th birthday was supposed to be a surprise party. Unfortunately, it did not work out like that. Three days after I sent out invitations, she figured out that I was planning a surprise party. But she was kind and played along, acting surprised when the guests arrived and all along she was the only one who knew it was *not* a surprise party. We met at Soho's, a neighborhood bistro in Vinings. About 40 guests showed up and it was a super atmosphere. We had great food. A highlight of the evening was the calamari in an open container with chop sticks. What a trooper Audrey is. We had a great evening even though the surprise did not work. I am so lucky to have a partner with whom I get along so well. After celebrating all these 70th birthday parties, I asked myself what are we going to do when we are 75 or 80, but I guess we'll worry about that when we get there.

It was time that we planned another trip with George and Jenny Mumenthaler. One night when we met we decided to go to France. I told George why don't you plan our trip for about two weeks especially since you know France better than I do and you speak the language; plan whatever you like, it's fine with me. The two are such nice people. I call Jenny "Mother Theresa" because she is so nice and giving. George is a good businessman, so I figured he would plan a great trip for us. We said we wanted to see some castles, different cities, and stay in a castle or manor.

The time came for us to go to Switzerland and begin our summer vacation. In about three weeks we would start our "tour de France." Unfortunately, George had some heart problems ten days before our trip. But our plan was still on until a few days before our departure. That was when the doctor told George he could not do the trip as he had other heart issues and needed a stent. Audrey and I decided we would cancel, but George said not to since we could not get our money back from the travel agency and we would lose all our prepaid vacation. So, after a long discussion Audrey and I decided we would go ahead and complete the trip alone; boy what a trip that was. It started in Paris when we went to pick-up the car that Mr. Mumenthaler had reserved; however, they told me I could not since it was in George's name. Even though I explained that he was ill, they would not give me his reservation. They cancelled the reservation and rented a car to me at a much higher rate because it was a "last minute reservation." Then I had a second argument with the clerk because of credit cards and the fact that I wanted to pay for the rental in cash. Finally, we were able to start out trip; however, with no proper GPS, after 30 minutes of driving around we ended up back at the Paris airport. On the second try we actually got out of the city. What a frustration we went through; Schatzi and I were about ready to kill each other. But as always after frustration comes sunshine. We eventually arrived at our first destination to stay over for the night.

We spent three nights there and took side trips during the day. Since we were in the Loire area, we had a plethora of castles to visit with over 600 located in the Loire Valley. One we had to see was Chateau Chambord, which is unique in Europe and has been designated a World Heritage Site by UNESCO. Chambord was intended as a hunting lodge, but its architecture makes it an extravagant chateau since it is 156 meters long and 56 meters tall with 77 staircases, 282 fireplaces, and 426 rooms. Despite these wild dimensions, from the outside the chateau appears delightfully graceful and well-balanced. Francis I reigned for 32 years, during which time he spent only 72 nights at Chambord and never saw his project finished prior to his death in 1547. He only witnessed completion of the royal wing. It was his sons, Henry II and Louis XIV, who were both very fond of hunting like their father, who were responsible for making Chambord look the way we see it today. Chambord and its park are hands down the most beautiful castle I have ever seen, and I have visited many in several different countries, but Chambord beats them all. Our next drive was to Brittany. With over 1,500 km of coastline, Brittany is almost completely surrounded by water. We stayed for two nights at the Château de la Sébinièr. Our first impression was a bit disappointing, but that changed fast. The chateau is in the vineyard of muscadels, 15 km southeast of Nantes, with the country estate of a wealthy wine merchant built in the 18th century.

Madame Cannaferina, the humorous hostess at the chateau, has succeeded marvelously in blending antique and modern elements with a meticulous attention to detail, and guests are welcomed with a glass of wine. Audrey and I were walking in the park talking with a young Swiss couple, when all of a sudden we heard a big roar and an old Jeep came driving next to us. Elegantly dressed, Madame Cannaferina stopped and asked us to hop in. We rode with her in this 1940s U.S. Army Jeep down to a quiet place next to a pond where she stopped and to our surprise unloaded a table, chairs and served us an Apero. Another memory I have of this place was I only had 500 Euro notes with us which meant I could not get a cup of coffee or simple items like a cookie. Each time I tried to pay the clerk they refused to take the large bank notes. I asked our hostess if she could help me. She was so nice saying it was not a problem, but I would have to go to the local bank to clear my money. That did not work either since the bank wanted four days to make sure the 500 Euro notes were okay. Then our hostess suggested that I go to the post office and purchase some postage stamps. She even called the post master whom she knew well to make certain this would work. Finally, Audrey and I found the post office asked for some stamps, gave them the 500 Euro note. As you can guess, the clerk said she could not take my money, either. I asked the clerk for the postmaster, who came out and said he was able to get some change. At that moment I decided there would be no more large bank notes for Hermann in Europe. Our stay at Château de la Sébinièr was fabulous.

On September 20, 2014, we drove to our next destination near La Roche- Bernard, still in the Brittany area. We stayed for one night. It was an ivy-covered manor house from the 19th century which was located in the large park with mature trees, located close to the idyllic port of La Roche-Bernard. It was about 20 kilometers from the coast of Brittany. The interior of the manor was elegant and typically French. The hosts provided helpful tips for day trips, boat rides, hiking, and golf.

After Le Domaine de Bodeuc, we drove around a long time until we found our next stop for the evening. It is so difficult to find these castles since most of them are located in the boondocks. So you go around for hours on country roads until you finally find the accommodations. Our next stop was Chateau du Guilguiffin. The enchanting chateau is a gorgeous stone manor house accented by white shutters. It has steeply pitched slate roof with dormer windows and a profusion of chimneys. The elegant décor features beamed ceilings, mellow wood paneling, and heirloom antiques. Some look more like worn out furniture. Also, in the lobby the stones are all green from moss and need to be cleaned. In our room I had a problem with the hot water, so I called the lady of the castle to fix it. She kicked the pipe and when the hot water came she said in a rude manner "What do you expect? This is a castle." The gardens are stunning, and in the spring guests can admire the spectacle of 350,000 daffodils followed by thousands of azaleas and rhododendrons. Philippe Davy is supposed to be an exceptional host and the chateau has been owned by his family for over 900 years. Although the place had high ratings, in my opinion something was missing and as I frequently say, it has no "heart beat."

Staying there was okay, but it was not comfortable like a simple well-managed motel in the USA. Quite often I have noticed these chateaus and manor homes have kind of a musty smell, like mildew. The drapes, linen, tapestry, furniture, pictures, etc. just do not give me a feeling of being clean. Perhaps I am being too critical since I am married to a Director of Housekeeping who keeps everything so nice and clean. I had to remind myself to close one eye and enjoy the good things instead.

Our trip on small side streets continued. The country road brought us to Chateau de Bouceel. This chateau is a true treasure. Surrounded by a vast park, it sits on the crest of a hill facing a lawn that rolls gently down to a small lake, replete with white swans and a little bridge. This handsome stone mansion was built in 1763 but has roots in the 12th century. It has been owned by the same family from the beginning. The charming host, Comte de Roquefeuil, can tell fascinating stores of the chateau's colorful past and the role of his ancestors in various battles. The hotel's interesting interior is impeccably maintained. All of the rooms are decorated with antique furniture and family portraits line the walls. On the ground floor there is a foyer with a sweeping staircase on one side and a cozy library, billiard room, and an elegant dining room on the other side. The bedrooms have the same elegant décor and are decorated with family antiques.

The Count has studied in the USA, where he received most of his education. He is a real nice fellow, as we would say. Since the chateau is close to Mont Saint Michel and the landing beaches of Normandy, we had three nights at this destination which enabled us to visit both of these places. The beaches of Normandy were of course our first visit and it was an unforgettable experience. We saw the landing beaches of Omaha, as well as Gold and Juno Beach. I took several nice photos of me standing on the beach where the landing on D Day, June 6, 1944 took place. With all the war memorials and the signs explaining the battle, it really touched your heart. We visited the Brittany American Cemetery and Memorial in Saint-James. First, we went to the visitors center, where we received a welcome from an American service person who gave us an overview. Some interesting facts: 28 acres, headstones 4,408, Latin crosses 4,327, Stars of David 81, Missing in Action 498, Unknowns 97. Our host, the Count at the chateau, had adopted an American soldier many years ago and gave us a fresh bouquet of flowers which he asked us to lay at this soldier's grave. When we did, Audrey and I got tears in our eyes because we were so touched. The cemetery is so well laid out and organized even with the thousands of graves it was relatively easy to find this one soldier's gravesite.

We also visited the Normandy American Cemetery and Memorial in Colleville-sur-Mer, France, which is even more impressive. It is 172.5 acres, with 9,387 headstones, Latin crosses 9,238, Stars of David 149, and Missing in Action 1,557.

We made another great trip from Chateau de Bouceel to visit Mont Saint Michel. That too was a very unique and unusual experience. Mont Saint Michel is an unusual Benedictine abbey jutting out of the waters of the English Channel and is considered the most important monastic structure of the European Middle Ages. Built between the 11th and 16th centuries, it occupies most of a one-kilometer diameter clump of rocks which was originally connected to the mainland by a thin natural bridge. According to legend it was the Archangel Michael himself who was ordered to found the monastery. The best way to describe Mont Saint Michel is to divide it into five groups. The abbey is a monument of international reputation and is one of the main attractions in the Mont Saint Michel visit. It offers the visitors a glorious view of the bay. Resting on top of the Mont Saint Michel rock are 20 rooms which can be visited. The brothers and sisters of the Jerusalem Community provide a spiritual presence which has supported the abbey with their prayers for years. While we were there, we received blessings and were able to participate in one of their services.

SOUVENIRS

In this medieval town men and women uphold the tradition of the shopkeepers of the Middle Ages, who for over a thousand years have looked after visitors and pilgrims in search of a memento of their stay at the "Wonder of the West." Specialties include copperware, pottery and chinaware.

GASTRONOMY

Mont Saint Michel is also famous for its excellent hotels and its many fine restaurants with the traditional omelets, leg of lamb, and local specialties of fish and seafood from the bay.

THE STREET

At the entrance through the Bavole Gate, built in 1590, you find on the left the Burghers Guardroom and on the right are the "Michelettes," English bombards recovered in 1434. At the King's Gate the portcullis is visible. Above this gate, the King's House today is the Town Hall. The whole area is a very exciting place and walking these streets is just amazing.

MUSEUM

The museum in the village of Mont Saint Michel recalls the history of the place, with historical re-enactments, old collections of weapons, paintings, sculptures, watches, and a unique collection of 250 old model ships.

d'Ar Run was where we spent September 23, 2014. It was interesting when we arrived and one of the owners told us that we were to be the last guests they would have in their life. At first I almost got scared, but our visit was absolutely wonderful. The home was run by two gay fellows who were very nice and pleasant. The one who seemed to do all the work told us they had been running this place for many years, but they were tired of working and the government took so many taxes they had decided to spend the rest of their lives on the beach. While we were there, each day some prospective buyers came by and looked at the place. I can only say this "Maison de charm" is a place where everything was very fine. This former farmhouse stands alone between meadows and hedges just ten kilometers from the Brittany coast. In the distance you can see the Castle Rosanbo. In the summer the social life tends to happen outside in the lawn around the house where garden furniture and a barbecue area are provided. The interior is stylish and the rooms are decorated with fine materials. In the bathrooms there are jacuzzis. Breakfast is unusually abundant for French standards. Everything is so nice, the table set-ups, the yogurts are covered with a pretty cloth, and all the items are fresh and wonderful. The hospitality in this place was hands down the best we had during our trip and we had many nice places with good service. The two fellows were just extraordinary. We felt so lucky that we were able to experience this fine stay at d'Ar Run and I must say it is a shame that they went out of business.

On the last two nights of our castle tour we stayed at Le Mas Normand. The lovely 18th century house is done in a modern rustic style. A fun place, with warm and colorful bedrooms, it was a sheer delight. They have done a great job on this 18th century house: old stonework and beams, modern showers, and a real cozy place. It was hard to find, plus we had to carry our luggage up two floors, but it was all well worth it. The breakfast was served in a glass decorated Florida room and the food was excellent.

There is one other castle I have to write about even though we could not stay there. It is the Chateau du Luce in Parc Leonardo da Vinci. This place is really something to see. It was bought by Charles VIII in 1490. For over 200 years it served as the residence and summer home of the Kings of France. Francois I held Leonardo in high esteem and appointed him "First Painter, Architect and Engineer" of the King. He made this residence available to him, as well as a princely allowance of 700 gold ecus a year and financed all of Leonardo's work. The only thing he asked in return was that he could enjoy the pleasure of hearing him talk, which he did on an almost daily basis. Protected by the great affection that both the King and his sister, Marguerite de Navarre, bore for him, Leonardo was free to dream and to work. There would be so much to write to describe the castle when taking a tour, but I don't want to bore the reader by statistics. However, there are two rooms which I would like to particularly like to mention.

LEONARDO DA VINCI'S BEDROOM

He loved the view of the royal castle of his friend Francois I from his bedroom window. His drawing of this fine view is in the Windsor collection. Leonardo da Vinci spent the last three years of his life in this room. Here in 1519 he wrote his will, leaving his manuscripts and his notebooks of drawings and sketches to his beloved disciple, Francesco Melzi. It was here that he died at the age of 67 on May 2, 1519, after receiving the holy sacraments. I have some wonderful photos of Leonardo's bedroom, including his red bed with curtains and Audrey standing in front of it.

THE MODEL ROOM

This place really peaked my fascination. I always figured Leonardo was a famous painter and did some sculptures. Nothing could be further from the truth. Going down the stairs you will meet Leonardo the engineer. The four rooms in the basement are devoted to Leonardo's inventions. Forty fabulous machines, five centuries ahead of their time, are exhibited. There are models produced by IBM from Leonardo's original drawings using material of the period. You can admire his inventions in the field of civil and military engineering, mechanics, optics, hydraulics, and even aeronautics. On display are examples of the first tank, the first automobile, the swing bridge, the paddle boat, and the flying machine which was the forerunner of the airplane, the helicopter, the parachute and many more. Today, Leonardo is widely considered one of the most diversely talented individuals ever to have lived.

All good things must come to an end. We missed Jenny and George Mumenthaler on this trip, but I must say we had an excellent experience. The two of us driving hundreds of miles on freeways and back roads through France without any major incidents was a blessing. The crazy French drivers, the trucks, and the challenges we met were a good experience and provided us with unforgettable memories. But after all these castles and antiques, I must say it was nice to stay in our own castle.

In 2013 Audrey felt we would like to do another trip with the kids, their husbands and our grandkids. She did a great job planning a trip to Switzerland, Italy, and France. We booked a little bus with a driver, got airline tickets for everybody, and got ready to refine the trip. We were shocked when the owner of the travel agency told us he did not have a bus or driver. What a jerk! We went to see him and begged him to help us since we had purchased all the plane tickets, but no luck. At the last minute we found another operator and they were so nice and helpful. At the end it worked out just great. The family came to Switzerland and stayed at Vitznau, the village next to Weggis where our home was. We had a super time. Then one morning our driver with the Mercedes bus showed up and drove us toward Ticino over the Gotthard Pass.

Menaggio at Lake Como, Italy was our first overnight stop. The hotel was very nice with a little garden outside our rooms. After a delicious dinner and a good night's rest, our journey continued to Milan, Pavia to the Italian Riviera, passing San Remo. San Remo is the absolute flower capital for Italy, with millions of carnations which can be seen when you drive through this area. There are many, many other flowers as well, in bloom according to which season you visit. We then visited Menton at the French Riviera and Monaco and stayed there overnight. We had a booking for several nights and would take day trips in the area to Nice, Antibes, Cannes, Eze, and Saint Paul. Audrey and I made this tour a few times before because we love this area. One of the trips was with our friends, the Beloins.

There are a couple of things I should note about this trip. We wanted to visit Nice, which I thought was a big mistake. The day we arrived the Tour de France arrived in town, which made for a traffic nightmare. The kids loved it as they felt they participated in the world's most famous bicycle race.

Saint-Paul is a commune in southeastern France. It is one of the oldest medieval towns on the French Riviera. The town is well known for its modern and contemporary art museums and galleries. The art pieces you find are very unique. Notable people who lived in Saint-Paul are Yves Montand, Simone Signoret, and Lino Ventura, as well as the poet Jacques Prevert. Saint-Paul is also well known for its artists such as Jacques Raverat, Gwen Raverat, and Marc Chagall. It is a cozy and romantic place.

Èze is another absolute darling of a village like you can only find in France. Èze is a commune in southeastern France not far from the city of Nice. The area surrounding Èze was first populated around 2000 BC as a commune situated near Mount Bastide. A hoard of ancient Greek silver phialae dating from the 3rd century BC was found in Èze in the last 19th century and is now part of the British Museum's collection. Èze had an interesting history although it saw turbulent times when the Spanish, French and Turkish troops seized the village at different times. Finally, in 1860, Èze was designated as part of France. It has been described as an "Eagle's Nest" because of its location overlooking a high cliff 1,401 feet above sea level on the French Mediterranean. Èze , renowned tourist site, is famous worldwide for the view of the sea from its hilltop. The small medieval village is famous for its beauty and charm. Its many shops, art galleries, hotels, and restaurants attract a large number of tourists and honeymooners. The local dialect is similar to the Monegasque language of the nearby principality of Monaco.

We spent a lot of time in Monte Carlo in Monaco. We even found a restaurant where we went back again because it was in an open piazza with excellent food and service. The kids liked it so much that they begged to go back since it was situated next to a kid's park. What a great time we had. Monaco is really a wonderful location featuring the Rue Princess Caroline, the Grimaldi Plaza, the principality, the castle, and the yacht harbor with the most exquisite yachts. The richness and luxury in that city is so obvious you could almost smell the money. It is a real fairytale city for a lady like Princess Grace Kelly; however, that dream passed and died way too soon. Andrea asked me what I was doing when I wrote down some of my thoughts. I told her I am old otherwise I forget what I have seen. Then I challenged her and said what about you, do you ever write something down? She said she did, and she showed me some of her notes. With over 30 years difference in our ages, although we have different styles, I was pleasantly surprised when I read some of her comments from our trip. I felt it was really great that she captured some of her experiences on the trip. Following are a few of her comments:

27 arrival, visit Swiss pa's condo. 28 Lucerne, went shopping, dinner on deck. 29 early breakfast, Gotthard Pass, show, dad's barracks from the Army, boat ride to Bellaggio, walk uphill from hotel to

Mezzegra, saw church, kids played on playground. 30 left Mezzegra for BeauSoleil, lunch at the small outdoor cafe in San Remo. Arrived in BeauSoleil. Went down long elevator to reach Monaco Marina. Had dinner at a nice outdoor café. I had a tomato and ham pasta and Sam had an asparagus risotto while we split both. 1 early break-fast in Monaco hotel, drove to Cannes, walked up LeSuquet to view Cannes from above and saw church, beautiful view. Walked through shopping area, grabbed some baguettes and cheese and meat at a gro-cery in Antibes the hit the beach. Cool water, kids had a great time. Had dinner at Belle Vita which was wonderful (Monaco). Had the best Bolognese. Restaurant was on a beautiful street with art hang-ing across the houses (tightrope guy). 2 started the day spending in St. Paul. Loved it. Beautiful buildings flowers, street, galleries, shops. Will definitely have to go back. Notable was the church which held the bones of the Pope of Avignon, St. Clements in the chapel. Next is Nice. Nice was a cluster because the Tour de France was coming through. We basically sat in traffic and then ate at a Kebab shop. Next we went back to Monaco and took a 30 minute tram tour. Saw the Grimaldi Palace, rode up to Monte Carlo to see the famous casino and drove back. Ate at Bella Vista again. We shared a pizza and a risotto. 3 ate breakfast at hotel. Went back to Nice to take the tram ride. Visited Castle Hill. Nice is the largest city on the French Riviera and the 5th largest city in France. Next we went to Ville France. Did a little look-ing around at the shops then went to the beach. The beach was pebbly with a jumping rock. Next was back to Monaco for a little last min-ute shopping and another Gelato. Had dinner at the hotel. Butter and sage ravioli and pizza. Bay of Angles (nice) talent show in Monaco. 4 bus all day. 5 Pilatus—took cogwheel up, overcast so we had no view but had an awesome soup, went down to the Roddelbahn where Tina and Annaliese both flew out. Dad took kids down to playground and we got lost and ended up taking the bike route down. Tina lost her tell pass, overpriced fondue. 6 kuorez, Gorse Onkel Peter. 7 Rigi, Jenny, George dinner. 8 Stanserhorn shopping in Lucerne, 9 Seebodenalp swimming in Lake Lucerne dinner at George and Jenny's.

I felt it interesting to see our trip through the eyes of my daughter Andrea, who is over 30 years younger than me.

We started our tour back via Italy and then home to Switzerland. As we got back I gave each grandchild $20 that they had to give to the driver. I asked them to say thank you for all the help and good driving. I explained to the driver this should be a lesson of life for them. I added some extra money when he brought us to our home. It was a great trip and we were all thankful that it went well. We spent the next few days in Lucerne, made some trips like visiting Stanser Horn, which is a high mountain you can visit via the Cabriolet Gondola, a new sensation in Europe. Also, we had dinner with Jenny and George and spent an evening at my brother Peter's house with his wife Lotti. They presented us with a great evening and each kid got a gift packet including some money. Then they all went back to Atlanta while Audrey and I spent the rest of the summer at Lake Lucerne.

Another fabulous trip I want to write about is the summer that Audrey and I spent in Switzerland. We then flew to Amsterdam where we met Lena, her friend Gary, a real "Aussie Boy," as well as Helga and Joe Klein, our friends from Atlanta. Joe and Helga live in the same condo complex as Audrey and me. We spent a couple of days in Amsterdam, which is a very interesting city which I have visited on several occasions. We did the usual tourist tour where we found a neat pancake house where we enjoyed breakfast three days in a row since it was so good. We have also learned to love the Dutch honey wafers, which quickly became a favorite of ours. A year later, when I stopped in Amsterdam, I took the opportunity to pick up some for Helga. We visited a diamond factory outlet and for the longest time Audrey did not show up, so Helga asked what Audrey was doing, to which I replied she's probably purchasing a new diamond ring; of course, I later learned my assumption was correct.

We booked a ship from the Viking Cruise Line. The check-in was very easy since there were only about 150 guests on the ship. The cabins and accommodations were excellent as well as the service and the food. Our first stop was Kinderjik, a village in a South Holland province known for its iconic 18th century windmills. We had a chance to go into one of the unique windmills which was fascinating, and I was amazed at the excellent condition in which most of them appear to be kept. Our trip continued on the Rhine and then on to Cologne. Audrey and I have been there many times when we lived in Germany. This time Madame Gammeter got really mad at me because while they visited the famous Cologne Cathedral I went to the railroad station and looked for a hair tonic which I like but can only be found in Germany. This cathedral is Germany's most visited landmark, attracting an average of 20,000 people a day. After our separation while I shopped for hair tonic we made up with coffee and apple strudel. The next day was called Rhine River Koblenz. Our cruise took us down the middle Rhine, a UNESCO site, and we visited the Marksburg Castle. The weather was awful and with continued rain I slipped on the slate stairs, which was not fun. Some people could not even make the tour. The Marksburg Castle is above the town of Braubach. This fortress was used for protection rather than as a residence for any royal families. Of the 40 hill castles between Bingenam Rhein and Koblenz, the Marksburg was the only one which was never destroyed. Koblenz is another lovely place. It is an ancient city with terraced vineyards and the castle ruins of the Rhine gorge. It is the place where Rhine and Mosel meet and a wonderfully beautiful piece of geography.

The next day we stopped in Heidelberg and took a city tour. I went to meet the owner of the oldest restaurant and hotel in Heidelberg, Hotel Ritter, but Nick was not there since he was on vacation. I was sorry to miss him as he used to be my General Manager at the Renaissance Heidelberg when I lived in Germany. Heidelberg is a fabulous city. During World War II the Americans thought they bombed Heidelberg, but in actuality they bombed Mannheim, which is why the city is still a gorgeous old romantic city as opposed to Mannheim, which is all new. Of course, we visited the castle in Heidelberg and learned the city is a popular tourist destination due to its romantic cityscape. We spent the evening in Ruedesheim on Rhein. This was another UNESCO World Heritage Site and lies in a region that is totally surrounded by vineyards. Strolling the Drosselgasse, a lane in the heart of Ruedesheim's old town which is full of beautifully decorated restaurants, is a must. Along this long, narrow cobblestone pedestrian street tourists can enjoy live entertainment, brass instruments, and dance music playing all day and night during the summer in the many wine taverns and the open-air garden taverns. Built in the 15th century, the Drosselgasse was for boat owners to move items from the river to homes in the town. Since it is Ruedesheim's most famous attraction, it is almost always crowded with tourists.

The next day we visited Strasbourg, where the food is totally different from the usual German food. Strasbourg is the capital city of the eastern region, formerly Alsace, in northeastern France. It is also the formal seat of the European Parliament and sits near the German border. This city features the cultural and architectural blending of both German and French influences. Its gothic cathedral, Notre Dame, features daily shows for its astronomical clock. I was very familiar with Strasbourg since my father, who was fond of Alsace-Lorraine food because it was good and inexpensive, used to take me there after the war in the late 40s and 50s. The last day before landing in Basel, we stopped in Breisach and enjoyed a short visit to the Black Forest. Breisach is a town with about 16,500 inhabitants situated along the Rhine in the Rhine Valley. It is in the district Breisgau-Hochschwarzwald. Its name is Celtic and means breakwater and is another tourist town, but we did not spend much time there as we had signed up for a bus tour to the Schwarzwald (Black Forest). This was an exceptional experience. We visited a Gloathlet shop, where we found hundreds of Black Forest clocks. Also, we saw the women in their local costumes as well as numerous traditional artifacts. In a bakery a pastry chef demonstrated how to make a Black Forest cake with all the cherries and Kirshwasser (a local cherry liqueur). This sure brought back memories of my apprenticeship as a chef. I used to make hundreds of these cakes as it was one of our best sellers. The next day we ended our Viking River Cruise in Basel, Switzerland. Basel is the city which dominated the pharmaceutical industry. The most famous companies in this field base their headquarters in Basel.

After disembarking, we took a train to Zurich and boarded a plane to Berlin. Now Joe was in charge as he was a Berliner. We checked into the Crown Plaza and realized how nice it was to be back in a town again without having to go back to the ship each night. Audrey had visited Berlin before, but it was my first time. We all had a superb time while visiting KDW, an outstanding shop, comparable to Harrods in London. They have anything you could want. For me the food particularly attracted me. Any taste you could dream of you can find there. I enjoyed many of the German and French delicacies. We had to make the usual tour of Berlin which included Brandenburger Tour, the Berlin Wall, and the Olympic Stadium where Jesse Owens won four gold medals in 1936. This was an enormous accomplishment by a black athlete. Hitler was furious for a long time because of this. I saw the movie about Jesse Owens years later and only then did I realize what he had to go through for this victory, a fantastic story.

Our trip with Joe, Helga, Lena, and Gary was fantastic. It was great to see how well they all got along. They had a good time with lots of German beer, wine, and all the good food. Helga and Joe went back to Atlanta while Gary and Lena started their trip back to Australia leaving Audrey and I to spend the rest of the summer in Switzerland.

In February 2005 I received a phone call from my brother Peter telling me that Mom had passed away. It was a sad occasion since I was very close to her; however, it was a blessing for her. The past five years she did not recognize me as she just lay in bed looking at the ceiling. I was going to fly to Switzerland right away, but Peter said there was no need to. Lotti, his wife and he would take care of the arrangements. I waited for three days, then Christina came to Europe to support me, which was nice. Peter and Lottie made all the arrangements like we do in Switzerland, such as writing the newspaper announcement, in addition to designing and sending out the notices to family and friends. The pastor, who was born in Canada but lived in Switzerland for many years, did a nice service. After the church service, even though it was raining, we went outside to the gravesite for our prayer. Peter arranged for us to take the urn from Dad's grave and put it together with Mom's urn, something she always wanted to have done; now they are together forever. After the funeral, we went to a restaurant for lunch, which was nice, and we had the opportunity to meet with people we had not seen in years. I said a few words after the meal but must admit I was choking up, which I did not expect to happen. But I had to thank the pastor, the guests in attendance, and mention the many good things they did for Mother over the years. Of course, I thanked Peter and Lotti for making all the arrangements. Living in America for so many years, I felt so helpless with the whole situation. Thank God all went well and it was all over. Mother was a giving, really nice person and I hope now that she has peace being back with Dad.

Yes, we experience a lot even though we are retired; the show goes on. Last summer after Audrey got to Switzerland, she was hit by a mountain bike driver. It was bad, and I felt so sorry for her. The next day we went to the hospital and learned she had a broken collar bone and for six weeks I had to help dress and undress her. The pain was so bad that often at night she had to sit in a chair because she could not sleep. I did all the cooking, washing dishes, making the bed, etc. This was hard for her since she is such a perfectionist when it comes to home economics. When she was finally okay, I had a bad experience. I fell down an escalator and smashed three ribs and broke two. Now we had reversed roles; she had to take care of me. I cannot describe the pain I endured. When you break your ribs you cannot laugh, cough, or sneeze as it hurts so much. Even breath hurts, so I was not breathing properly, which affected my lungs and I ended up with pneumonia. It was a very uncomfortable time; but such is life and you get through it. The only thing that helps is the healing time. After about six weeks I was okay again, but what a genius I am. Three months later I broke another rib on the right side of my body.

I have to say how lucky we are in our retirement as so many friends work all their lives and at the end they have a short retirement. Audrey and I have traveled so much since I stopped working and look what fantastic trips we have taken. Audrey planned another great trip for us. This January we flew to Tokyo Japan 13 ½ hours non-stop where we changed planes and went on to Singapore for another 7 ½ hours. Even when you fly business class, being in a plane for 21 hours is a long time. I think in the future we will stay overnight and rest in a hotel before we go on. While in Singapore we visited friends and Audrey's family, then her sister from Kuala Lumpur joined us. Audrey and her sister Sue had not seen each other for over 20 years, so there were a lot of tears. Our next flight was to Sydney, Australia where we met Audrey's daughter Lena, as she has lived there for many years.

The same day we arrived in Sidney, we boarded the *Dawn Princess* with Princess Cruises. I realized right away there were not too many Americans on the ship. There were a few of us, some Canadians, but the majority of the passengers were from Australia and New Zealand. The Australians and New Zealanders reminded me a lot of Midwest farmers, not that there is anything wrong with farmers. My grandfather was a farmer and so was my mom in her early years. We had a fun group. Our cabin was nice and we had a balcony. We got a printed version of the captain's log book each day on our cruise. I don't want to reproduce each day's comments by the captain, but I thought it might be fun to show the first day's writing of that captain's log book.

16 January 2017 — Sidney Australia
Position at noon: Alongside White Bay Terminal, Sidney
Sky at noon: Mostly Sunny
Wind: Moderate Breeze
Temperature: 24C/75F
Air Pressure:1018.0mb

Today Dawn Princess welcomed onboard 2,140 guests and their luggage. At 15:56 with a total of 2,974 souls onboard and all our pre-departure checks complete, Dawn Princess began to single up her lines. Once all our lines were back onboard at 16:08, the Captain began to thrust the ship laterally. The berth using the ships thrusters and set the engines ahead, passed under the Sidney Harbor Bridge passed the Opera House at 16:29, then abeam of "Fort Denison" at 16:35.

We disembarked our Sidney Pilot at 17:04 using our pilot ladder rigged form the portside of Deck 4. Once the pilot disembarked the Captain made a broadcast to inform guests and crew about the decision to abort the scenic cruise in Fiordland due to adverse weather condition. So Dawn Princess set an easterly course to transit through the Cook Straight.

The Captain sent us the log book information each day and I thought it was interesting.

After two and a half days and nights of sailing we arrived in Port Chambers near the city of Dunedin. This is a charming and prominent regional port unlike any other thanks to the exceptional natural offerings that abound. From its dramatic scenery to its railway adventures, Dunedin offers the curious traveler a myriad of unspoiled environmental treasures, attracting tourists of all ages worldwide. Nicknamed the "Edinburgh of the South," Dunedin is rife with eclectic cultural zest. They say for the glimpse into the past you should visit the historic Taieri Gorge Railway. We decided to do the several hour trip through the green pastures of New Zealand up the mountain which was more like a hill for me. In a way it was a disappointment for us having taken so many train rides in Europe. It was kind of a tourist trap to us. I must say the workers were extremely nice and I learned later they were all volunteers. They served us tea, coffee, and cooked, then later served a cold picnic package which contained white wine from the region, plus coffee and sweets. At the top of the mountain we stopped for 45 minutes and met several locals who had stands selling sweaters, gloves, and jewelry, plus food and tourist items. For me the best of the whole trip was seeing the thousands and thousands of sheep which is so typical of New Zealand. We also visited the only castle in New Zealand, called the Larnach Castle. It was commissioned by William Larnach for his beloved first wife. The home is preserved in the baronial lifestyle of the 1800s. The views from the tour are spectacular and the gardens are nice. The castle went through some hard times and was almost empty and dilapidated. Now it is privately owned by the Barker family, who spent many years restoring it to its former self. Again, it was a disappointment for us, but it was okay.

Akaora was our next stop after cruising all night. Akaora is unlike any other town in New Zealand. Its picturesque charm exhibits a unique French flair in addition to the colonial 19th and 20th century dwellings. It was founded almost simultaneously by both the French and British. In 1838 the French bought the region from the natives for 240 pounds worth of goods, but a few months later the British claimed it. The setting of the city is very pretty with this quaint French/British influenced village nestled in the heart of an ancient volcano. It offers colonial architecture, art galleries, cafes, and dramatic seaside views. Akaora means "long harbor" in Maori.

Wellington, the city most south of the North Island, was our next stop. The area was inhabited by the indigenous Maori since the 10th century; however, Wellington was officially founded by European settlers in 1840. Set between rolling hills and a weather-beaten coastline, it's easy to think that New Zealand's capital city only suffers sunshine and scenery. But there's more to Wellington than just good looks. Nationally acclaimed museums have given the city the title of "Culture Capital of New Zealand." In the area a lot of filming was done for the *Lord of the Rings* movies. You can even take a tour called Lord of the Rings. The local hero here is Sir Edmund Hillary, the first man to reach the peak of Mount Everest. He was born in New Zealand and his face is on the New Zealand $5 bill.

January 2017 — a comment regarding the Captain's log book — during the night, *Dawn Princess* set a northeasterly course passing a beam of Cape Turnagain and Cape Kidnapper on our portside before altering our heading position of Napier. Well what the captain did not mention was that it was also Audrey's birthday, but our steward sure remembered it. We had balloons and a big sign saying "Happy Birthday" at the door. Also, Lena and Sue sent her some pretty roses. At dinner that night, which was a festive, nice affair each night, the waiters brought a cake with candles and sang "Happy Birthday" to Audrey which was a very nice touch. Napier was discovered by the explorer James Cook. Napier is loved and admired for its historical art deco architecture, award winning wines, and inviting nature. The city reminded me a lot of South Beach in Miami and their famous art deco city. The dramatic design elements of Napier such as sunbursts, fountains and chevrons and the innovative geometric shapes all add up to one of the world's most eclectic architectural styles. World renowned as the "Art Deco City," Napier boasts 123 stunning art deco buildings. The structure also pays homage to the

Maori by combining the linear symmetry of art deco with tribal Maori motifs.

The next stop was described as the best of Tauranga and Rotarua. We did not see much of Tauranga since the ladies wanted to make the trip to Rotarua instead. That was fine with me since I had visited it in the early 70s and knew it would be an exceptional journey. We took a bus ride for almost two hours to Rotarua. We could see the thermal wonderland of New Zealand. We hiked into the Wai-o-tapu thermal valley to see the spectacular mud pools, geysers, huge craters, colorful mineral terraces, and steaming volcanic lakes. Then we were treated to Maori dances and costumes and visited a museum which fascinated me. I was always intrigued by the Maoris, as they are called in New Zealand, but in Australia the natives are called Aborigines. It reminds me a lot of the American Indian culture.

We could see how Maori's rich heritage is being kept alive at Te Puia's Maori Arts Craft Institute. Dedicated to preserving the ancient skills of Maori, young people from across New Zealand are selected as apprentices. Here the students learn skills ranging from carving to weaving and creating flax skirts and patterned bodies. It is interesting to see these young people at work.

In the early 70s when I was in New Zealand I visited Auckland and this was our next stop on this cruise. I guess we can say Auckland is a good-sized city with a population of close to 1.5 million. This friendly city offers a diverse and exciting blend of European, Asian, and South Pacific charm as well as beautiful beaches, breathtaking scenery, and once in a lifetime experiences. From the dizzying heights of Sky Tower to undulating hillsides covered in vineyards, Auckland is a cosmopolitan city just waiting to be discovered. Around 1350, the first Maoris arrived in the Auckland area. The Maoris lived a relatively peaceful existence until the British arrived and established a colonial capital here in 1840. Just 12 years later gold fever swept through Auckland. Thousands arrived seeking their fortune and by 1900 Auckland was New Zealand's largest city. This reminds me of San Francisco when it was hit by the gold rush. When 19th century immigrants discovered Auckland's Mediterranean type of weather, fertile soil, and pastoral hillsides, vineyards were sure to follow. Today Auckland is home to many of the country's most respected award-winning wineries. I was so excited when I visited a wine shop that had a wine which displayed the medal of the Atlanta International Wine Festival.

Our last stop was way up in the Nord Island called Bay of Islands. Once the pilot was onboard at 6:00am we anchored the *Dawn Princess* then the passengers who wanted to go on an excursion commenced the tender operation and these vessels took us ashore. With descriptions such as sheltered beaches, craggy coves, and a myriad of outdoor activities and never-ending seascapes these are just a few of the phrases used to illustrate this country's finest maritime park. But the Bay is more than just a pretty face as it remains a home to the Maori whose ancestors arrived on these shores over 1,000 years ago.

We got back on a tender to our ship then cruised for another day and a half to Sydney. It was so exciting to get back and enjoy the view of the Opera House and the Sydney Bridge—what a wonderful site. Our trip was fantastic as we all had a great time.

I do have to write one more thing. The Executive Chef Gaetano Patamia and the Maitre d'hotel Silvio Zampieri, both Italian, gave a cooking presentation which was not only fabulous but also very, very entertaining. It was funny. They presented it as a comedy, but it was great. I had the chance to meet them both during the cruise. Following are some recipes which they presented. We really had a fun time.

LINGUINE AL PESTO ALLA MODA
(GREEN BEANS, RED BLISS POTATOES AND PINE NUTS)

- Serves 6
- 1 lb. red bliss potatoes
- 1/2 lb. fresh green beans
- 1 1/2 lb. dried linguine
- 3 Cups fresh basil leaves
- 4 large garlic cloves
- 1/2 cup pine nuts
- 1 1/4 cups Parmesan cheese, grated
- Salt & Pepper

The secret to an excellent pesto is to begin with the finest ingredients, to not over mix or pound the basil, and to prepare it as fresh as possible just before serving. A fresh sweet basil, good quality extra virgin olive oil and real Parmigiano-Reggiano cheese are ideal. If you have leftover pesto, place it in an airtight container with enough olive oil in it to cover completely and refrigerate for one or two days. Keeping the pesto for a longer period or freezing it will negatively affect its flavor.

METHOD

1. In a blender puree the basil, garlic, pine nuts and olive oil until a smooth paste is formed. Do not over blend or the mixture will get hot and darken. Transfer to a bowl, mix in the Parmesan cheese and season with the salt and pepper;
2. Place the red bliss potatoes in two quarts of cold, salted water and bring to a boil. Continue to boil until the potatoes are tender but not falling apart. Remove the water, slice and season with salt and pepper.

3. Meanwhile, blanch the green beans with two quarts of salted boiling water for approximately 6 minutes or until just tender, but still crisp. If the beans will not be served immediately, chill them in ice water to prevent them from over cooking and turning brown. Bring 6 quarts of salted water to a boil. Boil the pasta until al dente, approximately 8 minutes.

4. In a large sauté pan combine the cooked pasta, potato slices, green beans and a generous amount of pesto to coat well. Heat it all together thoroughly and adjust the seasoning.

5. Preheat the oven to 4000F. Toast the pine nuts for garnishing by placing them in the oven and cooking until light brown, turning often. The pine nuts will continue to darken slightly once removed from the oven.

6. Serve the pasta with the potatoes and beans in a large bowl or plate. Garnish with toasted whole pine nuts, fresh basil and grated Parmesan cheese.

SEARED DEEP SEA SCALLOPS (HERB RATATOUILLE AND POTATO NOISETTES) SERVES 6

- 36 large sea scallops
- Salt & Pepper
- Vegetable oil for searing
- 1 lemon, halves

RATATOUILLE:

- 1/2 cup olive oil
- 1/2 cup onion, large dice

- 4 garlic cloves, chopped
- 1 red bell pepper, large dice
- 1 green bell pepper, large dice
- 1 yellow bell pepper, large dice
- 1 cup zucchini, large dice
- 3/4 cup eggplant, large dice
- 1/2 cup black cured olives, pitted
- 2 cups tomato concassé
- 2 tablespoons tomato paste
- 1/2 tsp. rosemary, chopped
- 1 tsp. oregano, chopped
- 1/2 tsp. thyme chopped
- 1/2 tsp cinnamon stick
- 1/4 tsp cayenne pepper
- 3 bay leaves
- salt & pepper
- 3 large potatoes
- chopped fresh parsley

Although the base for a ratatouille or vegetable stew does not change, the outcome can be varied greatly by the introduction of unique ingredients such as olives or capers along with the use and combination of various spices such as cinnamon and cayenne pepper. Variations should be used subtly. Ratatouille can be served hot or cold as a side dish, appetizer or vegetarian main dish.

METHOD

1. Prepare the ratatouille by heating the olive oil in a large heavy pan over high heat. Add the onions and sauté. Add the garlic and pep-

per and sauté 4 minutes or more. Add the remaining ingredients and stir well. Reduce the heat, cover and stew. Change the seasoning after 15 minutes and adjust (the cinnamon stick may need to be removed at this stage). Continue to cook for approximately 15 minutes more or until all of the vegetables are tender and the flavors have combined well.

2. Meanwhile, peel the potatoes and cut into quarters. Using a small sharp knife, shape the potato quarters to resemble Brazil nuts. Place the potato Noisettes in a small pan, cover with salted water and bring to a boil. Reduce to a simmer and cook until the potatoes are tender, approximately 12 minutes. Drain and season.

3. In a sauté pan, heat a few tablespoons of oil over a high heat. Season the scallops well with salt and pepper. Sear the scallops on both sides until well-browned. Reduce the heat moderately and continue to cook until the scallops are just cooked, approximately 6 minutes. Squeeze the fresh lemon juice over the scallops when done. The scallops should be plump and juice when cooked. If over cooked, they will become dry and tough.

4. Serve the scallops with the ratatouille and potato Noisettes and garnish generously with chopped fresh parsley.

CHOCOLATE MOUSSE WITH RED FRUIT COMPOTE
SERVES 10

- 1 1/4 cups semi-sweet chocolate chips
- 2 1/2 cups heavy cream (whipping cream)
- 1 cup raspberries, fresh
- 1/4 cup strawberries, fresh
- 1/2 cup blueberries, fresh
- 1 1/2 tsp lemon juice

- 1/3 cup granulated sugar
- 1/2 cup raspberry sauce, pre-made

METHOD

1. In mixing bowl, whip 1¼ cups heavy cream using mixer on medium speed until soft peaks form, set aside.
2. In a saucepot, heat additional 1 ¼ cups of heavy cream to almost boiling. Place chocolate chips in separate bowl. Pour hot cream over chocolate chips. Stir to melt and mix well, set aside. When chocolate mixture is cool, fold whipped cream into chocolate using large spoon or whisk, incorporating air, set aside.
3. In a separate saucepot, combine raspberry sauce, sugar and lemon juice and bring to a boil. Add fresh fruits and let cook for one minute. Remove from heat and let cool.
4. In martini glass or dessert cup, layer fruit mixture and chocolate mousse. Serve chilled.

After the cruise, we spent a week in Sydney and visited many nice places. We also were able to spend time with Lena and enjoyed several great dinners. One such dinner was in an Indian restaurant which served authentic dishes which were quite different from Western food. We were served lamb with rice, a yogurt dressing, Indian bread as well as some spiced veggies. They also prepared chicken tandoori which is chicken marinated in yogurt and spices then cooked in a tandoor clay oven. Another night we had Italian that was really fantastic. All the pasta the guests ordered was cooked fresh behind a glass kitchen where you could view the chefs as they prepared the dish.

Since it was Chinese New Year, we drove to South Sydney to a restaurant that Lena was familiar with. We had an original Chinese dinner which started with a plate of raw fish and salad. We each received long chopsticks, stood up and mixed the salad while a server spoke Chinese. I understand it is a Chinese tradition to mix the fish and salad on New Year's Day and they believe it will bring good luck throughout the year. One day we were up in Sydney and experienced Chinese lion dancers as part of their New Year festivities. It was great to see all the excitement. For days I could not use my phone, email, nor Google — I missed it all. Then Lena found a repair shop and within an hour the old Samsung was kicking again. I was so happy. I figured it was over with my phone as I did not think it could be repaired. The last night we had dinner at Lena's home then the next day we continued our trip on to Singapore. We spent three days this time. Audrey's brother hosted us, and we stayed at the Tangling Club, one of Singapore's premier clubs. Its membership is made up of more than 41 nationalities. It is a fabulous club with tennis center, Olympic pool, outstanding gym plus restaurants and lounges, all featuring great service and fabulous food. The suite we had was very, very nice and we enjoyed their hospitality. On Sunday after lunch they had a group of Chinese lion dancers and while I have seen a lot of these before, this was without question the best group I had ever seen. Saturday night we hosted a family dinner with Audrey's brother, his wife Lucie and their three kids.

Sunday, we had a dim sum lunch in the Singapore Island Club, again it was fantastic. It was hosted by Tim Chan who used to be our Financial Controller at the Shangri La Hotel. He invited a few old timers and with good food we spoke about the good old days when we all worked together. At midnight we started our trip home — Singapore, Tokyo, and then back to Atlanta. We had enjoyed a super vacation and after almost seven weeks in other parts of the world, it was good to be back in Atlanta and the good old USA.

We are blessed that we can do all these great trips. In summer we always do our trip to Switzerland with hiking and visiting family and friends. It always starts with a week in Ticinino where we visit the music school. After coming back from Asia, I asked Audrey to organize a cruise in Europe for 2018. Our plan is to go to Copenhagen, then board a cruise ship so we can visit Stockholm, Sweden, then Oslo, Norway, followed by Helsinki, Finland, then on to St. Petersburg, Russia. This fall we have a trip planned with Andrea's family and Christina's family to Costa Rica. Audrey and I were looking forward to getting the whole gang together where we are all under the same roof since that will be a dozen people all together, so we rented a beautiful villa. Unfortunately, Andrea declined to join us, which I am really sorry about. In my family we always found a way to get along together. For some reason the past few months there is some friction between Andrea and Christina. Like always, there are two sides to every story. There is no question it is on both sides that they are experiencing friction. Each one says I love my sister and respect her; however, something is wrong. To Audrey and me it makes no sense, but what can you do since both are over 40 years old. I guess you have to let them do their own thing. We did the same things too and our parents had to let go of us when we grew up. What I am most sorry about is that we cannot do things together in the future, like going all to Europe, Hawaii, or on a cruise together.

We will not be able to enjoy the endless traveling, music, painting, meeting with friends; but at the same time, they should realize that life does not go on like this forever. Sooner or later there comes a moment where everything eventually and unfortunately changes. So, Audrey and I have prepared for this too with the best of our knowledge. We are so lucky that Audrey and I are so compatible and can come to agreements in the interest of everybody. We have a living will in which each of us specifies how our assets are to be controlled, how a trust is to be set up, and who is to control the trust. We hope we did the right thing by purchasing a plot at Arlington Memorial Gardens. It is a beautiful cemetery where Andrea is buried. It is quite interesting how you make these arrangements since it is similar to purchasing real estate. We have a black marble bench overlooking the lake. It is a nice plot where Audrey and I will be together forever. We also arranged the funeral, receptions, etc. and want it to be a celebration of life because we have had such a great life on this earth. Sometimes when I visit Andrea's grave I stop by our bench with the golden letters with our names, date of birth, etc. It is an eerie feeling when you see your own final stop; however, we must all be realistic. I used to say when I go to the big hotel in the sky (and I know I will because all hotel people go to heaven since they have already experienced hell on earth) I know I cannot be the General Manager there, so I want to be a doorman. As the doorman, when certain people show up that I knew in my life I could say, "Sorry, we are overbooked; you have to go downstairs." However, I have to realize that St. Peter already has that doorman's job. So, when I arrive at the Pearly Gates and St. Peter welcomes me there and he asks me who I would like to see my answer will be Cesar Ritz. I would like to meet him because I want to chat about hotel business with him a little bit.

Born and reared in Switzerland, after watching good ole American westerns Hermann yearned to visit the fabled land of "milk and honey" and daydreamed of riding horses and seeing real live cowboys and Indians. As you will see from this book, he was able to realize his dreams and not only visit America but ultimately become a citizen. From a Private in the Swiss Army to Sr. Vice President of the European, Middle Eastern, and African Division of an international hotel chain, his early apprenticeship as a chef eventually enabled him to fulfill each of the lofty goals he continuously set for himself. His love of this country continued to grow because it was so good to him.

CPSIA information can be obtained
at www.ICGtesting.com
Printed in the USA
FSHW010316140319
56285FS